Insight and experience

A manual of training in the technique and theory of psychodynamic counselling and therapy

Michael Jacobs

Open University Press
Milton Keynes · Philadelphia

Open University Press
Celtic Court
22 Ballmoor
Buckingham
MK18 1XW

and
1900 Frost Road, Suite 101
Bristol, PA 19007, USA

First Published 1991

British Library Cataloguing in Publication Data

Jacobs, Michael
Insight and experience: A manual of training in the technique and theory of psychodynamic counselling and therapy.
I. Title
361.3

ISBN 0-335-09792-8
ISBN 0-335-09791-X pbk

Library of Congress Cataloging-in-Publication Data

Jacobs, Michael.
Insight and experience: a manual of training in the technique and theory of psychodynamic counselling and therapy/Michael Jacobs.
p. cm.
Includes bibliographical references and indexes.
ISBN 0-335-09792-8. – ISBN 0-335-09791-X (pbk.)
1. Psychodynamic psychotherapy.
2. Psychodynamic psychotherapy – Problems, exercises, etc. I. Title.
RC489.P72J33 1991
616.89' 14–dc20 91-8245 CIP

Typeset by Type Study, Scarborough
Printed in Great Britain by Redwood Press Ltd

Contents

Preface

The exercises in this book have proved valuable in the training of counsellors studying on the Certificate courses run by the University of Leicester Department of Adult Education in Leicester and Northampton. I am glad that they can now be given the chance of wider application. Because teaching is a co-operative venture between tutors and students, and because most of our courses have been taught by two tutors, I take this opportunity of conveying my thanks to both of those who have co-tutored with me over the years and to those students who have participated in these exercises. Everyone I have worked with has made a positive contribution to the development and design of the courses for which the exercises in the book were designed. Feedback from students has shown what works and what misses the point, and has often led to simplification of over-elaborate 'rules' and to more effective means of translating an exercise into practical counselling experience or knowledge. Each of the tutors I have worked with has taught me something about communicating knowledge, thereby making me a more effective teacher.

Some of these tutors have made a particular contribution of materials which I have used or adapted in this book: Alan Lilley (Exercises 6.5.i and 10.4), Kate MacMahon (5.3.iii and 9.4), Mo Shapiro (6.5.iii), Jackie Smith and Jane Taylor (7.2), and Derek Wright (7.3.i). The person with whom I have worked most continuously and closely in recent years inevitably calls for a special mention: to acknowledge Exercise 7.1 as hers does scant justice to the way in which Moira Walker has co-designed some, and helped me refine many more of the exercises in the book. My other tutor colleagues will appreciate the special contribution she has made to my own teaching, in both style and content. Other people have taught from this material, although I have not always had the pleasure of working alongside them. They, too, have my sincere thanks for the hours of work they give to preparation, teaching and assessment.

I am extremely grateful to Dr Meredith Belbin for his permission, and his positive encouragement, to use my own adaptation of his self-perception inventory, which appears in its original form in his book *Management Teams*, and to his publishers, Heinemann, for their permission to use the material in this particular form. I am equally grateful to the estate of the late Dr Masud Khan, author of *Hidden Selves*, and to his publishers, Hogarth Press, for permission to use in a heavily adapted form material which can be found extensively in Chapter 8 of Dr Khan's book. Without the generous response of all those who hold the copyright of the original material upon which my Exercises 3.1.2 and 11 are based, the section on groupwork would be the weaker, and the concluding exercise unavailable to trainers and students.

Finally, I am glad of this opportunity to thank the secretarial staff at Vaughan College, Leicester, and the University Centre, Northampton. Some of them will recognize these exercises from their own experience of joining the courses; others will remember them from years of photocopying them before classes! But what they will be particularly remembered for themselves is the warm and clear way in which they deal with the queries of students and tutors alike, and the efficiency with which they handle the administration of a huge counselling training programme.

Michael Jacobs
Vaughan College, Leicester

1

Preconceptions: revising basic skills

Introduction

This manual of training exercises is designed to promote some of the more advanced skills used in counselling and therapy, as well as to further an understanding of many of the issues and concepts which underlie what is known as the *psychodynamic* approach. One of the features of the psychodynamic model of counselling and therapy is that there is a continuous interplay between what the client describes as happening in relationships and events and the therapeutic relationship itself; between past relationships and events experienced in reality and in fantasy by people (including client and counsellor), and their present situation; and between external relationships past and present and the different aspects or 'parts' of the 'inner' personality. Some of the exercises in this manual illustrate this interplay; others provide insight into the constituent elements that contribute to the development of people's relationships, attitudes, preconceptions, behaviours, beliefs and fantasies.

While this manual is designed in the first instance for use by those who train counsellors, I have also assumed that some students on counselling courses may wish to refer back to exercises in which they have taken part, in order to revise and reinforce what they have experienced and learned. It is, of course, desirable that students using this book refer to the various sections after participating in exercises rather than before. But it is also important that they should have acquired certain basic skills before attempting the exercises, some of which provide practice for more advanced counselling, others of which provide background knowledge which needs then to be translated into effective use in the counselling session.

Since trainers may also wish to have some indication of the prior knowledge expected of their students before these exercises can be used, this section recapitulates the basic skills referred to elsewhere, and provides some exercises which can be used to consolidate existing knowledge and experience.

Guidelines for listening and responding

There are many manuals of counselling skills which usefully seek to identify and teach the principles of listening and responding.[1] There is also much written about the basic attitudes expected of counsellors and therapists – for instance, positive regard, empathy and congruence.[2] The basic skills used in counselling have been described in different ways. I have myself summarized them elsewhere as: listening and observing; reflecting responses; exploratory responses; and information-seeking responses.[3] In an earlier manual of basic skills[4] I expanded these four headings into particular guidelines for listening and responding:

Listening

1. Listen with undivided attention, without interrupting.
2. Remember what has been said, including the details (the more you listen and the less you say the better your memory).
3. Listen to the 'bass line' – what is not openly said but possibly is being felt.
4. Watch for non-verbal clues to help you understand feelings.
5. Listen to yourself, and how you might feel in a described situation, as a way of further understanding and empathy.
6. Try to tolerate pauses and silences that are a little longer than is usual in conversation (and avoid asking lots of questions to break silences).
7. Help yourself and the other to feel comfortable and relaxed with each other; keep calm, even when you don't feel calm.

Responding

8. Be as accurate as possible in describing feelings and ideas that you perceive (do not just use descriptions such as 'depressed' or 'angry').
9. Use your empathic understanding, again making this accurate (but also tentative – you may be wrong).
10. Keep questions to a minimum unless:
    (a) you need information (in which case ask precise questions);
    (b) you want to open up an area (in which case use open-ended questions);
    (c) you wish to prompt (when rhetorical questions help);
    and avoid at all costs questions beginning 'why . . .?'

11 Use minimal prompts: 'mm', 'yes', or the last few words spoken.
12 Paraphrase or reflect accurately as:
  (a) a way of prompting;
  (b) an indication that you have been listening;
  (c) a way of checking that you have heard correctly.
13 Avoid making judgements or loaded remarks.
14 Where possible link reported experiences, events, reactions and ideas.
15 Avoid changing the subject or interrupting unnecessarily.
16 Avoid speaking too soon, too often, or for too long.
17 When you have responded, return to the listening mode; watch and listen for the reaction to your response, as well as anything new that emerges.

Another formulation of the skills used in some counselling training is that described by Egan.[5] For those who have learned Egan's approach this manual assumes acquaintance with Egan's Basic Communication Skills (giving attention, listening, empathy and probing), as well as with some of his Stage I skills (Step IA: helping clients tell their stories; Step IB: focusing, clarifying).

Egan's Step IC (challenging) and his Stage II skills (creating new scenarios, identifying themes, self-disclosure by the helper, using the relationship between helper and client, and goal-setting) I classify as more advanced skills. Challenging is a skill which I address in Exercise 2.4. The ability to identify themes in what the client is saying and experiencing might be said to be paralleled in the major themes I introduce in Chapters 4–6. The relationship between helper and client will be illustrated in many of the role plays, and particularly in the major concluding exercise in Chapter 11. But I think that in all the relevant exercises I mean something rather more comprehensive by 'themes' and something rather more complex by 'the relationship between helper and client' than is envisaged by Egan. Likewise, I do not see much place in the psychodynamic approach (as such, although all counsellors need to have a repertoire of other skills for certain situations) for Egan's Stage III skills (problem-solving and decision-making, planning action, and evaluating), which seem more applicable to short-term counselling than to longer-term counselling or therapy. In other words, while the basic skills training which many students will have had is an essential grounding to make proper use of the exercises in this manual, they will find that a psychodynamic approach puts a particular slant on many of the more advanced skills.

'Time out'

One feature of role-play work in particular, to which I refer at various points, needs recapitulating for those who have not come across it in my earlier manual of basic exercises.[6] Briefly described, the counsellor (but only the counsellor) in a role-play is permitted, and indeed actively encouraged, to call 'time out' at any point. The person playing the client leaves the group; and those observing can then assist the counsellor in reviewing how the counselling is going. When the counsellor is ready the client is asked to come back, and the session resumes, either where it left off, or as if it were the start of the next session. In all the exercises where I include 'time out' I assume that it is limited to no more than half the total time available for the role-play. In other words, where a role-play is set to continue for forty minutes, up to twenty minutes' 'time out' can be taken (and called for as many times as is necessary as long as the total of twenty minutes is not exceeded). A record can be kept of how counsellor and client use the allocated time, including where silences and 'time out' occur.[7]

Exercise 1.1: Revising basic skills

Purpose

To provide a relaxed opportunity for rehearsing and revising basic skills of listening and simple responding, and perhaps also to introduce 'time out' to students who are unfamiliar with its use.

Duration

2 hours.

Method

In small groups of four members, and over four twenty-minute sessions, participants take it in turns to practice listening, to speak about a subject, to record 'time out' and to observe.

Materials

A 'time out' chart could be useful.[8] Display the four topics the speaker may choose to talk about.

Exercise 1.1: Continued

Instructions

1 If introducing 'time out', explain its value in providing a breathing space for counsellor and observers to reflect on role-play work; and how 'time out' is used. If using a chart to record 'time out', hand it out at this point to all participants. Remind them that 'time out' can be called as often as the counsellor 'Listener' in this exercise) wishes; and that it will normally not exceed half the time allotted to the interchange between client and counsellor – although in this exercise, where the time is limited, 'time out' is limited to five minutes of each fifteen-minute period of listening.
2 Divide the class into small groups with four people in each. In every group each person takes it in turn to be the speaker, the listener, the time keeper and the general observer.
3 Instruct the groups that there will be four twenty-minute periods, each of which consists of fifteen minutes for speaker and listener to work together, and five minutes for immediate feedback from the observer, timekeeper and speaker on the listener's skills. Within the fifteen minutes up to five minutes' 'time out' is permitted.
4 The speaker each time chooses to talk about one of the four topics below. It is important that the speaker is at ease talking about that subject. Speakers should not choose any area which might trouble them:
   (a) My experience of education as a child and teenager.
   (b) Starting my first real job.
   (c) Someone who has strongly influenced the course of my life.
   (d) My memories of my grandparents.
5 Instruct the listener to assist the speaker to tell her or his story, including the feelings involved in it, and to keep the speaker to the topic chosen. Remind listeners again that they can call 'time out' when they like, but for no more than a total of five minutes. The timekeeper is to announce the start and end of the fifteen minutes for speaker and listener to work together; the tutor announces the start of each new period.
6 If there are any groups of three dispense with the role of the observer; and for the fourth period, split the three up so that they can be extra observers in any of the foursomes.

Exercise 1.1: Continued

Debriefing

Following all four periods, when everyone has had a turn at each of the roles, the remaining time is spent in fours or in small groups discussing what they have observed and learned from the exercise.

Comment

This essentially simple exercise provides a chance to practise skills, and for speakers to address a non-threatening personal experience. Sometimes, however, what seems like a straightforward topic to choose can uncover feelings which had been forgotten and which give rise to some pain. A perceptive listener may elicit such feelings. Tutors need to keep an eye open for anyone who is upset by their chosen topic, and on how the foursome handles such a situation. A further general exercise in putting together basic skills is described in Exercise 18 of *Swift to Hear*.[9]

Exercise 1.2: Role-play practice

Purpose

To provide a simulation of working with a client, particularly to avoid advice-giving, or attention to the surface question a client may ask; and to concentrate rather on listening to the different issues the client is really expressing.

Duration

45–60 minutes including debriefing.

Method

Using small groups of four to six persons, one takes the role of a counsellor, another the role of a client, and others observe, perhaps recording the use of time and types of

Exercise 1.2: Continued

intervention made by the counsellor.[10] For an initial role-play twenty minutes is allowed, of which ten minutes can be 'time out'. For more practised students the role-play can last thirty minutes, of which fifteen is allowed for 'time out'.

Materials

Sufficient role-play briefings below (Alice for women, Alistair for men), and (where used) a time chart and an intervention chart for each role-play group.

(i) Briefing for Alice (aged sixteen)

Before starting the interview, inform your counsellor of your name, gender and age. The counsellor knows nothing else about you at this stage. Agree with your counsellor what sort of helper it would be most appropriate and comfortable for her or him to play (a counsellor, teacher, social worker, etc.) and where the interview is taking place. The information below is yours to reveal as and when it feels right, and depending on how sensitive your counsellor is.

You moved into the area about ten weeks ago, and you are getting on well with a new group of friends. You are in the first year of the sixth form. You start your interview by asking the counsellor a direct question, to which you would like a direct answer: 'Is it dangerous to go on the pill?'

You want an answer, although if your counsellor is encouraging, you are prepared to talk more widely about the background to your question. If your counsellor is heavy-handed, moralistic, or more interested in giving you information than in the reasons for your question, you keep pressing for a black and white answer. If your counsellor encourages you to open the question out, you have further information to draw upon below.

Your question reveals that you like to have some clear idea of 'rules' for living, and you are actually concerned at first about whether the pill is dangerous. But the real danger is what your parents would say if they found out, because they are both rather rigid people; they are not so strict that you could really rebel against them, but you do feel a sense of frustration that they always tell you what is best for you, and always assume they are right.

You have recently moved to the city from a quiet part of the country, and meeting new friends has introduced you to all sorts of exciting possibilities. You do not yet have a boyfriend. But you are torn between what your parents would say and what your friends actually say; between being careful, and living a little dangerously; and in all this it is not easy to get away from your need to have an adult tell you what is right and wrong.

Exercise 1.2: Continued

(ii) **Briefing for Alistair** (aged sixteen)

Before starting the interview, inform your counsellor of your name, gender and age. The counsellor knows nothing else about you at this stage. Agree with your counsellor what sort of helper it would be most appropriate and comfortable for her or him to play (a counsellor, teacher, social worker, etc.) and where the interview is taking place. The information below is yours to reveal as and when it feels right, and depending on how sensitive your counsellor is.

You moved into the area about ten weeks ago, and you are getting on well with a new group of friends. You are in the first year of the sixth form. You start your interview by asking the counsellor a direct question, to which you would like a direct answer: 'Is it dangerous to smoke pot?'

You want an answer, although if your counsellor is encouraging, you are prepared to talk more widely about the background to your question. If your counsellor is heavy handed, moralistic, or more interested in giving you information than in the reasons for your question, you keep pressing for a black and white answer. If your counsellor encourages you to open the question out, you have further information to draw upon below.

Your question reveals that you like to have some clear idea of 'rules' for living, and you are actually concerned at first about whether smoking pot is dangerous. But the real danger is what your parents would say if they found out, because they are both rather rigid people; they are not so strict that you could really rebel against them, but you do feel a sense of frustration that they always tell you what is best for you, and always assume they are right.

You have recently moved to the city from a quiet part of the country, and meeting new friends has introduced you to all sorts of exciting possibilities. But you are torn between what your parents would say and what your friends actually say; between being careful, and living a little dangerously; and in all this it is not easy to get away from your need to have an adult to tell you what is right and wrong.

Instructions

1. Where possible hand out client briefings the session before, briefing enough clients so that there is one for each small group of four to six persons.
2. Set up small groups, one for each client; the person playing the client chooses a counsellor, and tells the counsellor any prior information indicated at the top of the brief. Where time and intervention charts are used, two others arrange to complete these. Any remaining people become general observers.

Exercise 1.2: Continued

3 Remind the counsellors of the value of 'time out', and how much 'time out' is available to them in this role-play. Make clear the time allowed for the role-play, and the amount of 'time out' within that period.
4 Groups start and finish the role-play in their own time, although the tutor will need to remind them about debriefing after the time allowed for the role-play has elapsed.

Debriefing

Participants remain in the small role-play groups. Ensure that client and counsellor have sufficient time to share their experience of the role-play, what they felt and thought but did not say, and any information on the briefing not revealed during the role-play. Client and counsellor also need the chance to become themselves again, particularly disowning features of their role which are not actually them. Tutors need to be careful that those playing clients in particular are called by their proper name and not by the client name during debriefing and thereafter; and that the client is spoken about in the past as someone who no longer exists. When client and counsellor have had sufficient time to unpack their own experience, and to remind the group of who they are in real life, the observers can show the charts that they have completed to the others, giving them to the counsellor at the end; and other observers can join in with their own reflections upon what they saw. Remind groups before debriefing that those playing the counsellor will learn more when their colleagues and observers are honest in their observations, and not afraid to be critical of bad practice, as well as supportive of good practice.

Comment

The general instructions for conducting and debriefing this exercise also apply to role-plays in later sections of this manual. Later role-plays are included in this manual to illustrate the way clients present themselves and their difficulties in relation to the major themes of Chapters 4–6. Alice and Alistair test the ability of the counsellor to stay with basic skills of listening and responding, when under pressure to answer questions or to give advice. It may be observed that the way Alice or Alistair look for a clear answer is a reflection of their position as teenagers in their families, where they experience their parents as providing black and white rules for living. The counsellor may recognize this from the persistence with which the client asks for clear answers. These role-plays may also be used as illustrations of working with adolescents (see also Chapter 7).

Exercise 1.3: A multiple role-play[11]

Purpose

(a) To provide a large group of students with simultaneous experience of role-play practice. It is particularly suitable as an ice-breaker or refresher exercise when starting with a new group of students already familiar with the basic skills.
(b) To provide experience of some of the techniques used in psychodrama.
(c) To illustrate the complexities of counselling one person alone, when the person presenting often represents the dynamics within a couple, family or close group.
(d) To provide a glimpse of what might be involved in working with a whole family.

Duration

2 hours, or more if using all the possibilities.

Method

Following an improvised scene at breakfast, four family members each seek some counselling from an appropriate helper. After these separate but simultaneous role-plays the family members have the chance to talk with each other in pairs, and at the evening meal; and as part of the debriefing their counsellors have a chance to take their clients' roles as they imagine them to have been at the original breakfast scene. Two stages in the instructions can be omitted where time is short.

Materials

A table and five chairs. The exercise requires a large hall or at least four small rooms. Briefing papers are needed as follows: a general briefing (i) for every person except those playing the helpers and their assistants; (ii) depending on how many are taking part in the exercise, eight or ten instruction sheets for helpers and assistants; and two each of (iii) – (vii) for the person playing the family member, and her or his alter ego.

Exercise 1.3: Continued

(i) General briefing

Storm over the breakfast table

The Jones family live in the suburbs – just a typical family of four, with Mrs Jones's mother (Mrs Williams) living with them. Mary and Bill have a son and daughter. David is away studying Economics in London, while Brenda is fifteen and still at school. Bill works as a maintenance engineer for a widely scattered group of works, and is constantly called out for emergency repairs; so home for him is a place to find some peace and quiet.

But trouble is brewing. Brenda has dropped hints that she wants to do a paper round, which Mary Jones does not approve of. Her exams come first. Grandma Williams does approve – she left school at thirteen and it never did her any harm. Bill would just like some peace and quiet.

It is breakfast time on a typical school day; everyone is up because it's shopping day for Mary, Grandma is expecting the new health visitor, and Bill hasn't got to go in quite so early. . .

(ii) Briefing for the counsellor/helpers

There are four (or five) counsellor/helpers, and, if numbers permit, each helper will have an assistant with whom to discuss the help they are giving during 'time out', which can be taken as usual. There will be others observing you, but only your assistant is permitted to comment during 'time out' on your counselling skills or on what might be happening for the client.

During your briefing there is a family breakfast taking place in the Jones home; after breakfast, sometime during the day that follows, each member of the family will have the chance of talking over their feelings with one of the counsellor/helpers, as follows:

Mrs Mary Jones goes shopping in town, and sees the local counselling centre. She comes in on the off-chance of talking to one of the volunteer counsellors.

Mr Bill Jones goes to work, and takes the opportunity of bringing up the situation with the personnel manager, to whom he goes to talk over some aspect of his job.

Brenda Jones asks to see her form tutor and talks over the situation in the lunch break.

Mrs Williams is visited at home by the health visitor who is new to the area.

David Jones, if he is an actual part in this exercise, has been rung up by his mother before leaving for lectures, and goes in to see the student counsellor, worried about the family at home.

During the time you are waiting to be called back into the main room, decide between yourselves which counsellor/helper you are going to play. You might also discuss the factors you will want to bear in mind, knowing as you do that this is a

Exercise 1.3: Continued

family situation, and that the other members of the family are seeing helpers (although when it comes to your counselling session, you do not of course 'know' this in your role).

You will have thirty minutes for the counselling session, and you can use up to half of that for 'time out'. Apart from your assistant, there will be others watching as observers, who will not comment during 'time out', since they know more than you do about this situation.

The end of the counselling sessions will be called centrally, and if time permits there may follow a period of negotiation, when different pairs in the family can meet and talk before dinner. It might be helpful to bear this in mind since it may give you the opportunity to encourage your client to talk to other members of the family. During this period of negotiation, and during the following evening meal, you and your assistants will once more be asked to leave the room. You first debrief with your assistant, discussing how it went, and then can share your experiences with other counsellor/helpers.

You will be called back for a review of the exercise in small groups, although, if time permits, there may be one small task for you before then . . .

Assistants to helpers: Your task will be clear from the above briefing.

(iii) Briefing for Bill Jones

You run your work on the principle of delegation of labour, and you expect your home life to follow the same pattern. It is your wife's concern to manage the kids, while you earn the money. Girls' education is not all that important as far as you can see, but you are concerned at the thought of a fifteen-year-old girl being alone on the street when it's dark.

When you go to work you have the chance of seeing your personnel manager to talk about staffing, and can bring up any concerns you have about the home situation.

(iv) Briefing for Brenda Jones

You obviously want to get some extra money to enjoy yourself, buy make-up and clothes, records, etc. Some of your friends have newspaper rounds. But you are not really in any mood to bargain: this is a bid to be independent. You were 'talked to' by David recently, but told him that how he ran his life was his bloody funeral. If he wanted to stick around on your parents' apron strings he could do, but you wanted some fun, like those friends who were going to leave school at the first opportunity. Play the role as you wish, but you want to leave the breakfast table for school with a bang!

Exercise 1.3: Continued

When you go to school, you have the chance in the lunch break of talking to your form tutor about the way things are at home.

(v) Briefing for Mary Jones

You do not yourself have a job, although you have in the past worked for extra money for the kids, and you feel it is important that Brenda should have opportunities you never had. You feel that you and Bill have made sacrifices to give her a good education, and that Brenda should at least repay this by making this small sacrifice herself. You had a word with David when he was last home and asked him to speak to Brenda about the advantages of education, but heard no more. He supports you, although of course he is not here to say so.

When you go into town shopping you give David a ring to tell him what has happened (although in reality he will have witnessed the scene so you do not literally have to do this). You then see the counselling centre, and drop in on the off-chance of talking to someone about the situation.

(vi) Briefing for Grandma Williams

You are not keen on modern education. You feel it would be OK for Brenda to have her newspaper round, and might indeed envy her her youth and her chance of being free. You too feel that you have to depend too much on Bill and Mary.

During the day your new health visitor calls, giving you the opportunity to talk about things.

(vii) Briefing for David Jones

Last time you were home you sensed trouble brewing, because your mother asked you to speak to Brenda about the advantages of education. When you did so she told you in no uncertain terms that you were still tied to your parents' apron strings, and that the way you run your life was your bloody funeral. It was pointless speaking to her.

Since you are away at university, you only hear about what has happened when your mother phones you after breakfast (in reality shes does not need to do this because you witness the scene as a member of the audience). You are worried about the situation at home, and go to see the student counsellor; in fact you're not sure you enjoy education that much yourself, although you couldn't tell her, since it means lots of hard work, being away from home in a strange and expensive city where you can't afford to do anything, and perhaps you wish you were at home now, if only there weren't the rows there.

Exercise 1.3: Continued

Instructions

Two stages (11 and 13) are supplementary, for use should time permit.

1 Depending on the numbers in your group, there can be four or five main characters. Having a fifth (David) introduces the need for five extra roles or responsibilities. The exercise works best with four characters where there are up to twenty-four students in the group. Where there are more the fifth character enables more people to play an active part. Smaller classes need not include timekeepers, or 'alter egos'. References to 'four or five' below depend upon whether the character David is included, or left as an absent member of the family.
2 Select or get volunteers for the following tasks: four or five to be the 'counsellor/helpers', and four or five to be their assistants (in the initial briefing, 'time out' and debriefing). These counsellors and assistants are asked to leave the room (preferably with a second tutor), after they have been given their briefing sheet (ii); they are called back at the appropriate time.
3 Hand out the short summary of the Jones family (i) to all remaining students.
4 Select or get volunteers for the following tasks: four or five to be the family members; four or five to be each family member's 'alter ego' (see below); four or five to be timekeepers during the role-play. Give family members and their alter egos the relevant briefing (iii)–(vii). Any students left over become observers.
5 The role of the 'alter ego' is to act as the inner voice of the family member – assisting the person to get into the role, adding other dimensions to what the person might be experiencing; watching the breakfast scene and conveying other feelings the person may have before the counselling session; and during 'time out', acting as a go-between in stage 11, if time permits; and in the final dinner scene quietly prompting the family member with thoughts which might or might not be expressed.
6 Allow each family member, with her or his alter ego, five minutes to read through their individual roles and discuss together how to play the part.
7 Meanwhile, set up table and five chairs around the table (one chair stays empty whether four or five parts are played); and ask timekeepers to set up a small set of chairs elsewhere in the room ready for the counselling session to which they will be attached. Each timekeeper should be assigned to a family member, and will be responsible for ensuring that, when the

Exercise 1.3: Continued

counselling begins, family member, counsellor/helper, alter ego and counsellor's assistant are brought together as follows:
(a) Brenda and the form tutor.
(b) Mary Jones and the volunteer counsellor.
(c) Bill Jones and his personnel manager.
(d) Grandma Williams and the health visitor.
(e) (David and the student counsellor).

8 Enact the breakfast scene for as long as at least two of the family stay round the table, or until enough heat has been generated! (David, if taking part, watches from the sidelines.)

9 Call in the counsellors and their assistants; timekeepers will guide them to their 'corners'. Start the counselling role-plays – thirty minutes' duration, including up to fifteen minutes' 'time out'. During 'time out' the family member and alter ego leave, and only the assistant speaks to the counsellor; any others observe.

10 Following the counselling role-plays the counsellors/helpers and their assistants once more leave the room, so that their assistants can help debrief the counsellors.

[11 If there is time, there can now be a period of negotiation when any family member, through their alter egos acting as go-betweens, can contact any other family member to ask 'for a chat'. If the family member approached does not wish to talk to that person, then she or he sends a message back through the alter ego. There can be as many changes of pairing during this period (up to fifteen minutes) as necessary, before dinner is called.]

12 The family members (less David whether there are four or five parts) sit round the table for dinner that evening: they resume relations as they wish. Call this scene to an end when enough has been said to illustrate either the success or the failure or the complexities of a first session of counselling! During this scene each alter ego sits behind and beside the appropriate family member, and whispers prompts that might give expression to what is being thought if not necessarily being openly said.

[13 If there is time the counsellor/helpers can now be called back, with their assistants, and asked to re-enact the scene at the breakfast table that morning as they imagine it, playing the character whom they counselled, and drawing upon what they learned in the counselling interview as their script. It is interesting to refrain from indicating to them who sat where, and to see how even the seating arrangements work out. David's counsellor does not join in this.]

Exercise 1.3: Continued

Debriefing

Debriefing of the family members, their alter egos, and eventually of the whole exercise must be done thoroughly in small groups, perhaps those which formed for the role-plays themselves. (See debriefing instructions for Exercise 1.2.) It is essential that the family members are thoroughly debriefed, and that there is some follow-up in the next session, to check whether they have really left the role behind them. Simple though the preliminary situation is, this exercise sometimes generates very strong feelings, and there is always the danger that family members will go on being identified by the class as 'Brenda', 'Mary', 'Bill' or 'Grandma', particularly if they have allowed their angry feelings to come through.

Comment

This exercise often generates quite a lot of heat in the family members, and demonstrates, partly through the later evening meal, that one session of counselling does not immediately alter the situation. It also shows how much one member of the family may be carrying for others – Brenda, for instance, carries the flag of freedom not only for herself but also for Grandma, who may also resent being in a dependent position; Brenda may be expected to do well to please her mother, who did not have similar chances; Mary may find that this act of testing-out by Brenda needs more than her own response, and the role-play may throw up how passive her husband Bill has been in family matters. Finally, the complexities of even such a simple situation exposing family dynamics over three generations may suggest the value of other approaches, such as systems theory, or other forms of family therapy, which look at the whole, rather than one-to-one counselling that seeks to help individuals somewhat in isolation from the family unit.

Exercise 1.4: Images and perceptions

Purpose

(a) To provide a new group of students with openings to get to know each other and the tutor – an ice-breaker exercise.

Exercise 1.4: Continued

(b) To examine the similarities and differences between perceptions of self and perceptions by others.
(c) To consider the way in which images are used to express various, idiosyncratic meanings by different clients.

Duration

Up to 2 hours, depending on how many parts of the exercise are used.

Method

Students describe themselves through their selection of given images, and then have the chance to meet and describe each other on the basis of their description. The match and mismatch between self-perception and perception by the other is explored in pairs; and in small groups comparison is made of the different meanings given to the images. The exercise also includes an opportunity for students to consider how they would like to be; and how they view their tutor(s).

Materials

Handouts including word lists and four sections for description/self-description. These can by typed on one A4 sheet for photocopying, but the different sections are cut and handed out one by one.

Instructions

1 Hand out the word lists and Section 1 only. Students use each word list to complete the first and subsequent statements: 'If I were a colour I would be . . .', etc. Note that they are indicating how they actually see themselves at that moment, not as how they would like to be. That comes later.
2 Ask the students to find a partner, preferably someone whom they do not already know, or do not know well. They are given fifteen minutes to talk with each other about any subjects other than colours, animals, flowers, transport or music! But during this time they are instructed to try and assess how the person they are talking with might have described her or himself.
3 Call time, hand out Section 2 and provide a few minutes for each person to write down in Section 2 their profile of the person they were talking with.

Handout for Exercise 1.4

Images and perceptions

colours	*animals*	*flowers*	*transport*	*instruments*
signal red	cat	poppy	penny-farthing	guitar
lemon yellow	monkey	delphinium	rowing-boat	clarinet
lime green	leopard	rose	galleon	cello
turquoise	otter	hyacinth	motorbike	piano
royal blue	horse	sunflower	Morris Minor	harp
magenta	hedgehog	primrose	helicopter	violin
burnt sienna	dolphin	waterlily	jet aeroplane	trumpet
light grey	sheepdog	daffodil	steam engine	flute
tangerine	Jersey cow	snowdrop	Porsche	cymbal
dusky pink	deer	anemone	speedboat	organ

Section 1 How I see myself as I am: colour__________ animal__________ flower__________ transport__________ instrument__________	*Section 2* How I see my fellow student: colour__________ animal__________ flower__________ transport__________ instrument__________
Section 3 How I would like to see myself: colour__________ animal__________ flower__________ transport__________ instrument__________	*Section 4* How I see my tutor: colour__________ animal__________ flower__________ transport__________ instrument__________

Exercise 1.4: Continued

4 Each pair now has a further fifteen minutes to compare the profiles made by them with those made of them by the other: what made each describe themselves and the other as they did?

5 The exercise now uses the self-descriptions (Section 1) to look at the meaning different people give to the same images. (It also provides a splendid opportunity for people to meet a lot of the others in the group.) All those who described themselves as the same colour meet together – i.e. all the 'reds', all the 'yellows', etc. When they meet together they are to note down the names of those who are in the same 'colour group'. Singletons meet together but do not make a note of names, since they are in this category the only person identifying with that colour. The colour groups meet for five minutes, sharing with other members of the same group why they described themselves as red or yellow or whatever colour they chose, and what the image or symbol means to them.

6 Repeat this for all four remaining word lists. All the animals of one kind get together and compare notes for five minutes, again noting down the names of those with whom they are meeting each time. And so on, for the flowers, means of transport, and instruments.

7 When all five categories have been discussed, suggest students get together with the person or persons they have met most frequently during the five blocks of five minutes. Where students have a number of people they have met an equal number of times (for example, just twice) they can choose just one with whom to discuss the following questions. They should find out something about each other: do they mirror each other as personalities, in background, etc. – or are they very different? If the exercise is being used for deeper exploration of relationships, they can also ask whether they could complement one another to their mutual benefit, or would they find it difficult to get much from each other's company? There is no reason why we should get on with everyone!

8 If time permits, or the next part of the exercise seems appropriate, ask students to find a partner with whom they feel comfortable – it may be a pairing they have already had during this exercise, or a completely new one. Hand out Section 3.

9 Provide a few minutes for the completion of Section 3: this time they should choose not the image that represents them as they are, but the image that represents how they would like to be. This may be the same as or different from the one recorded on Section 1.

10 As both partners complete this, they have time to discuss the following two areas:

Exercise 1.4: Continued

(a) what these images mean to them, and what they are saying about how they would like to be; and
(b) what changes in them, and/or in the way they relate to others, or in the way others relate to them, would enable them to move from the one self-description image (Section 1) to the other (Section 3).

The tutor brings this discussion to a close.

11 The last part of the exercise, which again can be used where there is time, or if it feels appropriate, involves the students completing Section 4 (or two of these if there are two tutors). What image would they use to describe their perceptions of their tutor? During this time, if not completed earlier, the tutor should complete Section 1 and Section 3 for her or himself.

12 To round off the exercise, take a straw poll on how many have described the tutor(s) as particular colours, animals, flowers, etc. The tutor can reveal her or his own profile, how he or she feels that day, and how he or she would like to be, as part of the equalizing process of self-disclosure involved in this preliminary exercise.

Debriefing

No debriefing is required for this exercise, since it is essentially an ice-breaker. But students may be encouraged at the end to reflect upon the way in which people see each other and themselves differently. The tutor can usefully stress the different interpretations which have been made of the various images used in the exercise, and how this reflects upon the way in which there can be different understandings of the same images and material presented by the client. The Comment section below provides a graphic example of this in therapy, which can be used in summing up the exercise.

Comment

It has been difficult to know where to place this exercise in the manual. It is an ice-breaker, and so appropriately can be placed here, following the multiple role-play (Exercise 1.3), which likewise can double up as an ice-breaker. It is about the preconceptions people have about each other, and how these need to be tested. It therefore forms a useful basis for all subsequent learning about advanced counselling

Exercise 1.4: Continued

skills, and about the way therapists and counsellors try to understand their clients as well as themselves.

My own use of this exercise has been as an ice-breaker for teaching about therapeutic relationships, and for that reason I have used it as a preliminary to the more taxing Exercise 9.1 on differences and similarities in relationships, which can be therapeutic.

Yet a third place for Exercise 1.4 is in conjunction with Exercise 2.7 on transference and counter-transference. Used prior to Exercise 2.7, it provides an opportunity for students to describe their perceptions of self and others, but indirectly, and therefore more safely, through the use of images and symbols. Exercise 2.7 then follows well, since it involves much more direct sharing of perceptions and self-perceptions, yet with some understanding from Exercise 1.4 of the room for error there is in the way people perceive one another.

At whatever point the exercise is used, it can be used to ask the question of how much we can ever know another person. The following account is pertinent to this point.

The American psychotherapist Yalom tells of a single hour's session in which he asked a consultant hypnotherapist in to work with his client.[12] Yalom was present for the whole session. In the course of this man's work with Yalom's client, Marie, she smiled at two apparently significant moments. Yalom asked the consultant afterwards what he felt the two smiles meant. Yalom himself thought, from what he knew of the client, that they meant something different. Later he asked the client herself what the two smiles had meant, and she gave yet a third interpretation.

When she first smiled, the hypnotherapist Dr C had suggested Marie discuss the pains in her jaw with her oral surgeon, so that he could tell her what pain was functional and what pain might be of some other origin. Dr C thought that her smile meant that she had received his message.

Yalom felt she had smiled because her oral surgeon was an old college friend who had, and still made, sexual advances – but he was very good at his job and essential for a law-suit she was conducting about the accident in which her jaw was damaged. Yalom felt that the hypnotherapist's innocent suggestion evoked a smile at the complex relationship she was already in.

When Yalom later asked Marie what the smile meant, she said the smile was embarrassment – that she felt ashamed, because she thought Yalom had told the hypnotherapist about the relationship with the oral surgeon. She liked the hypnotherapist, and indeed would like to have had a relationship with a man like that. So the smile said: 'Please Dr C, go on to something else. Don't ask me any more about the oral surgeon. I hope you don't know about it.'

Likewise the second smile meant something different to each of the participants. It

Exercise 1.4: Continued

came when the hypnotherapist, Dr C suggested that Marie's smoking was harming her body as much as if she fed her dog poisoned meat. Again Dr C thought her smile meant that she understood, and he reinforced the point.

Yalom thought the smile was at a joke she and Yalom had between them. Her awful-smelling dog put men off coming to her house – and Yalom had tried to support a suggestion from her friends and family that she have the dog put to sleep. So her smile meant, rather like the first one, 'If only you knew what you were saying, Dr C'.

For Marie the smile meant something else again. She appreciated all Dr Yalom had done – and she felt he had made things work for her, partly by pressing her on areas like the dog, which was almost like him giving her direct advice. But she thought psychotherapists were not meant to give direct advice, so her smile meant 'Yes, Dr C, got it, let's get on to something else. I don't want to be questioned like that any more. I might make Dr Yalom look bad.'

On both occasions the hypnotherapist thought the smile meant that he had got each point right; Yalom thought the smiles meant recognition of two complex situations (which he thought he had got right?); and Marie thought her smile was one of embarrassment, protective of herself or of Dr Yalom.

Yalom comments that this particular hour was 'a testament to the limits of knowing . . . A series of distorting prisms block the knowing of the other'.[13] He lists these prisms as:

(a) a barrier between image and language: we always have to translate image into language to communicate.
(b) selectivity about what we choose to disclose to each other.
(c) translation by the receiver of the speaker's language back into images: 'the translation error is compounded by bias error'.[14] We see people through our own reading of them.
(d) 'the vast richness and intricacy of each individual being'.[15]

2

The facilitating environment: further skills

Introduction

The exercises in this chapter begin to face the trainee counsellor with some of the more complex situations which arise in the therapeutic setting. There are many occasions, of course, when clients speak freely, thoughtfully and with feeling, and find great support and help in the counselling interview. Nevertheless, there are also other times when the counsellor or therapist feels stuck, threatened, or uncertain how to proceed – a feeling which may or may not be obviously shared by the client. At some level what the sensitive counsellor perceives is nearly always also a part of the client's experience, although it takes a more experienced counsellor – who is aware of her or his own blind spots and anxieties – to distinguish when such are not a reflection of what is happening within and to the client.

Even sessions which apparently proceed satisfactorily from both the client's and the counsellor's point of view may contain moments when a sharper perception of the issues, or a different way of handling a remark or a question by the counsellor, takes the client into new ground. Responding to certain remarks from an alternative angle to that suggested by the basic skills alone yields the possibility of fresh and fuller insight. The various exercises in this chapter demonstrate the choice of more productive and often challenging ways of responding to what clients say, express or feel during counselling sessions.

Exercise 2.1: Alternative to questions[1]

Purpose

To show ways of eliciting information other than through asking direct questions.

Duration

30 minutes.

Method

A briefing sheet containing some suggestions for alternatives to questions is given to each individual. After the tutor has explained the alternatives to questions which are listed, a brief exercise is completed in pairs, and demonstrated by each pair before other pairs, showing how a conversation can take place without using direct questions.

Materials

Briefing sheet as follows:

Alternatives to questions

Asking questions is such a common feature of interviewing and of ordinary conversations that it is not surprising that counsellors are conditioned to make too much use of them in responding to clients. This conditioning to ask questions also applies to answering them, so that clients may feel that a question demands an answer, although the effect of a question (however well-intentioned) may be to put the one questioned on the defensive. Counsellors could usefully pause to think of alternative and less threatening ways of gaining the information they believe would be helpful to them. Some alternatives to asking questions include:

(a) Observing the non-verbal clues. Instead of asking 'What's upsetting you?' the counsellor can say 'you appear to be upset', inviting but not demanding the client to say what he or she is feeling upset about.
(b) Closely related are 'seem to be' statements, which observe non-verbal clues,

Exercise 2.1: Continued

or draw upon empathic understanding of what lies behind the client's tone of voice or choice of words. Instead of asking: 'What's troubling you?' the counsellor chooses an empathic comment, again inviting the client to take it further if he or she wishes: 'You seem to be troubled.'

(c) The use of 'I' statements. Here the counsellor uses a modified form of self-disclosure in order to draw the client into explaining more about a situation. Instead of asking 'Why didn't you get angry with him?' a counsellor can describe her or his own reaction: 'I found myself getting angry as you told me that.' Or instead of asking 'What happened in your childhood?' the counsellor can express a more personal interest: 'I think I would find it helpful to know more about what life was like for you as a child, if you feel you could tell me.'

(d) It ought to go without saying that an invitation to answer a question is always far less threatening than asking even the most necessary question: 'Only answer this if you feel you want to, but what was the relationship with your mother like?' Although the shorthand 'Tell me about' statements sounds as bald as a question, it is softer to combine it with an invitation: instead of asking 'What about your father?' a counsellor might say 'Perhaps you could tell me about your father' or (still a question, but much softer): 'Would you like to tell me about your father?'

(e) Use minimal responses, inviting the client to take on what he or she has just been saying, perhaps (though perhaps not, it is up to the client) in the direction the counsellor's question might have moved it. Thus, instead of asking a supplementary question, the counsellor simply says 'Yes . . .' or 'No . . .' or (gently) 'Go on . . .'.

(f) An additional way of minimally inviting the client to say more is to use a gesture or facial expression, a slight movement of the hand, or raising the eyebrows a little in a questioning expression.

In pairs devise a brief conversation in which the questions below are replaced by other forms of gaining the same information. Write a brief script, where one partner is the 'questioner' and the other is invited to say more. Try using a different alternative to a question for each of the five parts of the conversation.

1 How did you get that plaster on your arm?
2 What speed were you doing at the time?
3 What happened after you hit the car?
4 Did you feel angry about that?
5 Did you think it was his fault?

Exercise 2.1: Continued

Instructions

1 Distribute the explanatory sheet above to each student. Go through the alternatives to questions with them.
2 Form the class into pairs. Each pair devises a brief scenario using alternatives to the five questions listed.
3 The pairs rehearse the short script briefly, and then form into small groups consisting of three or four pairs. The pairs demonstrate to each other their alternatives to questions, and their version of how the conversation might go.

Debriefing

Not necessary.

Comment

One possible conversation, avoiding explicit questions, might run as follows:

[1. How did you get that plaster on your arm?]

A: *(Noticing plaster on B's arm)* You look as if you've been in the wars.
B: Well, it feels like it. Actually I was involved in an accident. I collided with another car.

[2. What speed were you doing at the time?]

A: One of you must have been going quite fast to get an injury like that.
B: Well, it was only forty miles an hour, but he swerved out in front of me.

[3. What happened after you hit the car?]

A: Uh-huh . . .
B: He got out and walked over to me as right as rain and asked me whether I was hurt. It was my new car; I could have wept.

[4. Did you feel angry about that?]

A: I'd have felt furious about that.
B: Yes I suppose I was, too, although at the time my main worry was that I of course was the person coming up behind him.

Exercise 2.1: Continued

[5. Did you think it was his fault?]

A: You sound concerned in case you're blamed for the accident.
B: Yes, it was quite clearly his fault.

Exercise 2.2: Answering clients' questions

Purpose

To suggest other ways (than the obvious) of understanding the questions which clients sometimes ask; and to give practice in devising more useful responses to them than just addressing them at face value.

Duration

30–45 minutes.

Method

A briefing sheet explaining ways of understanding clients' questions is given to each individual. After the tutor has explained these a brief exercise is carried out in pairs. Feedback from the pairs illustrates the variety of ways of interpreting some of the questions clients ask.

Materials

A briefing sheet as follows:

Answering clients' questions

When a client asks a question it nearly always has another level to it. It may suggest a straight answer is all that is required, but it can mean something else. In everyday conversations people have learned to ask questions rather than communicate more

Exercise 2.2: Continued

directly what they would like to say. For example, a parent may ask a teenager 'Where are you going?' when the parent really wants to say 'I wish you'd stay and help me with the washing-up'. Or someone may say to a friend 'What are you doing tonight?' when he or she would prefer to say 'I rather like you and would like to go out with you'. Or in a committee one member may ask 'What's the time?' when he or she really means 'What a boring meeting! How much longer is it going on for?'.

Sometimes it is important not to frustrate a client unnecessarily and so it is necessary to answer a question. But at other times it is either not appropriate for the counsellor to answer the question, or it is more important, at least for the time being, to get at what the question might signify. There are, therefore, three ways of responding to a client's question. One is to answer it, and then look at what it might mean. A second way is to look at what it might mean and answer it after that. A third way, which is perhaps the most common, is to look at what the question might mean, and in doing so render the original answer to it unnecessary.

There is a great difference between answering a client's question, and actually responding to it. The best response is the one which in some way meets what the client is really trying to get at. In this context a client's question might, of course, be met with a question, although, as the previous exercise illustrates, it is less combative when the alternative answer which the counsellor makes is also an alternative to a question!

In order to illustrate what a client might be saying when asking a question, consider some possible responses to some possible meanings behind a client asking the counsellor the question 'How much longer have I got to go on coming here?':

(a) The counsellor may respond with a statement about intent: 'You seem to think you've got to come to see me.'
(b) The counsellor may respond with a statement about an emotional state of the client: 'You sound rather annoyed with me for not making things better.'
(c) The counsellor may respond with a generic, inclusive comment: 'That's a common question for people to ask when they have been sent by someone else.'
(d) The counsellor may comment on the process: 'I notice you ask me that whenever I have to alter the time of the session.'
(e) Or the counsellor may not be clear about the meaning and ask for clarification, putting the question back: 'I wonder what you mean by 'got to?'

In pairs consider what the client might be asking in each of the following questions; and devise one alternative response to each question that might be used by the counsellor in reply to the client. Where possible, use a variety of responses, which

Exercise 2.2: Continued

between them demonstrate each of the possible meanings behind a question which are illustrated above.

1 Do you think I'm crazy?
2 Would you suggest I change my job?
3 What sort of training have you had for counselling?
4 Do you ever shout at your children?
5 How much longer have I got this session?

Instructions

1 Distribute briefing sheets and go through the alternative ways of understanding questions.
2 Allow fifteen to twenty minutes for pairs or small groups to consider ways of understanding what the client may be asking, and possible responses to the client's question.
3 Take feedback in the whole group from various pairs, for each of the five questions.

Debriefing

Not necessary.

Comment

The following are possible responses, demonstrating samples of the five ways of interpreting the client's question:

1 Do you think I'm crazy?
   (b) You appear very frightened by how you are feeling.
   (d) You always seem to worry about that when you talk about your family.
   (e) What do you mean by 'crazy'?
2 Would you suggest I change my job?
   (a) You seem to want me to give you definite advice.
   (b) You look anxious about that possibility.
   (c) People sometimes ask that rather than look at what they might change about their present work.
3 What sort of training have you had for counselling?
   (a) Perhaps you are wondering whether I will be able to help.

Exercise 2.2: Continued

(c) People sometimes ask me that when they've got something really worrying on their minds.
(e) I wonder what you're really saying when you ask that?

4 Do you ever shout at your children?
(b) You're looking cross with me at the moment.
(c) Nearly everybody does. Perhaps it worries you?
(d) Do I appear to be angry with you?

5 How much longer have I got this session?
(a) You seem to think you have to stay.
(b) You look worried at having to leave.
(d) I notice you tend to ask that when there's something you're not sure about mentioning.

Exercise 2.3: Awkward customers

Purpose

To practice the handling of various awkward situations that can arise in counselling, particularly those concerned with boundaries of time, of responsibility and of competence.

Duration

At least 2 hours.

Method

The exercise looks at six situations which might arise in counselling, in the form of miniature role-plays. These give each person the chance to be the counsellor, the client and the observer twice. Each one presents the counsellor with a different dilemma, often to do with boundaries of one sort or another.

Exercise 2.3: Continued

Materials

General briefing sheets for each participant (i), plus sufficient separate briefings, A, B and C (typed on separate sheets), for each of the six miniature role-plays (ii) – (vii).

(i) Instructions for all participants

Awkward customers: situations which might arise in counselling
You will be formed into threes, with the threesomes themselves forming a large circle around the edge of the room. Between 'sessions' two of the three always move. Although A stays each time, B moves clockwise and C anti-clockwise; this means that for each 'session' you will work with a new threesome. You will be given your personal instructions for each 'session'. You will take it in turns to be client, counsellor and observer.

Each session is divided into three (or four) parts. During the first three or four minutes, clients move into the middle, where they can share with each other how to play their role. Counsellors and observers use this time to prepare how to handle the situation – especially if they are given any clues about it. The clients then return to the threesome for the second part, a role-play lasting up to five minutes – the tutors will keep time. In the third part, for five minutes or so, the threesome discuss how the situation was handled, and what it felt like on each side. A fourth part, if there is time, may consist of the tutor giving some guidelines on how such a situation might best be handled. Threesomes then change for the next session, clients into the middle, etc.

(ii) Briefings for Session 1

C: You play a new client who asked to see a counsellor. A time was arranged, which is due to take place. You now have cold feet, and so use a number of ploys in the opening five minutes, perhaps in this order:

'I don't know where to begin.'
'But it's such a long story I don't know whether to start with now or the past.'
'I don't know quite how to put it.'
'Do you think talking about it is going to help?'
'I think I'm going to waste your time.'
'I think it doesn't really trouble now as when I first made a time to see you.'
'Perhaps I could see you another time.'
'I do feel awful taking up your time like this', etc.

Put in any other similar phrases, as you wish. But if you feel the counsellor presses

Exercise 2.3: Continued

home the point that you are uncertain, or in some other way encourages you to make a start, you can then begin to start your story: that you are a person who worries about making decisions – and here you can put in your own ideas, such as whether to change jobs, move house, etc.

B: You are the counsellor. It is the very beginning of a counselling interview, arranged by you with someone who asked to see you; and you have forty-five minutes set aside for the session. [Although you will only play the first five minutes of it].

A: In this session you are the observer. Assist the counsellor during the briefing time. Observe during the role-play, making notes if you wish; and in the debriefing time share your observations, particularly on how you felt about the way the counsellor coped with the situation.

(iii) Briefings for Session 2

A: You play the client, a demanding person, coming to the end of the first session with a counsellor, who has already arranged with you to meet next week. When she or he says it is time to finish you ask whether you could 'just go on for another half hour or so' because there are some things which you haven't yet had a chance to say. See how the counsellor responds, but have up your sleeve remarks like: 'But it can't wait till next week'; 'I might not want to say these things then'; and as a last resort, as you begin to get angry, 'But you call yourself a counsellor; I thought counsellors were meant to be caring', I don't think you really care', etc.

If the counsellor is able to bring the session to a close within the five minutes allowed, either by brute force, or by saying the right thing, then you go along with it; and in that case get into the discussion period on the mini role-play earlier.

C: You are the counsellor. It is the end of the first session, and you have already arranged to meet again next week. You start the mini role-play with the words 'We do have to stop there. So we'll meet again next week, same time', or something similar.

B: In this session you are the observer. Assist the counsellor during the briefing time. Observe during the role-play, making notes if you wish; and in the debriefing time share your observations, particularly on how you felt about the way the counsellor coped with the situation.

(iv) Briefings for Session 3

B: You play a very 'panicky' person, who rings up the counsellor, in an awful state; you must speak to her or him now. If you don't do so you don't know what you will

Exercise 2.3: Continued

do. You woke this morning with dreadful palpitations, and you know it's nerves, because you've had them before; you've rung the doctor, who says come to surgery, but you can't leave the house; and the doctor can't call until this afternoon. You must see the counsellor – can she or he call? It must be her or him – a friend has told you this counsellor is very good. You are due to go and see your mother for coffee, but you can't ring her in this state – her heart's not good, and it might kill her; etc. etc. – embroider as much as you like.

If the counsellor brings the call to an end before the five minutes is up, either by not answering, or putting the phone down, or by saying the right thing, then you go along with it. You will then have more time for the discussion period. (Conduct this interview face to face, assuming that it is a phone call, without troubling too much about authenticity about being on the phone.)

A: You are the counsellor. You are just about to leave the office or study to catch a train to London, and you are already a little late; under no circumstances can you afford to miss the train. The phone rings . . . (Conduct this interview face to face, assuming that it is a phone call, without troubling too much about authenticity about being on the phone.)

C: In this session you are the observer. Assist the counsellor during the briefing time. Observe during the role-play, making notes if you wish; and in the debriefing time share your observations, particularly on how you felt about the way the counsellor coped with the situation.

(v) Briefings for Session 4

C: You play the client, who is a young person, who has just spent some forty-five minutes telling the counsellor about the blazing rows you have at home with your father; and that this last week he got at you for not yet having a job, and contributing nothing therefore to the household income. The counsellor suggests that you meet another time, which you are happy to agree to.

But you then bring out more information: not in an effort to prolong the session, but just in a matter-of-fact way; as though you accept the situation, that you have to leave now. You are not a demanding person, in fact the opposite, rather passive; but at the same time you are at the end of your tether and wonder whether there's any point going on living. The thing is that as a result of the row this week, your father told you to 'get out and not come home until you've found a job'. You said that you were going for a job interview today, but it was a lie, and you just dare not go home. But you have got nowhere else to go, nowhere to sleep, no money for anything to eat. 'I don't know what I'm going to do', you say, although not actually asking for the counsellor to do

Exercise 2.3: Continued

anything. A sensitive counsellor may feel this is one time that the session should be extended a little, or some action taken to get you help, although you are not expecting this.

B: The young person with you (you are the counsellor) has presented with the problem that she or he does not get on with her or his father; and that there was a blazing row this week about this young person not yet having a job, and therefore not contributing anything to the household income. The time has come to conclude this particular interview, and you start the mini role-play by suggesting another meeting next week.

A: In this session you are the observer. Assist the counsellor during the briefing time. Observe during the role-play, making notes if you wish; and in the debriefing time share your observations, particularly on how you felt about the way the counsellor coped with the situation.

(vi) Briefings for Session 5

A: You play the client, a person who has seen the counsellor several times. Your problem is that you find it difficult to relate to people, and that you are always on the edge of groups. Your counsellor has just come back from holiday, and this is the opening of the first session after this break. You play a person who wants to find out as much as you can about the counsellor's holiday, so you start with a phrase like 'How are you?'; and go on to questions like 'Did you have a good holiday?', 'Where did you go?', 'Was the weather good?', 'Did you stay in a hotel?', 'Did you go with the family?', etc. The counsellor, if she or he responds well, will try to get the subject back to you; but you try and keep up the pressure on the counsellor; unless the counsellor is able to bring out the possibility that you have once again felt 'on the edge' because of her or his holiday.

C: You are the counsellor. You have seen your client a few times before – her or his difficulty is one of finding it hard to relate to people, and of always being on the edge of groups, etc. You have just come back from holiday, and this is the opening of the first meeting arranged after that.

B: In this session you are the observer. Assist the counsellor during the briefing time. Observe during the role play, making notes if you wish; and in the debriefing time share your observations, particularly on how you felt about the way the counsellor coped with the situation.

Exercise 2.3: Continued

(vii) Briefings for Session 6

B: You play the client, who has been referred to the counsellor, whom you are meeting for the first time. Mr Smith referred you. You went to see him once, and he suggested this counsellor would be a better person than him to help you.

This is a difficult person to play, but try to be someone who on one level is very earnest, and apparently talks in a very knowledgeable way; but who is proverbially 'as mad as a hatter'. You are delighted to be able to meet the counsellor – you knew she or he would be the right person to see, because you had a vision, in which the figure of Christ sitting in judgement told you that you would go on a long journey, and that you would meet a person who would help you save the world. And this counsellor is clearly the person – the world has been taken over by doctors, who meddle with your mind, and set themselves up as healers, when they know nothing about spiritual healing. This counsellor is the person you are destined to meet and work with – the signs are all coming true. The key thing is to get in a phrase like 'I know you are the one chosen to assist me – are you prepared to help me?'.

A: A colleague, Mr Smith, rang you up and asked whether you would see one of his parishioners – he gathers you have done some counselling training, and this should prove a very interesting little case for you. You meet the person referred to you, for what you have made clear is an initial interview to see whether you may be able to help; and the client opens the session . . .

C: In this session you are the observer. Assist the counsellor during the briefing time. Observe during the role-play, making notes if you wish; and in the debriefing time share your observations, particularly on how you felt about the way the counsellor coped with the situation.

Instructions

1 The exercise can be set up in a variety of ways, but one particularly effective method is to use the model of a progressive barn-dance. Form the large group into threes, in each of which the participants are lettered A, B or C.
2 As the instruction sheet indicates, A is asked to stay in the same place for all six sessions, while after each session B moves round clockwise, and C anti-clockwise, thus altering the composition of the threes for each mini role-play.
3 At the start of each mini-session A, B and C are given their separate instructions. (Alternatively the instruction sheets for As, Bs and Cs can be

Exercise 2.3: Continued

made up beforehand in the form of a small booklet, with a separate page for each session, not to be turned over until instructed to do so!)

4 Some hints on the handling of each of the six situations are included in the comment section on the exercise below. Such hints can be shared by the tutor either following the debriefing after each miniature role-play, or at the end of the whole exercise, or the following week.

Debriefing

This takes place during the exercise, after each miniature role-play. But experience of conducting this exercise suggests that it often faces counsellors in training with just how difficult some clients can be. The exercise may make them more realistic about the difficulties of counselling, but at the same time set them back a little in their confidence. While such realism is no bad thing, the exercise may need more than the two hours allowed for it, in debriefing and reviewing how the counsellors have felt.

Comment

The following notes might be useful for debriefing the counsellors in this exercise, either after each mini session, or at the end of the whole exercise.

Session 1

If a new client, having made an appointment and come, is then reluctant to talk it is not necessarily helpful to try and coax them into conversation. Better to grasp the nettle and look at their reluctance with them. So 'You seem hesitant', 'You have changed your mind since you made the appointment', 'But you still decided to come and see me?', 'You're not sure now about whether you can talk to me', 'Perhaps it's something about me – I'm not how you expected me to be?' and similar responses show the client that the counsellor is listening to what the client is saying, while at the same time encouraging the client to reflect on what it is that is blocking them from opening up what troubles them.

Session 2

When it is the end of the session and the client urgently wants more time, and gets angry or upset, the temptation is to feel guilty and give the client a little more time, or to try and persuade the client to be reasonable about the end of the session. But what

Exercise 2.3: Continued

needs to be grasped here is how it might feel to the client: 'I guess that it seems very uncaring of me to say we have to stop there'; 'You obviously feel angry because it feels like I am throwing you out'; 'You will probably feel rejected that I am saying we have to stop, but we do have to'; 'I realize that you want to go on, and waiting till next week seems impossible; you may not feel like coming back to tell me then more about what it feels like to have to finish now', etc. In fact it is often a relief to a demanding person that someone will gently but firmly set limits, and not ultimately reject them for being too greedy.

Session 3

The first question to ask when the phone rings, and you answer it when you have a train to catch, is why you answered it at all! Two minutes later, having left the room, the counsellor would not even have known about this client. Similarly, had the counsellor had another client in the room already, the phone call would be kept very brief. It is important to take the initiative early if the call has been taken, and to set a limit immediately: 'I'm very sorry, but I am just this minute leaving: please give me your telephone number and I will ring you back in . . .'; or 'I will get my colleague to ring you'; or 'I suggest you ring this number instead'. If that doesn't work, there may just be time to say 'I know this is going to feel very rejecting, but I have to leave, and I am already late; please give me your number . . . I am sorry I have to put the phone down, I will ring you later.'

Session 4

This situation (where the young person has had a row with her or his father and is prepared to leave the session, but cannot go home) is different from Session 2. Here the counsellor should recognize the need for other resources, at least that can be offered. It is probably necessary to stop at that point, but the counsellor can give a number for the young person to contact; and/or can ask the young person to contact the counsellor later in the day. By then the counsellor may have had a chance to find resources which can offer some management of the young person's difficulty; or may discover that the problem has been resolved in some other way by the young person. Clearly counsellors need information on the different welfare and other resources that are available locally, especially emergency services, so that they are to hand to draw upon as necessary.

Exercise 2.3: Continued

Session 5

It is tempting in this situation (where the normally reticent client is trying hard to be warm and friendly about the counsellor's holiday) to allow a few pleasantries at the beginning of a session, especially after a break; but then to find that the situation has been turned on its head. The client's questions come thick and fast. While it seems churlish to put some questions back, it is important to do this early on, and to get firmer about it if the client continues to ask questions. At the same time observe how it might have felt to the client when the counsellor was away. A series of interventions with a persistent client might therefore run as follows: 'Yes, I had a lovely time; I wonder how you have been?'; 'I could tell you where I've been, but I feel we are slipping away from what has been happening to you'; 'I think you have felt really left out with my being away'; 'I wonder if you are asking me these questions so that you can feel you belong with me again. Does that make any sense to you?'

Session 6

This near-psychotic, religious fanatic is probably the hardest situation to deal with, although the person playing the client may find the power implicit in the role quite 'heady'. It helps us to understand why 'madness' can feel safer than apparently sane relationships. It is, of course, possible for therapists to work with clients who are deluded, borderline or psychotic personalities, as Laing and Searles have amply demonstrated.[2] It is equally possible for less experienced therapists to make sense of apparently 'crazy' communications. This means steering a delicate path between not being seen as agreeing with or colluding with the delusion; yet also not arguing for a different ('normal') kind of reality or perception. Neither 'Of course you are right' nor 'No, you are wrong' are helpful interventions. Such communication often has an internal logic – this client, for instance, may have fared badly at the hands of some psychiatrists or through inhumane methods of treatment. The referral is a bad one; it is unlikely that a trainee counsellor will feel capable of taking this client on. Referring this client on is also tricky, partly because it is then a second referral, partly because the very help the counsellor may want to suggest – a good psychiatric or psychotherapeutic assessment – is virtually ruled out by the client in the paranoia about medicine. There are no easy answers to the handling of this situation. What can be said is that it is important not to offer ongoing sessions before the counsellor has really assessed the situation; if there is some doubt, and this client makes the counsellor feel uneasy straight away, then promise no more than can be given: 'I can see you today, but this meeting is to see whether or not I can help you. I cannot tell you anymore at this stage.' Later the truth will have to be spoken: 'I'm sorry to tell you, because I guess it will be very disappointing to you, that I do not think myself that I am the right person to see

Exercise 2.3: Continued

you. I know it may be difficult for us to find the right person who can, but I would like your help in working out who it might be best to see. Can you first tell me what makes you feel so angry about the medical profession?' Here the counsellor sets firm limits, but also tries to tap both the disappointment and the adult rational side in looking for the best means of securing help.

Exercise 2.4: Facing people with themselves

Purpose

This series of exercises is designed to help counsellors enable their clients to face more painful, uncomfortable, unpleasant or similarly difficult aspects of their own thoughts, feelings or behaviour. Such skills are known as *confrontational* or *challenging* skills.

Duration

Each part to the exercise has been given an approximate timing in the Instructions below.

Method

A variety of methods (chiefly discussion and miniature role-plays) are used, progressively building up the skills and also the confidence of the counsellor in facing people with themselves.

Materials

General briefing paper (i) and printed instructions for Exercises 2.4.2 (ii), and 2.4.3 (iii).

Exercise 2.4: Continued

(i) Facing people with themselves

A particular feature of counselling from a psychodynamic perspective is the recognition of 'repression' and the way in which people sometimes cannot experience themselves as they really are: they do not always hear what they are saying or see what they are doing in relationships. An outside observer, such as a counsellor or therapist, is often aware of ways in which people could change their behaviour or attitudes, and believes that if such people could see these for themselves, they might relate better to others. Other people find it difficult to face certain aspects of themselves, and they either hide the truth from themselves (which can be unconscious inasmuch as they are not aware that they are kidding themselves) or they try to hide the truth from the helper (normally a more conscious move).

The term for helping people to face themselves, which is often used in books on counselling skills is *confrontation* or *challenging*. It is not altogether a helpful expression, because it implies that a counsellor is blunt. What is important is that counsellors can be assertive without being punitive or judgemental. But it is not always easy to get the balance right in telling a client something which not only the client finds difficult to hear, but the counsellor might also find difficult to say.

(ii) Instructions for Exercise 2.4.2

A good way of learning how to help people face things is first of all to say to yourself what you'd really like to say to a 'difficult client'. This gives you the main thrust of what you want to get across. Then analyse the main thrust of this 'confrontation', disentangle any strong feelings you may have about this aspect of the client, and work out how to put across the main thrust in a form which the client may actually listen to – sugar the pill!

Jim, for example, agrees to make a regular time to see you, but he always turns up late, getting later and later each time. The time has come to help him face his lateness.

(a) What would you really like to say – no holds barred?
(b) Analyse the main thrust of your confrontation.
(c) Disentangle what you are feeling. (But remember, too, that there are times when what you are feeling gives you clues to what your client might also be feeling.)
(d) Compose a more acceptable way of putting across the main thrust of what you originally really wanted to say. But don't soften it by asking a question!

Exercise 2.4: Continued

Mabel talks too much in a discussion group; she dominates the other members, and they cannot interrupt her, yet they are clearly getting bored with her and the group. As group leader how would you help her see this? Go through steps (a)–(d).

Brian has been to see you twice about his marriage. He has so far put all the responsibility on to his depressed wife, and speaks of himself as innocent of any blame. How can you help him face what his attitude might be doing to his wife? Go through steps (a)–(d).

(iii) Instructions for Exercise 2.4.3

Practising it 'live'

Split into pairs, and divide the next four situations between you. Let one partner 'get into' the character A, while the other partner works out how to 'confront' the character (using steps (a)–(d) as earlier). When both are ready, play out a few moments of a counselling interview, with the 'counsellor' at some point confronting or challenging the 'client', and the client reacting as he or she might. Stop the scene, and monitor how it felt to say what you did as counsellor and to receive what you heard as client. Then swap roles as counsellor and client as you move on to do the same with characters B, C and D.

A: You have come to ask for help for your friend who is pregnant/has got a girl pregnant. In fact you are talking about yourself, but you daren't admit it. (Does the counsellor help you to speak the truth?)

B: You have come to the helper because you are really fed up because you can't make friends. You are depressed very badly, you are untidy, and your clothes don't appear to have been washed for weeks. You complain that nobody wants to know you. (Does the counsellor help you to look at yourself?)

C: You've been kicked out of college because you haven't done any work. Instead of expressing any real feelings about this, you make light of the whole incident, and talk about surface issues, like what a laugh college was, that you don't mind about this or that consequence, etc. (Does the counsellor help to acknowledge deeper feelings?).

D: You don't want to criticize your counsellor, because you are afraid you will look bad in the helper's eyes; but you feel really let down by him or her, for not being around last week when you wanted extra help. You can't say this: instead you insist on saying what a pity it was that you couldn't see the counsellor, who is so very helpful, and that another person you contacted last week instead was useless. (Does the counsellor help you acknowledge your true feelings towards him or her?)

Exercise 2.4: Continued

Instructions

1 Hand out the general instruction paper (i) on 'Facing People with Themselves', and explain what is meant by confrontation.
2 Carry out **Exercise 2.4.1** (duration 10–15 minutes). This involves the following two questions for discussion in small groups: What makes it difficult for helpers to say what they'd really like to? What makes it difficult for clients to hear such remarks? Only brief feedback is necessary, to acknowledge the main points made in discussion.
3 Move on to **Exercise 2.4.2** (duration: 30 minutes), handing out the instruction sheet, and taking feedback after part (a), parts (b) and (c), and part (d) in the 'Jim' example, and then feedback on parts (a) and (d) only for the 'Mabel' and 'Brian' examples. The comment on this whole exercise below contains an example of (a), (b), (c) and (d) in relation to Jim and Mabel and Brian.
4 Split the class into pairs and move on to **Exercise 2.4.3** (duration 20–30 minutes), handing out the instruction sheets, and taking general feedback at the end of the exercise. The comment on this whole exercise below also suggests some examples of what the counsellor might say.
5 Join the pairs formed already together into fours. This part can also be used for a review of the whole course of which this Exercise may be an element. The fours are invited to practise their learning of confrontational skills on a real issue. They should decide what they would like to say to the tutor about the course they are on, or about the teaching. Ideally it should be something which initially seems too negative and critical, and therefore difficult to say directly to the tutor. They need to go through the same sequence as in Exercise 2.4.2 above, from (a) to (d), and frame a confrontation (d). Although they are not asked to feed back their initial comments (a), they are told they will be given the chance to face the tutor with their more 'polished' comments (d)!

Debriefing

Feedback from the different parts of this exercise has been indicated at various points.

Comment

The following are examples of what might be said to Jim, Mabel and Brian in Exercise 2.4.2.

Exercise 2.4: Continued

Jim agrees to make a regular time to see you, but he always turns up late, getting later and later each time. The time has come to help him face his lateness.

(a) 'I'm getting really fed up with you playing me around.'
(b) It is the playing around with my time that I want to put to him.
(c) I feel very angry. I need to confront him without using an angry tone of voice. Jim may also be feeling angry with me for some reason.
(d) 'Jim, I am wondering whether you are feeling annoyed with me perhaps because you aren't sure I am taking you seriously enough. I wonder too whether coming late is your way of telling me that?'

Mabel talks too much in a discussion group; she dominates the other members, and they cannot interrupt her, yet they are clearly getting bored with her and the group.

(a) 'Will you shut up! You are ruining this group.'
(b) I think Mabel may have taken over what she thinks is my role, imagining she is keeping the group going, because the others are silent – partly, of course, due to her talking too much as well.
(c) In fact I think I am also feeling annoyed with other group members for not interrupting Mabel more. I could easily get too angry with Mabel when I am feeling it in a more general way.
(d) 'I think that as a group we are making you, Mabel, take on all the responsibility for talking here, as though it is the one way of making the group feel it is working; but I guess we all find it frustrating in our different ways, including you, Mabel.'

Brian has been to see you twice about his marriage. He has so far put all the responsibility on to his depressed wife, and speaks of himself as innocent of any blame.

(a) 'No wonder your wife is depressed; you're making me feel depressed, too, that I can't help you if you won't accept your part in it.'
(b) I want to get Brian to look at his part in all this.
(c) My helplessness is something I mustn't convey, but it may tell me something about the way Brian or his wife are feeling.
(d) 'I think it must be very difficult, when your wife feels depressed, and this makes you angry; and you feel you do nothing to cause this, which might make her feel even more depressed. It must be difficult to know how to start helping herself or yourself in this situation.'

The following interventions might be made in relation to the clients in Exercise 2.4.3:

A [The pregnant girl] I'm wondering whether it would be very difficult for you to tell me if it was really you who was pregnant?

Exercise 2.4: Continued

B [The unwashed client] I know this may sound odd, but I wonder whether there is actually a strong part of you that isn't at all sure about letting anyone get close to you as a real friend? What might you do that could perhaps put some people off?

C [The nonchalant failed student] You seem to me to feel very light-hearted about something which you could also find rather worrying. Perhaps it is difficult to admit that this also has a more serious side to it.

D [The timid but critical and let down client] I think you are finding it hard to tell me that you feel disappointed in me for not being here when you really wanted me. Last week my absence made me just as useless as you say the other person was.

Exercise 2.5: Defences

Purpose

To show how the various forms of defence identified in psychodynamic theory are seen as conscious or unconscious resistance in counselling and therapy; and to find ways of using the identification of defences to help clients to acknowledge painful but feared feelings and thoughts.

Duration

The exercise is in various parts, and the timing is indicated at appropriate points in the Instructions.

Method

Working in small groups, identifying defences, and using miniature role-plays to practice making accurate interventions.

Exercise 2.5: Continued

Materials

Handout on defences (i); instruction sheets for Exercises 2.5.1 (ii), 2.5.2 (iii), 2.5.3 (iv) and (v), and 2.5.4 (vi).

(i) General handout for Exercise 2.5

Defences

Defences are strategies which are employed, sometimes knowingly but often unknowingly, in order to avoid facing aspects of the self or of relationships with others that feel threatening. These aspects differ: what is felt threatening to one person (e.g., becoming dependent) may feel less threatening to another (e.g., to someone who fears becoming *in*dependent). Resistance is another name given to the way defences are seen at work in counselling itself, but it may confuse the picture to make too definite a distinction between the two terms defence and resistance.

Common *defences* include: repression, projection, introjection, turning against self, denial, isolation, splitting, idealization, reaction-formation, undoing, asceticism, regression, fixation, rationalization, and displacement. In practice, many of the defences overlap one another. What is important is recognizing when defences might be employed, rather than naming them with great precision. Technical terms can be useful for shorthand communication between counsellors and in training and supervision, but are less necessary in counselling itself.

In actual counselling, therefore, it is important to be able to identify defences when they appear. They can be often seen in passivity and silence, rejecting everything the counsellor (or indeed the client!) says, talking about trivia, intellectualizing, lateness or leaving early, missing sessions, terminating a counselling arrangement early, acting out, flight into health, or even what has been called the 'gain from illness'.

While it is not essential, in actual counselling, to label defences accurately, what is important is to be able to identify them when they happen, and, when the time is right, to draw attention to (a) the defence and (b) the reason for it. The reason often involves the person's fear, for one reason or another, of expressing or even feeling particular feelings or thoughts.

If counsellors can identify defences as they happen, they can then begin to look for an explanation for their use. What is important is to help clients see that the counsellor understands their difficulties in facing up to themselves. Sometimes counsellors can explain to clients what they think is the reason for the client's responses or reactions; or they can invite the client to examine the difficulty with them, in a combined effort to understand what is going on.

Exercise 2.5: Continued

(ii) Instruction sheet for Exercise 2.5.1

Identifying defences
What defences might be at work when:

Alan qualifies everything you say with 'Yes, but . . .'?
Betty tells you she is better now, after last week you had begun to touch on painful feelings of loss?
Charlie tells you of a row with his boss after the last session?
Doris tells you how helpful you are compared to your colleague?
Eddie says he can't be upset at his father's death because he had such a good innings?
Fiona goes over the time you should have stopped, telling you how demanding her husband is?

(iii) Instruction sheet for Exercise 2.5.2

In the following examples, expanded from the earlier Exercise 2.4.2, see if you can spot (a) what form the defence takes, as well as (b) a possible reason for the person being defensive? In each example identify (a) and (b); and then (c) work out the words you might use to help the client see what she or he is doing, as well as her or his reason for doing it.

For example, Jim agrees to make a regular time to see you, but he always turns up late, getting later and later each time. He starts today by telling you that he's getting more and more frustrated at work, but can't tell his boss that.

(a) Defences: turning up late; and displacement when he talks about his work and his boss instead of his frustration with the counsellor.
(b) Reasons: both defences seem to be an (un?)conscious expression of what he feels about the counsellor, but cannot directly express.
(c) Counsellor: 'Jim, I wonder whether you are feeling pretty frustrated with the work we're doing here, too, and you can only tell me that by coming late?'

Now try the same approach with Mabel and Brian.

Mabel is talking too much in your discussion group; she is talking about modern education, and the way in which children are allowed to speak to their teachers and parents. When she was young the motto was that children should be seen and not heard. She dominates the other members, and they cannot interrupt her, yet they are clearly getting bored with her and the group.

Brian has been to see you twice about his marriage. He has so far put all the

Exercise 2.5: Continued

responsibility on to his depressed wife, and speaks of himself as innocent of any blame. He says that she is always complaining about him, just like his mother always did; he felt and feels that he can't do anything right.

(iv) Instruction sheet for Exercise 2.5.3

Mini role-plays

Your tutor will give each of you a slightly expanded version of one of the four mini situations used in Exercise 2.4.3. Everyone should refer back to the relevant character in that exercise before starting each mini role-play.

Role-play each situation in turn (briefly) with client, counsellor, and one or two observers. When the counsellor has heard enough new information from the client the counsellor must call a 'time out'. During 'time out' discuss with the observers what the defence is, and what its explanation might be. Frame how to put this to the client, and then call the client back, simply to try out the intervention. If the client looks perplexed, or reacts badly, or shows in some way that the intervention hasn't worked, then immediately say 'Cut' and have a further 'time out'; discuss an alternative intervention and then try that out. If the first version 'works' (i.e. makes sense to the client), or even if the second version does not, stop at that point, and discuss with the client how the intervention(s) felt, and whether it (they) would have worked in a real situation. Allow about fifteen minutes for each mini situation.

(v) Individual briefings for Exercise 2.5.3

A: You have come to ask for help for your friend who is pregnant/has got a girl pregnant. In fact you are talking about yourself, but you daren't admit it. You insist on confidentiality because you don't want any of the friend's family or friends finding out. The parents will be particularly angry if they know, because they have very strict moral views.

B: You have come to the helper because you are really fed up because you can't make friends. This is your first term at college away from home, although you are glad to be away from home because your mother fussed over you all the time at home, wouldn't let you do anything for yourself, was very protective, and always worried about the sort of people you might mix with. You are dressed very badly, you are untidy, and your clothes don't appear to have been washed for weeks. You complain that nobody wants to know you.

C: You've been kicked out of college because you haven't done any work. Instead of expressing any real feelings about this, you make light of the whole incident, and talk

Exercise 2.5: Continued

about surface issues, like what a laugh college was, that you don't mind about this or that consequence, etc. Anyway, you slip in, among all the bravado, that at least it's different from your brother, who went to Oxford, got a first, and is now doing research. You've always had to struggle to keep up with his achievements.

D: You don't want to criticize your counsellor, because you are afraid you will look bad in the helper's eyes; but you feel really let down by him or her, for not being around last week when you wanted extra help. What you do say is that it was a pity you couldn't see the counsellor for an extra session last week, because you had the most awful nightmares after seeing a violent film at the cinema. You wouldn't have gone if you had known what it was going to be like; you want more peace around in the world. You had contacted someone else when you couldn't see your counsellor but he was not at all helpful, not like your counsellor is.

(vi) Instruction sheet for Exercise 2.5.4

Divide into pairs: take it in turns to discuss a piece of counselling work you are doing, where you feel there is some defensiveness around – a feeling of being stuck perhaps. Describe the person to your partner, and together try to work out:

(a) What you would really like to say to your client. Be completely honest.
(b) What form the defence is or might be taking.
(c) What feelings or thoughts the client might be defending against.
(d) What reasons there might be for the defence(s).
(e) How to 'confront' the client, suggesting a possible reason for their defence(s).

Then it is your partner's turn to describe a situation.

Instructions

1 Hand out and go through the general paper introducing the concept of defences and resistance.
2 Form small groups of four, and hand out instruction sheets for Exercise 2.5.1 (duration: 10 minutes). Take brief feedback on the results of the identification of defences. The comment section on this exercise suggests what defences might be employed in these vignettes.
3 Staying in small groups of four, move on to Exercise 2.5.2 (duration: 30 minutes), again using the instruction sheets. The comment section on this exercise again gives examples which can be used as a check for this part of the exercise.

Exercise 2.5: Continued

4. Staying in small groups of four, move on to Exercise 2.5.3 (duration: 1 hour). For this exercise it is very useful for all students to have their copy of the parallel Exercise 2.4.3 to refer to during the exercise itself, especially during any 'time out'. Each student needs a copy of the instruction sheet for Exercise 2.5.3. They should letter themselves A, B, C and D; each then receives the appropriate part for the four miniature role-plays (see Materials section). Some suggestions for interpretations of these types of defence are included in the Comment section below.
5. Form pairs, and hand out the instruction sheets for Exercise 2.5.4 (duration: 20–30 minutes).
6. Staying in pairs, students are finally invited to look at their own defences, and the way they may resist seeing things about themselves or their clients which are important to the therapeutic relationship; or may find certain areas difficult to talk about; or find some of the techniques they have learned about (such as observation of time boundaries) difficult to put into practice. About thirty minutes can be allowed for them to discuss any aspects of their counselling practice which need facing up to, looking at reasons for any difficulties, and the defences they themselves put up when counselling clients, or some types of client.

Debriefing

Feedback from the different parts of this exercise has been indicated at various points.

Comment

The following are typical descriptions of the defences which appear in Exercise 2.5.1:

Alan qualifies everything you say with 'Yes, but . . .', signifying *denial*, *rationalization* or *rejecting* what the counsellor says.

Betty tells you she is better now, after last week you had begun to touch on painful feelings of loss; this signifies *flight into health* or *repression*.

Charlie tells you of a row with his boss after the last session; this is a *displacement* or *acting-out* strategy.

Doris tells you how helpful you are compared to your colleague; this is *idealization* or *splitting*.

Eddie says he can't be upset at his father's death because he had such a good innings; this is a form of *intellectualization* or *rationalization*.

Fiona goes over the time you should have stopped; her telling you how her

Exercise 2.5: Continued

husband is demanding is *projection* (it is not just the husband who is demanding).

The following are examples of how the vignettes in Exercise 2.5.2 might be tackled, including a reference to the possible defences:

Mabel (who will not stop talking): I wonder whether the members of this group are thinking that really I should be doing all the talking, and you should all be sitting listening to me like obedient children listening to teacher. I suspect that makes you, Mabel, take on what everyone thinks I should be doing; you fill the silence, while others feel fed up that I'm not saying more. So they let you get on with it, thinking they shouldn't interrupt you either.

Brian (who will not see that he contributes to his wife's depression) : I think there is a danger that you are going to think that I am criticizing you, just like you feel first that your mother did and now that your wife does. But I guess that it is difficult for you to admit that there are some things you don't do right, because you're afraid that means that someone like me is going to jump on you and blame you.

The following are examples of the type of intervention which might be made in Exercise 2.5.3, again incorporating some reference to the defensive position adopted by the client:

A [The pregnant girl]: I think you may be worried that I, too, would get very angry like these parents you are talking about, so you would find it very difficult to tell me if it was really you who was pregnant?

B [The unwashed client]: I know this may sound odd, but I wonder whether there is actually a strong part of you that isn't at all sure about letting anyone close to you, in case they try and take you over as you feel your mother does. Or even in case they are the wrong sort of person she warned you about? I wonder if you are needing to be very independent, but actually finding it difficult to look after yourself?

C [The nonchalant failed student]: You seem to me to feel very light-hearted about something which you could also find rather worrying – in case you now get compared once more with your clever brother. Perhaps it's important for you to be completely different.

D [The timid but critical and let-down client]: I think you are finding it hard to tell me that you feel disappointed in me for not being here when you really wanted me. Actually I think you are more than disappointed: I think you might feel very angry with me for letting you down, but you are very frightened of getting angry, in case being angry proves as destructive as the film you saw or the nightmare you had afterwards.

Exercise 2.6: First and last words

Purpose

To show the possible significance of apparently throw-away phrases, particularly those which are often spoken at the beginnings and ends of sessions.

Duration

30 minutes to 1 hour, depending on the number of examples used.

Method

Working in pairs or in small groups, students are asked to look beneath the obvious meaning of phrases to the possible underlying meaning; and in some instances to frame a response to what has been said.

Materials

A briefing sheet for each student:

First and last words

Work through as many examples of these first and last words as there is time for. Suggest what these first and last words might mean. In the case of last words generally, or with these specific examples, you might also consider how you would respond – remembering that they were nearly all spoken at the very end of the session. Do not be afraid to guess, to free-associate and to speculate about the meanings of these phrases: you may well come up with ways of understanding which are close to the original situations. Your tutor will tell you later what these situations were, although your own explanations, if they are different, may refer to other aspects which the counsellor did not spot at the time.

First words

(a) I'm sorry I'm late. I came what I thought was a quick way, but I got hemmed in and had to turn back.
(b) It's very hot – I think there's going to be a storm.
(c) The bell doesn't work. I couldn't reach you.

Exercise 2.6: Continued

(d) It's a battle having to open all these doors on the way in here, isn't it?
(e) How are you?
(f) (*It is midsummer*) The leaves on that tree are beginning to turn.

Last words
(g) I had a very interesting dream last night.
(h) Here's a Christmas present for you. See you in the New Year.
(i) I think I'll stop there and leave early if you don't mind.
(j) God! What a pathetic session!
(k) Is it all right if I bring my friend with me next week?
(l) (*Having just fixed the times for three further sessions*) Is it a trouble for you to see me?

Instructions

1 Explain how the opening words or the closing (door-handle) remarks of a counselling session are often significant, even if at the time they do not appear to be any more than pleasantries – the sort of things people say to each other to break the ice, or something to say as they part. While recognizing the temptation to interpret everything and anything, give an example to illustrate how often first and last words have something important to communicate. Let the groups suggest what these first and last words might mean to them. They may need to be encouraged to make guesses, to free-associate and to speculate, since the amount of information they are given is deliberately very small.
2 Hand out the briefing sheet for this exercise.

Debriefing

Either after each example, or at such a time as pairs or groups have discussed a number of examples in sequence, take feedback. Taking feedback from all the groups on all the phrases is likely to be too time-consuming and can get boring: instead ask a different group or pair each time. The Comment section on the following page contains possible interpretations of the phrases as they were originally used in a particular context.

Exercise 2.6: Continued

Comment

Everyone will have their own examples of these types of 'door-handle' remark, but the following serves as an illustration which can be used to introduce the idea of meanings behind apparently everyday features or phrases. A middle-aged man walked into the counsellor's room with a white polythene bag in his hand. He placed it by the front leg of his chair as he sat down, and said to the counsellor: 'That's my lunch.' The counsellor was inwardly amused at the firmness with which the man told him this, and wondered what it was about. About half way through the session the man was talking about the time in his life when the person who was to become his step-father first came for meals with his mother and the family. 'When he came we had to make a meal for three do for four, so I didn't get as much to eat as I used to. I think that's one of the reasons I resented him even then.' The counsellor was able to point out that he had made his ownership of his lunch very plain when he came into the room; and the counsellor went to talk about how the step-father coming in to the family also meant having to share his mother with one more person. Incidentally, this man also found difficulty keeping his counselling for himself – he felt obliged at first to tell his partner everything he had said when she asked what went on.

It is surprising how often groups come up with ways of understanding which are close to the original situation explained below. It is good to encourage speculative thinking, although it needs to be made clear that care is necessary in using speculation openly. Often it is necessary to wait before the meaning of a phrase becomes clearer, or until there is some confirmation or disconfirmation of what the counsellor originally suspected might be its significance.

The original circumstances, and the possible meaning behind the phrases used in this exercise, were as follows:

(a) 'I'm sorry I'm late. I came what I thought was a quick way, but I got hemmed in and had to turn back'. This client had seen two counsellors already, each time for only one session; she was looking for a quick solution, and went away each time apparently satisfied. At the end of their second session together, this third counsellor had suggested meeting regularly, and the client's words were spoken when the third session began late. She had indeed tried to take a short cut to the building, but found herself in a cul-de-sac, and had to turn back. So the counsellor did not pick up the deeper significance of these words, and at the end of the session, when the client said that she did not need to come again, it was too late to look at her difficulties staying in counselling.

(b) 'It's very hot – I think there's going to be a storm.' It was actually a hot day, although not a close one where a storm might be expected; this person was

Exercise 2.6: Continued

very upset about something that had happened outside the session, but the remark about the storm helped the counsellor to refer to, and draw out, just how angry the client was, too.

(c) 'The bell doesn't work. I couldn't reach you.' In fact the bell to say she had arrived did work, but unusually this client did not press it hard enough. She was concerned in the session that followed (with a male counsellor) that she was not attractive to men. Of course, 'belle' also means an attractive woman.

(d) 'It's a battle having to open all these doors on the way in here, isn't it?' There were indeed four doors to go through to get into the counselling room, but this remark also seemed to refer to the struggle this person was experiencing in opening the doors to his own feelings.

(e) 'How are you?' This is naturally a common phrase, but it can have many other meanings than a mere pleasantry. In this instance the counsellor asked the question back and was told that things were not at all good.

(f) 'The leaves on that tree are beginning to turn.' This client was due to finish counselling in the autumn after seeing the counsellor weekly for two years, and seemed both to be anticipating the season of autumn, and to be saying something about their relationship coming to a close.

(g) 'I had a very interesting dream last night.' An attempt to hold the counsellor's interest either at the time, or over the next week until they meet again.

(h) 'Here's a Christmas present for you. See you in the New Year.' With this particular client, the gift felt like a way of ensuring that she would not be forgotten over the break, but it could also have been an attempt to be kind to the counsellor when the client actually felt angry at being left over the long Christmas break. The question of handling such gifts is, of course, another issue, which this exercise does not look at.

(i) 'I think I'll stop there and leave early, if you don't mind.' Like most of these phrases this one could have many meanings, although in this instance the client was afraid of being rejected, and always finished the counselling session himself, rather than feel hurt lest the counsellor should say (which she never got a chance to) that it was time to finish.

(j) 'God! What a pathetic session!' This might have been a reference to the work by the counsellor, but it seemed more to refer to the client and how she felt she had wasted her time. In fact she had spent much of it complaining justifiably about things which she normally felt she shouldn't complain about, so the session was only pathetic to her 'be quiet and don't complain' side!

Exercise 2.6: Continued

(k) 'Is it all right if I bring my friend with me next week?' This client found it very difficult to talk about himself, and wanted his friend to do the talking. He was very dependent upon his friend; and although at the time these words were said they were not homosexual partners, they later became so. The question of seeing the other person as well obviously depends to some extent on the nature of the relationship between the client and the third person.

(l) 'Is it a trouble for you to see me?' The counsellor had a cold, and this may have elicited the remark; but this client had talked in the session of not having lived anywhere for more than a few months at a time. She also easily became defensive, and denied anything that might prove to be a painful insight. So while she may have seen herself as troubling for the counsellor, perhaps the client was more 'troubled' about what counselling would do to her.

Exercise 2.7: Transference, counter-transference and projections

Purpose

This exercise introduces counsellors to the difference between real perceptions and those which arise from projection, transference and counter-transference. It also helps counsellors look at their own self-perceptions, and the perceptions they think others have of them; and to check the accuracy of their own perceptions of others. Furthermore, it has the potential for considerably opening up the feelings and preconceptions which members of the training group have about each other.

Duration

30 minutes to 1 hour, depending on the amount of time needed for introduction and debriefing.

Worksheet for Exercise 2.7: Transference, counter-transference and projections

Stage 1 In this column draw up a list of ways you tend to be seen by people who do not know you well or at all, whether in your public role or as a private individual. It does not matter if some are contradictions: include them all whether or not people are right to see you in any of these ways:	*Stage 2* Now tick any of these statements which are in your view accurate perceptions of you; put a cross by any which you think are inaccurate; and a question-mark by any where you are not sure. Finally, add in any spaces left ways you would describe your real self, if not already included in column 1.	*Stage 3* Mix with the rest of the group, asking people one at a time for their first impressions of you – tick in column 3a where you have already listed these in columns 1 or 2, or add them as statements in column 1. Then ask them for their considered impressions of you and tick them in column 3b, or add in column 2.	
		3a	3b

Exercise 2.7: Continued

Method

The exercise uses a form of self-analysis, which is then checked with the perceptions of other members of the group.

Materials

Worksheets for each student, as the sample on page 56:

Instructions

1 The exercise is best prefaced with an explanation of the value of using the relationship between client and counsellor, as a way of understanding aspects of the client's relationships, past and present; and of the difference between transference and projection.
2 Explain also that by understanding how others normally perceive them, counsellors are in a better position to judge the reality or the transferential aspects of a client's perceptions of the therapist. The exercise also helps them look at how perceptive they themselves are of themselves and of others.
3 Hand out the worksheet, and take the students through it, column by column, using the instructions on the worksheet itself. Enough time needs to be allowed for each stage to be satisfactorily completed, the first two alone, the third by mixing with the others in the class. Encourage people to be really honest with each other. The exercise works best in a group where members have got to know and trust one another well.
4 Encourage participants to mix, to meet with others in the class they know and do not know, and to get as many perceptions as they can from others.
5 When the exercise has provided an opportunity for participants to meet and talk with several others, move on to debriefing in small, familiar groups.

Debriefing

Allow plenty of time for discussion following the exercise, particularly looking for people who may be distressed by others' perceptions of them. This exercise, at its best, encourages students to be open with each other about how they perceive each other. While most students are careful how they phrase their comments, some of those who receive comments may feel criticized or hurt. It is, therefore, important that participants in this exercise have the chance to reflect, with people with whom they

Exercise 2.7: Continued

feel comfortable, upon where the exercise has left them, as well as upon the central learning points about transference, counter-transference and projection.

Comment

Some of the examples in Exercise 2.6 (such as the leaves on the tree beginning to turn) demonstrate what is technically known as *displacement*: the client refers to a situation outside therapy which reflects upon the relationship within therapy. It is useful to draw a distinction between displacement (too often called 'transference') and transference proper, where a former or existing relationship outside therapy is transferred at least in some respects on to the therapist.

The psychodynamic model of counselling and therapy, true to its analytic roots, suggests four aspects of that relationship: the working relationship, the real relationship of two people who are essentially equal in their humanity and vulnerability, the transference by the client of former styles of relationships on to the counselling relationship, and the same process in the counsellor, which is called counter-transference. Clients and counsellors can also project unacceptable aspects of themselves on to others, or on to each other, which may or may not be different from transference perceptions.

For other aspects of the therapeutic relationship, see also Exercise 9.1, which illustrates styles of relating at different developmental stages and in various settings in adult life. It contains aspects of transference and counter-transference within it, which could be more explicitly explored if used in connection with this aspect of psychodynamic theory. The final exercise in this manual, in Chapter 11, illustrates the importance both of the therapeutic relationship, and of the use of transference and counter-transference, in highlighting the major issues present in the client's relationship to himself and others.

3

Working in and working with groups

Introduction

There are special skills necessary for facilitating therapy groups, but some of these same skills are just as necessary in other types of group, such as those often used for discussion and feedback in training courses. There are many management training exercises available, often of the 'survival' type, in which a group has to decide what items it would need to survive if stranded in the Arctic or on the moon. However, the following exercises make more obvious use of the actual situation in which small discussion or therapy groups can find themselves. There are other exercises in later chapters which also provide experience in groupwork or group relationships, but the three main exercises in this chapter (3.1.1, 3.2 and 3.3) provide very different experiences of taking responsibility within small groups, and, in the case of the third exercise, of coping with larger leaderless groups as well.[1]

Exercise 3.1.1: Facilitating groups

Purpose

To provide practice in facilitating small groups, including the handling of different types of group behaviour which can prevent groups from fulfilling their task.

Duration

2 hours.

Method

In groups of six or seven members, each person has an opportunity to facilitate a small group for about ten minutes, and to experience, experiment and work with some of the difficulties that arise in groups. Some of these difficulties are built into the exercise by asking group members to take on roles which deliberately tax the skill of the person facilitating the group at the time.

Materials

Each participant in each small group is given a numbered label (1–7) which matches the number of the mini session she or he will facilitate, and a briefing sheet outlining her or his role in each session. The briefing sheet for Facilitator 1 is given below (i). Note that there are four key phrases marked [A], [B], [C] and [D]: these must be replaced in the briefing sheets for Facilitators 2–7 according to the scheme in (ii). For groups of five members, see (iii).

(i) Facilitating groups: Facilitator 1

You have been divided into small groups. First read these instructions through carefully, and ask the tutor if you do not understand anything.

1 During the period of this exercise, each person will have a turn in leading or facilitating the small group.

[A] Your turn is in mini-session 1.

Exercise 3.1.1: Continued

2 When you introduce the session allocated to you, you need to announce the topic for discussion to the group. In your session the topic is:

[B] Introductions if people do not know each other, and feelings about doing this exercise.

3 Lead the group in the way you are used to. Of course, if you feel the discussion is going well, you may not need to intervene at all.
4 In each mini session there are one or two people who have been briefed to be 'flies in the ointment'. They have been asked, for that particular session, to display a particular facet of individual behaviour in groups. As group facilitator you need to spot the flies, and deal with them in the most helpful and unobtrusive way, so that the group continues to function well.
5 You will yourself have a turn at being a 'fly in the ointment'.

[C] This will be in mini session 3.

In that session you are asked to:

[D] Look distracted or bored, looking away or down, not at all interested in the group.

6 During the sessions when you are neither group leader nor a 'fly', try to be yourself, as you are in any group, and treat the group as you would any other of which you are a member.
7 The tutor(s) will keep time, and call the beginnings of the next mini session. Following the exercise there will be a chance to relax, and to debrief on how you felt as facilitator, as 'fly' and as a member of the group; you will also be able to comment on how you saw others in the group in their various roles.

(ii) Briefings for facilitators 2–7:

The inserts [A], [B], [C] and [D] for each facilitator are as follows:

Facilitator 2

[A] Your turn is in mini session 2.

[B] The advantages and disadvantages of groupwork.

[C] This will be in mini session 5.

[D] Engage with the person who was facilitator no. 3 in an argument or discussion which excludes the rest of the group.

Exercise 3.1.1: Continued

Facilitator 3

[A] Your turn is in mini session 3.

[B] Some good and bad groups of which you have been a member.

[C] This will be in mini session 5.

[D] Engage with the person who was facilitator no. 2 in an argument of discussion which excludes the rest of the group.

Facilitator 4

[A] Your turn is in mini session 4.

[B] Some good and bad group leaders you have known.

[C] This will be in mini session 2.

[D] Try and get the group facilitator to talk as much as possible.

Facilitator 5

[A] Your turn is in mini session 5.

[B] What it is that makes a good group facilitator.

[C] This will be in mini session 6.

[D] Try to take over the leadership of the group from the designated facilitator.

Facilitator 6

[A] Your turn is in mini session 6.

[B] Our own weak spots in being in groups and in leading them.

[C] This will be in mini session 4.

[D] Try and get the group off the subject introduced and on to

Exercise 3.1.1: Continued

the one above, which you will eventually lead, without the group realizing what you are doing.

Facilitator 7

[A] Your turn is in mini session 7.

[B] Feelings in the group as the exercise comes to a close.

[C] This will be in mini session 3.

[D] Look distracted or bored, looking away or down, not at all interested in the group.

(iii)

Occasionally a set of five will be necessary, in which case the briefing details for facilitators 4 and 5 are as follows (1–3 are the same as above):

Facilitator 4 (group of 5)

[A] Your turn is in mini session 4.

[B] What it is that makes a good group facilitator.

[C] This will be in mini session 2.

[D] Try and get the group facilitator to talk as much as possible.

Facilitator 5 (group of 5)

[A] Your turn is in mini session 5.

[B] Our own weak spots in being in groups and in leading them.

[C] This will be in mini session 4.

[D] Try and get the group off the subject introduced and on to the one above, which you will eventually lead, without the group realizing what you are doing.

Exercise 3.1.1: Continued

Instructions

1 The small groups are set up with six or seven members in each. Occasionally the numbers will dictate the inclusion of a group of five. Each member of the group is given a numbered label (1–5, 1–6, or 1–7), and a briefing paper upon which the number of the session for facilitating matches the numbered label. It is best to distribute these at random around the group, rather than clockwise or anti-clockwise.
2 Point out that the general instructions for the whole exercise are the same for each person, but that the individual briefings differ in relation to the mini session each person leads, the topic they are to introduce, and their role in a second mini session, when they are asked to be 'the fly in the ointment'.
3 It is important to stress that the facilitator is not asked to point out the 'fly' but to *deal with* that person as they might in any group, in a tactful but effective manner.
4 The tutor keeps the time for each mini session, which is twelve minutes in the case of groups of six, or ten minutes for each mini-session in groups of seven. If there are two tutors, one can keep the time of mini-sessions for the groups of six, and the other for the groups of seven. In instances where groups of five are used allow fourteen minutes for each mini session. By keeping to these times all groups, whatever their size, will start and finish at nearly the same moment.

Debriefing

Following the exercise, groups need the remaining time first to relax and then to debrief, reflecting upon the way in which each person facilitated the group, as well as how people felt playing the 'fly in the ointment'. Exercise 3.1.2 below (the questionnaire on types of group membership) can be handed out for 'homework' and scored at a later session, allowing further space then for discussion on personal behaviour in groups, as well as some of the principles of group facilitating.

Comment

This exercise is complicated to prepare, but if well prepared with individual briefing sheets as indicated above, it is easy to set up. Bear in mind that other people will become 'flies in the ointment' without realizing it – since they in some way exhibit these or other types of behaviour in groups without the need to be briefed to do so!

Exercise 3.1.2: Self-perception inventory on group roles

Purpose

To provide a means of reflecting upon personal styles of group membership, and to provide a means of debriefing group exercises.

Duration

The questionnaire itself can be completed beforehand outside the session. If it is completed in a session it takes about 15 minutes. Subsequent scoring and discussion of the results can take anything from 30 minutes to 1 hour.

Method

Students complete a self-perception inventory, in their own time or in the session; and they are then instructed in scoring it, and provided with a key to their scores. The inventory provides a way in to discussing individual roles and behaviours in groups.

Materials

One each of the following items for each student:

(i) Groupwork – self-perception inventory

Within each separate section distribute ten points among the sentences you think best describe your behaviour in groups. These points may be distributed among several sentences; in extreme cases they might be spread among all the sentences; or all ten points can be given to a single sentence. You will score this exercise at a later session.

Section I: *What I believe I can contribute in a group*

(a) I can respond quickly to other individuals who have something interesting to say.
(b) I can get on with a wide range of people.
(c) Producing ideas is one of my natural assets.

I	
a	
b	
c	

Exercise 3.1.2: Continued

(d) I can draw people out when I see they have something of value to contribute to the group.	d	
(e) I have the capacity to help the group follow through its task.	e	
(f) I am ready to face temporary unpopularity if it leads to something worthwhile in the end.	f	
(g) I can usually sense what is relevant and likely to be of value.	g	
(h) I can offer a reasonable case for alternative ways of thinking without introducing bias or prejudice.	h	
Section II: *If I have a possible shortcoming in groupwork, it could be that:*	II	
(a) I am not at ease unless groups are well structured and controlled and generally well conducted.	a	
(b) I am inclined to be too generous towards those who have a valid viewpoint that has not been given a proper airing.	b	
(c) I have a tendency to talk too much.	c	
(d) My reticence makes it difficult for me to share readily in the feelings that other group members express.	d	
(e) I am sometimes seen as forceful and authoritarian.	e	
(f) I find it difficult to lead from the front, perhaps because I am over-responsive to group atmosphere.	f	
(g) I am apt to get too caught up in ideas that occur to me and so lose track of what is happening.	g	
(h) Others see me as worrying unnecessarily over detail.	h	
Section III: *When involved in a group with other people:*	III	
(a) I am good at influencing people without pressurizing them.	a	
(b) My general vigilance prevents careless conclusions or significant omissions being accepted.	b	
(c) I am ready to press to make sure that the group does not waste time or lose sight of the main task.	c	
(d) I can be counted on to contribute something original.	d	
(e) I am always ready to back a good suggestion in the common interest.	e	
(f) I am keen to look out for those who have new ideas and insights.	f	
(g) I believe my capacity for judgement can help bring about the right conclusions.	g	

Exercise 3.1.2: Continued

(h) I can be relied upon to see that the essential task is carried out.

h	

Section IV: *My characteristic approach to group work is that:*

(a) I have a quiet interest in getting to know others better.
(b) I am not reluctant to challenge the views of others or to hold a minority view myself.
(c) I can usually find a line of argument to refute unsound propositions.
(d) I think I have a talent for getting things done once people agree on the task.
(e) I have a tendency to ignore others' contributions and to come out with the unexpected.
(f) I bring a touch of perfectionism to my contributions to the group.
(g) I am ready to make use of the experience of like-minded individuals in the group.
(h) I am interested in all views, but I have no hesitation in making up my mind when I've heard what others have to say.

IV	
a	
b	
c	
d	
e	
f	
g	
h	

Section V: *I gain satisfaction in a group because:*

(a) I enjoy analysing problems and weighing up all the possible choices.
(b) I am interested in finding practical solutions to problems.
(c) I like to feel I am fostering good relations.
(d) I can have a strong influence on the discussion.
(e) I get on well with people who are ready to express themselves in the group.
(f) I can get people to agree.
(g) I feel in my element where I can give a task my full attention.
(h) I like to find a subject that stretches my mind.

V	
a	
b	
c	
d	
e	
f	
g	
h	

Section VI: *If I am suddenly given a difficult task with limited time and unfamiliar people:*

(a) I feel like retiring to a corner to devise a way out of the impasse before putting my ideas to the group.
(b) I prefer to work with the person who shows the most positive approach.

VI	
a	
b	

Exercise 3.1.2: Continued

(c) I find some way of reducing the size of the problem by establishing what different individuals might best contribute.

(d) My natural sense of urgency helps to ensure we clarify the task.

(e) I keep cool and maintain my capacity to think straight.

(f) I retain a steadiness of purpose in spite of pressure.

(g) I am prepared to take a positive lead if I feel the group is making no progress.

(h) I open up the issues with someone who might stimulate thoughts and get things moving.

c	
d	
e	
f	
g	
h	

Section VII: *Amongst the problems I have in working in groups are:*

(a) I tend to show my impatience with those who are obstructing progress.

(b) Others may criticize me for being too analytical and insufficiently intuitive.

(c) My desire to ensure terms are properly defined can hold up proceedings.

(d) I tend to get bored rather easily and rely on one or two stimulating members to spark me off.

(e) I find it difficult to get involved unless the goals are clear.

(f) I am sometimes poor at explaining and clarifying complex points that occur to me.

(g) I expect from others the things I cannot give myself.

(h) I hesitate to get my points across when I run up against real opposition.

VII	
a	
b	
c	
d	
e	
f	
g	
h	

(ii) Self-perception Inventory Analysis Sheet

Enter the scores in each separate section of the Self-perception Inventory on the table below. For example, if in Section I you scored yourself 5 for (a), 3 for (d) and 1 each for (f) and (h), enter each of these scores in the first row 'I', on the right of each letter, and '0' for the remaining unscored letters in the row. When you have completed entering all seven sections add up the points in each column, to give a total group-role distribution score. Your high scores appear to indicate that you are a particular type of group participant. The initials stand for these types; you will be given a description of these when you have completed this table.

Exercise 3.1.2: Continued

Exercise 3.1.2: Self-perception inventory analysis

Section	*PP*		*GF*		*DL*		*II*		*PC*		*GM*		*PM*		*GL*	
I	g		d		f		c		a		h		b		e	
II	a		b		e		g		c		d		f		h	
III	h		a		c		d		f		g		e		b	
IV	d		h		b		e		g		c		a		f	
V	b		f		d		h		e		a		c		g	
VI	f		c		g		a		h		e		b		d	
VII	e		g		a		f		d		b		h		c	
Totals																

(iii) Some types of group member

PP = practical person
Good at helping the group to get things done, especially if the task has a practical outcome. Looks for what will work rather than at ideas, especially if the ideas seem disconnected from the real issues. In fact probably prefers to be getting on and doing things rather than sitting around discussing them, and tends not to see the finer points about issues.

GF = group facilitator
Welcomes all potential contributions on their merits without prejudice, and has a good sense of what a group can achieve. Is able to control the discussion sensitively, and enjoys being able to promote group discussion. Feels confident in groups. But is probably not so good at contributing creative ideas as an individual, although can enable others to do so.

Exercise 3.1.2: Continued

DL = dominant leader
Shows a lot of drive and initiative; is dynamic, outgoing, and ready to challenge ineffectiveness, complacency, and inertia in the group. Is however prone to getting impatient with others, and can be pushed into either a dominating position because of her or his dynamism, or can be pushed into a minority, scapegoat position.

II = individual idealist
A potential genius, who has bright ideas in the group, but would perhaps prefer really to be thinking things out on her or his own, for which she or he is well suited. Tends to put ideas into the group without seeing where they fit, or whether others understand them; and can get bored with others' contributions. Is not so good at learning from others.

PC = pairing contributor
Has a capacity for making contact with others in the group and exploring new issues with them, but this tends to lead to communicating with one or two others, and excluding the others in the group. An enthusiastic member of the group, but one who can be left by others to keep the discussion going with another pairing contributor; and may even lose interest if too many people seem to be joining in.

GM = group mediator
Good at evaluating ideas and helping the group find a reasoned solution, which takes account of the different things that people have said; but less strong on group facilitating or motivating others, and less able to appreciate other people's or own feelings, tending to prefer head to heart.

PM = peacemaker
Tends to be one of the quieter members of the group, although actually very responsive to others, and helps them feel someone is interested in them. May at times be afraid of speaking out, especially if what she or he wants to say is likely to be thought of as contentious; and doesn't like too much conflict in the group. Is able to promote group harmony, although if too quiet, people may distrust the silent observer she or he sometimes becomes.

GL = group lawyer
Has the capacity to help a group to follow through its task in an efficient way, although tends to concentrate upon getting the thinking right, and can frustrate the practically minded or the intuitive members. Not so good at showing feelings, or in facilitating can't allow others to show feelings which hold up the task of the group.

Exercise 3.1.2: Continued

Conscientious, orders things well, makes people feel safe, although her or his perfectionism and tendency to worry about details and definitions may also annoy.

Instructions

1 On the completion of a group exercise, such as 3.1.1 above, provide each student with the Self-perception Inventory (i), with a reminder of the instructions for completing it, set out as at the head of the inventory.
2 At a later session, or when the inventory has been completed, hand out the Self-perception Inventory Analysis Sheet (ii).
3 When individuals have scored themselves, and have found the categories where they score highest (and lowest), distribute the descriptive sheet 'Some Types of Group Member' (iii).

Debriefing

Discussion in small groups will be valuable, especially to check out the accuracy of the Self-perception Inventory and its scores with other people's perceptions.

Comment

The inventory, scoring sheet, and handout on types of group member are adapted from, and heavily based on, Belbin's study of management teams, and are printed in this form with the author's permission.[2] Although Belbin uses the originals to identify the eight types of person who together can form a balanced and efficient management team with complementary attitudes, characteristics and team skills, much of what he has researched and analysed is of value in looking at the different types of membership seen in discussion groups or other similar groups. Used in this particular adapted form, the inventory has not been tested rigorously to see if it has any diagnostic or predictive value, but it does act as a trigger for self-analysis, discussion and potential personal insight. It is important to note that all these types of group member have an important contribution to make. There is no particular merit in being one sort rather than another; although some may find there are aspects of their behaviour in groups which they would wish to heighten or tone down.

Exercise 3.2: Gender composition in groups

Purpose

This exercise is designed to study how men and women function in single-gender and mixed groups, and how they experience varying ratios of men to women and women to men in mixed gender groups.

Duration

2–3 hours, depending on the size of the group.

Method

Starting with two single-gender groups in different rooms, one person from each changes places every ten minutes, until the groups completely change rooms. Each group is observed by members of the same gender at the start of the exercise, but since the observers stay in the same room, by the end of the exercise each single-gender group will be observed by members of the opposite gender.

Materials

There are no materials required, although two adjacent rooms are essential, and equal or near equal numbers of men and women are necessary for this exercise.

Instructions

1 The exercise requires roughly equal numbers of men and women, and at least six or seven of each. To describe the exercise, assume that a class has seven men and eight women. Form two equal size single-gender groups (in this case five men and five women) with observers (two men and three women). It is essential the groups are the same size, although the number of observers may slightly differ.
2 The single-gender groups meet in different rooms, with observers of the same gender present in the room – the men with the men, the women with the women, but sitting outside the group.
3 Explain the task of each group: to monitor its response to its changing

Exercise 3.2: Continued

composition. A subsidiary but vital task is also to decide who changes places when each mini session ends.

4 Two observers, one in each room, need to synchronize watches, and to call the start of the exercise and the end of each mini session. Each group starts on a period of discussion (in this case totalling one hour) divided into six mini sessions – always one more than the number in each small group.

5 After the first mini session of ten minutes one man and one woman from each group change places, making groups with four of one gender, and one of the other. After a further ten minutes another two change places, making groups of three and two.

6 And so the exercise goes on, until for the last mini session the groups have completely changed rooms – although the observers have not. The women's group now meets with two male observers, the men's group with three women observers. Not only does the gender of the observer(s) make for potential difference, but, of course, the men observers may view the all-women group differently from the way the women observers originally observed the same all-women group, and vice versa.

Debriefing

Following the end of the last mini session the groups can be split up (perhaps in mixed-gender pairs, with observers spread round the pairs) to discuss the experience, and to hear the observers' comments. An alternative is to get the women's group, the men's group, and all the observers to debrief in three separate groups. Whatever method is used, a plenary is essential to draw together and to compare and contrast the different observations and experiences, as perceived by the men, by the women and by the observers.

Comment

This simple but powerful exercise can throw up many different types of observation: the way in which the groups organize themselves, including decisions about who moves next; the way in which incoming members do or do not take part in such decisions; the seating and participation of the observers; the content of the discussion, and its inclusion or exclusion of feelings, depending on the composition of the groups at various times.

Exercise 3.3: Coping with the unexpected

Purpose

To provide a large-group experience of the issues of trust and dependency (Chapter 4), authority and autonomy (Chapter 5) and co-operation and competition (Chapter 6).

Duration

One 2-hour session, and a further hour's feedback a week later, with the option of at least a further 1½ hours for a video on a child's separation from his mother.

Method

The tutor fails to attend the major part of the session. Although the class has some warning of the session being unusual, the tutor's absence throws them back upon their own resources, and raises issues of authority and leadership, as well as feelings about being let down by the tutor.

Materials

Two briefing sheets. For most members of the group the briefing sheet is short and to the point: an A4 sheet for each person simply contains the words:

> This session is rather different. Some people have been asked to observe.

One in five members are given a coloured sheet (to distinguish them from ordinary members) as follows:

Observer's brief

One in every five of the class this session is being asked to act as an observer: these guidelines are to assist you carry out this function. The only definite guideline is not to allow anyone else (other than another observer) to read this actual paper.

You have a very important role to play in helping individuals, small groups, and indeed the whole class to reflect upon what is happening this session, and to learn from it. It may be valuable to share your observations with groups or the class as the session proceeds, although you may have to make a space for yourself to do this. You may

Exercise 3.3: Continued

share your observations with anyone else, individually, or as a small group, or with the whole class. To observe fully, it is probably best not to get too caught up in any actual activity which people choose to do, but to watch, and note, and share your observations either when asked or when you want to.

It will be very useful for evaluation of the session to make some notes, recording what happens as time passes (noting the time of your observations will help the collation of observers' reports).

The following questions are worth addressing, although other observations will occur to you:

How soon does the class catch on that something different is happening?
What fantasies or explanations are given?
What were the fantasies prior to the session of what might happen?
What feelings are shown or expressed by individuals or the class as a whole?
How are you treated as an observer?
What does being an observer do to you?
Does the mood change as time passes? What different feelings do you perceive?
How are these feelings expressed?
What is said or felt about the tutor(s)?
How does the class organize itself? Does it fragment, or stay together?
Is there much sign of co-operation, or competition?
What about practical matters like registers, coffee?
Does one individual take the initiative? Do others follow?
How are decisions arrived at?
How are you viewed as an authority figure, if at all?
How is conflict dealt with?
Do people want to learn from the observers?
Does anyone (other than observers) make links between what is happening to them and the various themes of trust and dependency; authority and autonomy; co-operation and competition; separation, change and loss?

Instructions

1 On my own courses this exercise takes place in the fifth week, as part of the theme 'trust and dependency' (see Chapter 4). It could be used at any time, although at such a point it suits the young age of the class but also allows for some sense of trust in the tutor to have been built up. This deeper sense of trust underpins the temporary testing of trust in the tutor which the exercise in some ways raises.

Exercise 3.3: Continued

2. It is important that the syllabus contains a reference to the session along these lines: 'Coping with the unexpected. Please note that you have been told of this beforehand.' The tutor must be careful at no time in the weeks prior to this exercise to refer to being present or absent that particular session. No references such as 'See you next week' or 'I can't see you then because I shall be away' should be made the week before. Anything that smacks of trickery or falsehood must be studiously avoided.
3. As the session in question begins an independent person is needed to stand by the entrance and hand out instruction sheets to class members as they arrive. Nearly everyone receives the simple instructions, on an otherwise blank piece of white paper, but one in five receive the coloured paper with the observer's brief.
4. About forty minutes before the end of a two-hour session the tutor enters the class. While it is impossible to predict what happens then, experience suggests that the tutor will be ignored and frozen out, except by a few individual students who may rush to make contact. The tutor is not in charge of this session, since he or she has already handed over responsibility for it to the class as a whole. The tutor is therefore partly in the hands of the class, although he or she is also a free agent, and may choose how to react and respond to any request. What is important is that, two or three minutes before the session ends, the tutor conveys by speech (or via an overhead projector slide or blackboard message) that 'Next week we shall return to normal, and will review this exercise then. Please make notes on your experience, and bring them with you next time.'

Debriefing

The following week at least an hour can be spent getting feedback from individuals, from any small groups they may have formed, from the observers, and from the tutor(s), who fully share his or her own feelings and experience, both in their absence and when they returned to the class. A deeply relevant conclusion to the exercise is to show the Robertsons' film *Young Children in Brief Separation: John, Aged 17 Months, for 9 Days in a Residential Nursery.*[3] This takes three-quarters of an hour to view, and requires plenty of time for discussion in pairs following the viewing. The combination of the exercise, the feedback and the video is extremely powerful, and special care needs to be taken to follow up those who are either absent themselves, and/or obviously deeply moved, following these two sessions.

Exercise 3.3: Continued

Comment

This exercise deserves a word of explanation, as well as a full description of what can happen when it is used.

Its origin lay in my what I knew would be an unavoidable absence from teaching a class fairly early in the course; together with the memory of an American campus chaplain way back in the 1960s telling how the chaplains had deliberately not turned up to take a communion service, to see how students reacted to the loss of the only people authorized to conduct their most important service of the week. The learning on that occasion had been immense, and I decided that since I could not turn up (because I would be away) I would build this absence into the programme, to look at what happened to a group when the person they trusted, on whom to some extent they depended, who fed them with a course programme and who was a key authority figure for them, failed to appear.

I first did a trial run with a class the previous term, on an evening when I could have been present (and was contactable by phone), but chose not to be. The only hint that my absence was planned was in the syllabus. The subject for that week read: 'Coping with the unexpected. Please note that you have been told of this beforehand.' I needed to make it clear, without giving the game away, that my absence (as it dawned upon them) was deliberate, and not due to illness or an accident; and that normally I would not let them down without a similar sort of warning or prior information. Had the wording been clearer it could have taken away the element of surprise; but anything less could have involved too profound a rejection for a class to take, with the real risk of losing all their trust.

On that first occasion I stayed away for the whole session. In the feedback I realized that it was a mistake to carry the idea right through to the bitter end; that it would have been better to fulfil the hope that had been expressed throughout the evening that I would appear before they went home. While the feedback was valuable, and much was learned from it, a whole session's absence was just too much, and put the value of the exercise in danger.

As it turned out my 'unavoidable absence' in the autumn had to take place another week, so when I arranged this exercise the second time I was able to make my appearance in the session forty minutes before its end. I and other tutors have since repeated the exercise with subsequent classes, from which experience comes the composite account of the reaction of different groups.

I am aware of just how difficult it is for tutors to carry out this exercise. It is one of the most stressful sessions of the course, especially during the time they are absent from the class. Although it has been shown to be educationally effective, and in the end not damaging to class members, it is usual for tutors to feel deeply guilty at not

Exercise 3.3: Continued

appearing, and anxious about what will happen to individuals and the class as a whole. They worry about the exercise for the whole week before it and the week after it, too. But I am convinced that as long as the 'secret' does not get out to later courses (thereby spoiling the element of surprise) this exercise is one of the most significant of all the exercises in this book.

It has a number of very important effects. First, there is no doubt that on each occasion it has made the class come together and gel, partly because closeness is important in the face of adversity. Second, it is often referred back to at later points in a course on personal development, in which it is included. It clearly provides illustrations of a number of aspects in all the themes (referred to in the observers' notes in the last listed question). Third, the exercise provides clear insight and experiential understanding into how a child or a client can feel and how they can react, when let down by a significant adult, such as a parent or counsellor. Fourth, it provides a real piece of class 'history' if the feedback can be collated by the tutor and written up as an account of what happened. Finally, if the video *Young Children in Brief Separation* is shown after the debriefing in the subsequent session, it has an even more profound effect than usual for a film which clearly moves most of its viewers. The young child's feelings as he copes with the distress caused by an absent mother and lack of a constant substitute are all too well understood from the students' own experience of, and reactions to being let down.

The experience of running this exercise has already produced some valuable observations on the behaviour of individuals, small groups and the whole class in coming to terms with the absence of their tutor, and then with his or her return. The following account draws upon a number of 'histories' written up by the tutors after the feedback sessions following the exercise.

Even before the session, there is speculation about what 'coping with the unexpected' will mean. Fantasies include having to do a party piece, or having to perform something physical. Some women have wondered if whether they should have worn trousers. In another instance there was reference to the session being about touching. Others think they may have to dress up, or that the tutors will arrive in fancy dress, like Father Christmas, or (more sinister) as SS officers. Dress, touch, and having to perform physically (sexually?) seem to figure high in fantasies. On balance, if people have thought about it at all, they do not believe the tutor will make the class do anything too fearful. Nevertheless, there can be anxiety as the session approaches and a wish to get it over and done with. Traces of paranoia are already evident.

In one session the person who gave out the instruction papers said that the tutor's car had broken down. This was contrary to her own briefing to say nothing, and was obviously not true: perhaps her anxiety was so strong that she could not simply and silently give out the papers. Her obvious lie did the exercise little good, especially since

Exercise 3.3: Continued

many thought it came from the tutor. It took on an element of teasing in the minds of some, and anger with the tutor for being blatantly dishonest. It is obviously important that the 'messenger' does not get the blame, but also that he or she hands out the papers silently, refusing to be drawn into the anxiety of the occasion.

In the absence of any other structure, certain familiar routines can initially be followed, or even persist throughout the session. Pairs may form; someone will probably organize the coffee and the attendance register – these rituals provide an air of normality. If there are existing small groups they can sometimes form in their usual way, partly out of habit but partly also because they offer greater safety than the large anonymous group. There is, of course, no agenda; and observers may not join their own groups, so they are not the same as usual; but they can provide a semblance of getting down to work. There is often a fairly relaxed mood to begin with, even a feeling of being able to play while the parents are away, although this quickly gives rise to some signs of distress, sometimes as soon as within ten minutes of the start of the session. Having freedom, and being able to do anything, does not feel so good after all.

Early on there is realization that the tutor is deliberately absent, but this does not prevent groups acting strangely. One group searched cupboards, and turned on the video, in case the tutor was in hiding, or had left a message. Some wondered whether the tutors were under the table or behind the door. In another group two people searched the flip chart. Some thought they were being filmed or recorded by the tutors. One group thought a workman sent to repair a door was a spy sent by the tutor! There can be a general feeling of disorientation although at the same time a rational calmness, knowing that the absence is relevant and is intended to teach something. In one class some described themselves as feeling sick, or anxious about 'doing something'. Others felt rebellious, disappointed, bewildered, let down, frustrated, excited, or pleasantly apprehensive. One person who felt ill wondered why she had come at all. Some had not wanted to come, but had been drawn by curiosity as much as by fear of what the unexpected would entail.

In an early exercise the group greeted a stray visiting lecturer who had come into the wrong room as their tutor for the evening, convinced he had been sent by the course tutor; they allowed him to start talking about his subject ('Stress') before informing him he had come to the wrong group.

One or two students show greater individuality – either going home, in a few instances, or going to the coffee lounge. When the group takes a break it has been known for them to consume a lot of alcohol, quite unusual in the normal run of things. There is sometimes speculation as to when the tutor will arrive: surely he or she will come after a while? In fact, the way the exercise is arranged suggests that the tutors stay away just long enough to convince the members that they might not come at all.

Some small groups see the vacant session as an opportunity. Others are interested in

Exercise 3.3: Continued

trying to organize the class as a whole. There can be power struggles, especially if the class is a manageable size and can work as a whole.

The way the observers are treated is fascinating. Since in the courses I have run the observers have a pink instruction paper this tends to mark them out as different; they have even been called 'pink-sheeters' or 'pinkies', and may still be identified as such in later sessions of the course. The observers experience immediate isolation because of their role. They can be ignored, or confronted and challenged to show their papers (one of the few rules is that they are not permitted to do this). The observers can also be seen in some respect as representatives of the missing tutor (which of course they are inasmuch as they are invited to make the type of observations a tutor makes). They can be attacked, as the tutor would be attacked were he or she to arrive. They are rarely seen during the exercise as having a valuable contribution to make; it is often only in the feedback that they get a chance to share their perceptive and detailed observations.

But there is more to the observer role than this, because the observers sometimes invite isolation, rejection or being treated 'as a race apart', because they use the opportunity to make the role into one of a distant and somewhat teasing authority figure. They do not readily assist the group as they have been asked to, nor do all of them make any real attempt to try and help other group members see what is happening. Although they can take on the role of alternative tutors, they do this mainly as alien figures, and it may not therefore be surprising that the anger felt for the tutor gets heaped on to the observers. This in turn can make the observers as punitive in the way they withhold their observations as the tutor is perceived in withholding him or herself from the group for that session.

One observer felt she was treated as an authority figure by the group; important questions were addressed to her which the group could have addressed themselves. But even when some observers have tried to take concerted action (such as trying to get everyone together to discuss the session) people do not respond to them.

The observers have reported experiencing a feeling of anxiety about their power, and some pressure to record accurately. Occasionally an observer can feel cross at having to be an observer, because that prevents him or her from joining in fully. Others find it safer to have a definite role, and to have a certain degree of inside knowledge. This can also feel like collusion with the tutor. One observer felt that she was 'in on the secret' and therefore closer to the tutor than others in the group; but this also made her feel quite responsible. It was difficult, however, to raise issues as an observer, in case it was too confrontational.

Some groups express anger openly – with the observers, with the absent tutor, or with each other. Some are angry that the tutors are being paid and yet are not there. Some intellectualize their anger, saying that the experiment is 'silly'. In one small group the tutors were felt to be playing games with the class, so that they could get

Exercise 3.3: Continued

information with which to write another book and make more money! 'We want something from them' was the cry. In another class, when everyone had gone to the lounge for coffee, one member came in and said 'He's back'. This caused some students to return to the room in order to find the tutor, only to find they had been hoaxed: written on the blackboard in giant letters was the word 'GOTCHA!'. When this happened some realized how easily vandalism and graffiti could occur when people were let down, frustrated and bored.

Contrary to the fantasies of some members of the class, that the tutors are having a good time, drinking coffee and sitting around doing nothing, the truth is that the absent tutors feel very anxious, and may even wonder why they agreed to the teach the course at all. Two tutors arrived outside the building where they were teaching and sat nervously in the car. They felt concerned for different reasons: one whether the class was doing anything, the other that it had been unfair to leave them. One tutor who arrived slightly earlier than the other and waited outside the building, was convinced that her fellow tutor was not going to turn up at all, but would leave her to carry the can. She would be let down in turn.

In fact, by this time there is often a great deal of hard work taking place in the class. The initial bemusement, anger or lack of organization gives way to different-sized groupings, where some earnest discussion can take place. One small group got to know each other better that session than they had throughout their first year. Another was able to help one of their number with a difficult personal problem. One large group struggled creatively, unafraid of disagreement and conflict, with what was happening to them, trying to make sense of it as well as to go on experiencing it. Only occasionally are there feelings of collapse, strain, defeat, and having to make a fresh start.

Nevertheless, hard work though there may be, some of it is a defence against some underlying feelings, which show themselves once more when the tutor arrives in the room. By the time the tutor arrives the group or groups may look highly organized, and indeed in some ways they are. They can make (and probably intend to make) the tutors feel superfluous when they appear. In one instance a class of sixteen students had formed themselves into the tightest circle imaginable, their knees almost touching, making it impossible for the tutor to enter the circle and join them when he entered the room. He was ignored by most of the students for the rest of the session, except by one who wanted the tutor to be allowed to join the group. Only at the end did the group relax its defensiveness when one member said she was tired and wanted to go home – the tone of her voice was plaintive, and she felt like a tired little child admitting defeat. At this the group visibly relaxed, half turned to the tutor, and allowed him to speak.

In another session two tutors arriving together were greeted by one person with the words 'Look! Mummy and Daddy have come back!', although the rest of the large

Exercise 3.3: Continued

class did not seem to want to know. In some people there are feelings of relief as the tutor arrives, but others expérience resentment; the tutor can even be seen as intruding, and returning to take over power. Some expressed the thought 'Who cares?' as the tutors returned, perhaps also hinting that they are not convinced that the tutors care enough, otherwise they would not have deserted the group. Some are quite aware of how much they exclude the tutors after their arrival; in one exercise a small group felt particularly anxious whether the tutor was all right. The tutor, who felt dreadful at having deserted the group, really appreciated the concern shown her by this group, not realizing that she looked as bad as she felt.

Some groups feel very uncomfortable with the tutors back, and rebellious against the returning authority who has abandoned them. Tit-for-tat games are not unusual. Sometimes a group will rarely look at the tutor, although they are animated and working hard. It makes one wonder whether they are trying to put on a show of not caring, or of working very hard as a way of excluding them. Groups have expressed some disappointment that the tutors have returned, since this threatens the responsibility they have established for themselves. Left to themselves, one large class, almost without a word being said, formed into a large circle, and started to take their own feedback on the exercise. But in another instance the arrival of the tutors was the signal for the observers to rush up and ask permission to debrief the exercise. They appeared to feel put out when they were told they could do what they liked. In that case their efforts to organize the students into a plenary group failed.

When the exercise finishes, with the tutors indicating that everything will return to normal the next week, there can be signs of evident tiredness. The session is a strain for students, observers and tutors. Some students stay on, talking about the session for a long while. Others indicate in their notes that there was a lot more going on in them as they went home, and as they went to sleep; the session stirs up many different types of feeling and experience, both negative and positive, which are underlined by the feedback and by the moving film of John's separation from his mother.

4

Trust and dependency

Introduction

In this and the following chapters the emphasis in the experiential exercises largely shifts from practice of technical skills to the acquisition of insight, through experience of the situations, thoughts and feelings which arise in the course of human development. In many cases the situations in the exercises have an imaginative quality to them, designed to engender experiences of different kinds, and then, through debriefing and discussion, to assist the relating of these experiences to actual life events.

This and the next two chapters concentrate upon three major themes which appear time and again, sometimes singly, but more often in various combinations, in every counselling or therapy session: trust and dependency, autonomy and authority, and co-operation and competition. My book *The Presenting Past*[1] concentrates upon these three themes, relating them (as psychodynamic writing does) to the first three stages of human development. Since that book was written some years ago, and my own thinking has clarified further since it was published, I briefly amplify the significance of these themes and their relationship to developmental stages as an introduction to the various exercises that follow.

The model upon which the themes were originally based is that set out by Erikson[2] in what he calls 'The Eight Ages of Man' (*sic*). It needs to be said that Erikson, as might be expected of his generation, presents a male-dominated model, not only obviously formulated by a man, but also largely emphasizing the male perspective. It is certainly open to criticism on that score in a way which is not fully acknowledged in my book. The model's other drawback is one which I touch upon in *The Presenting Past*,[3] but one I see even more clearly now. Models can be taken literally. The 'Eight Ages' can become compartments; trust and dependency, the key concepts in the first stage of child development, are in danger of being seen as achieved or not achieved once and for all in the first year of life. Trust and dependency in later stages, whether experienced positively or negatively, reflect the experience of the earliest stage, but cease to be contemporary issues.

Such a use of the model is over-simplified, and not at all what Erikson intended. Erikson writes of the misuses of his whole conception which must 'be avoided. Among them is the assumption that the sense of trust (and all the other "positive" senses postulated) is an *achievement*, secured once and for all at a given state'.[4] It is tempting, faced with the complexities of understanding human development, to compartmentalize trust and to confine it to the oral stage. Yet there is already a precedent in the Erikson model for including trust as an issue in adolescence and in old age. Erikson writes of identity (the issue he isolates as belonging to adolescent development) as 'accrued confidence [in] inner sameness and continuity of one's meaning for others'.[5] And of old age he writes of 'the relation of adult integrity and infantile trust'.[6] Both references are clear indications of the relationship between different stages as well as between different generations.

I believe it is important to state much more forcibly than I do in *The Presenting Past* that the value of any model of stages of human development is to provide a series of pegs upon which to hook understanding and insight. To my mind the appendices[7] in that book illustrate most vividly, in a way which I have only a slight wish to change, how the themes (trust and dependency, autonomy and authority issues, and what I would prefer now to call co-operation and competition issues rather than social and rivalry issues) are clusters (complexes in the original use of the term). They are essentially convenient ways of grouping ways of identifying and understanding styles of relating, types of behaviour and patterns of thinking and feeling. Issues of trust and dependency occur at every point in life, from the oral stage onwards. Issues of autonomy and authority occur similarly at every turn, although more obviously from the anal stage onwards: the issue of autonomy in relation to early infancy is more difficult to conceptualize, although I guess that it is in many ways just as present in the feelings engendered when the baby wants attention, and the nurturing figure wants some peace and quiet. Similarly, issues of co-operation and competition arise at every moment of development, primarily from the time when the child begins to relate to more than one other person, but already with clear signs of them in the younger child, and, if Klein's work on envy is accepted, even at the breast.[8]

It is essential to come to understand that such terminology, about stages, about oral, anal and genital development, about trust and dependency, autonomy and authority, co-operation and competition, is more valuable as metaphor than when taken literally. These phrases help us to make sense of human experience, in babies and young children, in older children, in adolescents and in adults. The purpose of the exercises that follow is primarily to provide moments of insight into how such issues and themes can be and are experienced both in childhood and in adult life. The exercises are designed in one way to illustrate some of the matters raised in the literature on human development. But since the literature tends to convey only intellectual knowledge, perhaps the exercises also complement the reading, and provide the possibility of those moments of insight which are so essential for the training of counsellors and therapists.

Exercise 4.1: Fancy meeting you!

Purpose

To provide an understanding of the unconscious processes at work in relationships, particularly in the coming together of people in close relationships, and in the influence of one generation upon another. The exercise also acts as a very effective ice-breaker for experienced students starting on an advanced-level course.

Duration

1 hour.

Method

Participants are invited to pair up with someone who reminds them of a member of their family of origin, or who fills a gap in the family of origin; then pairs are invited to join in fours on the same basis. By comparing notes concerning their family backgrounds they often discover they have things in common which the other fours do not.

Materials

The exercise is found in *Families and How to Survive Them* by Skynner and Cleese.[9]

Exercise 4.1: Continued

Instructions

For obvious copyright reasons I refer the reader to the original exercise in *Families and How to Survive Them*.

Debriefing

Once the groups of four have drawn up a list of aspects of their family background which all four members have in common, feedback consists of reporting these features, one group at a time. An important additional feature of feedback, not mentioned in the original, is checking out how many other people in the rest of the larger group share the particular feature mentioned (e.g. 'We have all lived abroad at some time'). The exercise works best when it can be shown that in addition to finding something all four have in common (not in itself unlikely) that feature is not actually true of others in the room, or if it is, only in isolated examples; or, as sometimes happens, in three or four members of another small group, who discover they also have this in common, even though it did not occur to them in their discussion.

Comment

The conclusions from this exercise cannot be pressed too far. Some similarities are to be expected, and some may be rather contrived. Nevertheless, remarkable aspects occur. Skynner mentions the 'wallflowers', those who are last to choose partners and are forced into choices, and their backgrounds reflecting this 'left out' quality. Just as dramatic, although apparently ordinary, was one group which found they had in common that they came from families where they were one of two children. The tutor was tempted to dismiss this finding as so common as not to be worth checking out with the other groups. To his amazement, and that of the class, only two isolated members in other groups also had this family background. The few 'conventional-size family' members had found each other!

Exercise 4.2: Family trees

Purpose

To introduce students to the significance of the past, including past generations, and of family history, in the formation of character and in personal development. The exercise is also a good ice-breaker for a new group of experienced students who are comfortable with talking about themselves and their backgrounds.

Duration

Up to 2 hours.

Method

Where possible participants are asked to do some research into their family trees; they are given time to draw their own family tree, and then find a partner with whom to describe and discuss it. The exercise is finished in small groups in which the feelings evoked by the exercise can be shared and supported.

Materials

Participants will need pen and paper. To preface the exercise the tutor may wish to introduce a family tree or genogram of her or his own family, or of a client's family, on a hand-out or overhead projector slide.

Instructions

1 Where possible give students the week before the session to research their own family tree, particularly concentrating upon relationships between family members, and the patterns that tend to repeat in families.
2 Use a personal family tree, or a client's family tree, or demonstrate the use of genograms in family therapy as an introduction to the exercise.[10]
3 Students are given time to draw their family trees and, as they finish, to look around for someone else to work with in a pair, explaining to each other something of their family and personal histories. This part of the exercise may require more than an hour, since students on an advanced course frequently enter deeply into their histories with each other.

Exercise 4.2: Continued

Debriefing

Before the end of the session, provide at least half an hour for pairs to come together, or other small groups to form, in which the participants can share how the exercise has made them feel, and where it leaves them at the end.

Comment

Together with Exercise 4.1, this one creates an awareness of the significance of the past, of its relevance in the present, and of the importance of unconscious patterns in different generations and successive stages of life, and sets the scene for exploration of the issues of trust and dependency.[11]

Exercise 4.3: Learning about trust

Purpose

To simulate the experience of the very young baby in the gradual extension of its world and its dependency upon the nurturing parent, and to provide a metaphor of the trust relationship between client and counsellor.

Duration

1 hour.

Method

Students are guided through a series of movements alone and with each other, experiencing particularly their sense of the importance of touch and their ability (or lack of it) to trust another person, in pairs and in small groups.

Exercise 4.3: Continued

Materials

Taped music (such as Vaughan Williams's *The Lark Ascending*) is a valuable background to the first seven stages of the exercise.

Instructions

The following series of instructions (which speak for themselves) are slowly and calmly conveyed to the group members, who ideally need to have been forewarned to wear comfortable clothing:

1 Find a space in the room where you are free from contact with others. Lie down on the floor, roll yourself into a tight ball, and close your eyes. Keep your eyes closed throughout, until I tell you to open them. Spend some time in silence exploring what this tightly closed up world feels like, inside yourself.
2 Now gradually unroll; and staying lying down slowly begin to experience the space immediately with your arms and legs – if you touch anyone else, just draw gently back.
3 Now slowly rise to your feet, keeping your eyes closed the whole time; stay on the same spot but begin to feel space upwards and around you too. Again if you touch someone else, just gently withdraw from contact.
4 As you feel ready, and still with your eyes close, begin to move away from your spot, and slowly explore this new experience, as you move around the room. If you meet anyone else, just gently pass them by and move on.
5 The next time you touch someone, still keeping your eyes closed, I want you to form a pair; and with your eyes closed, without speaking to one another, and without any need for embarrassment, get to know each other through the feel of their face and head, and of their hands, gently finding out about the other person with whom you are standing.
6 Still with your eyes closed, and without saying anything in words, decide which of you is to be the first leader. Now the leader can open her or his eyes, and lead the other partner, still with her or his eyes closed, around the room. Try and give your partner as varied a group of experiences as possible; for example, feeling different textures and objects.
7 Now, first leader, close your eyes; and the person who has been led, open yours, and guide your partner round the room – introducing her or him to different experiences, too.
8 Now you can both open your eyes; sit down somewhere comfortable and share with each other how this exercise has felt.

Exercise 4.3: Continued

Following a period of feedback in pairs, the instructions continue:

9 Now I want the pairs to form into sixes (eights), and for one person to take the lead, while everyone else in the small group once more closes their eyes. Form a human chain; the leader, with eyes open, will lead you round the room – and outside the room, too. (It is valuable for the group to be led through doors, up or down stairs, round large objects, in light or dark, warm or cold atmospheres – keeping their eyes closed throughout.)

Debriefing

When the groups return to the room, they open their eyes, and share with each other how this part of the exercise felt. They are then asked to discuss what they have learned from the whole exercise about:

(a) experiences of trust or lack of trust which a baby or child might have in relation to the 'world'/mother/parents/adults;
(b) issues and problems about trust in the context of counselling and therapy.

Comment

This exercise provides an opportunity to create and experience a sense of trust in the group. It is equally valuable in providing some insight into the slowly awakening consciousness of the baby, and the enormous importance of a safe relationship with someone who can be completely trusted, and who is utterly dependable. The parallel of this early relationship with the sense of trust and dependability created for the client by the counsellor is obvious.

Exercise 4.4: Many selves, my self

Purpose

To initiate thinking about the inner world, and the different 'parts' of the personality; with an opportunity to compare and contrast how this is variously described in different psychodynamic theories.

Duration

45 minutes.

Method

Self-reflection, brief analysis of some theoretical concepts, and discussion.

Materials

A briefing sheet for each student as follows:

Who or what is 'the self'?

1 In small groups make a list of as many expressions as you can think of which illustrates the different aspects of 'self'. For example:
 I don't know what came over me'
 'I wasn't myself'
 'I was so angry with myself'
 'I am my old self again'
2 Different psychological theories speak of these parts of the self in various technical terms. For example:
 ego/id/superego [or I/It/over-I] (Freud)
 ego/persona/shadow/Self (Jung)
 internal objects such as the good object or the persecutory object (Klein)
 parent/adult/child (Berne and TA)
 true self/false self (Winnicott)
 central experiencing ego/libidinal ego/anti-libidinal ego (Fairbairn)

Exercise 4.4: Continued

In some instances each of these parts of the self are described as having both conscious and unconscious aspects.

Without necessarily using technical terms, analyse some of the phrases you have already listed. How many 'parts' of the personality or 'the self' do you think there might be?

Discuss this in your small group.

3 For these last questions you can stay as a small group or split into twos or threes:

Who or what is the real you? Discuss this without going into your innermost secrets.

Is there an inner self which is distinct from all the different external influences there have been upon you throughout your life?

How, if at all, would you distinguish the real you from your total personality?

Instructions

Introduce the briefing sheet to small groups. The main task of the tutor is to move the groups through the various parts of the exercise.

Debriefing

Feedback can be taken after any of the sections of the exercise.

Comment

The argument for placing this exercise where it is linked to an early developmental stage is that it appears that a baby has only a dimly formed sense of self, or what is sometimes called a *primitive ego*. While not quite the *tabula rasa* upon which impressions of personality are printed, the primitive sense of self gradually expands through experience of the external world, and also by internalizing features of significant others. In the end my 'self' is a rich amalgam of my own and of others' creating. It is something of this towards which this exercise reaches.

The following quotation might be a useful introduction to the exercise:

> What then, we can ask, is me? Me consists of a number of me's and I can make the mistake of identifying myself entirely with only one of them. There is, first of all, the me I put on for the benefit of other people. Then there is the me I put on

Exercise 4.4: Continued

for my own benefit. Then there is the me I have locked away out of sight (my own sight) in a dark cupboard because it is too painful to look at, since it is a me damaged and made ugly by the adverse chances of life. But this me, locked out of sight though he may be, can still exercise a malign influence on the me's I put on for my own benefit and that of others. . . .

But there is also another me – the me in which there is something infinite, the me where God and fullness dwell, and dwell not as a stranger or a visitor or a permanent guest but as more fully myself than the other me's.[12]

Exercise 4.5: Fantasy and fairy tales

Purpose

To encourage students to play with images, stories and fantasies, to look for meanings other than those on the surface; and to show the significance of stories both for children and adults.

Duration

1 hour.

Method

In this exercise small groups try to understand some of the underlying meanings in one particular fairy story. The story lines of up to six fairy stories are given out, one to each small group. Using their common experience and existing knowledge of psychological development, particularly when viewed from a typically Freudian perspective, the group members are invited to work out what they think the story they have been given might be about on a psychological level; and to share their speculations with the class in a plenary session.

Exercise 4.5: Continued

Materials

Copies of each of the following outlines of a fairy story, a different set for each small group.

(i) Goldilocks and the Three Bears

A little girl gets lost in the forest; she finds a house, peeps through the window, knocks three times, and enters uninvited. The house belongs to the three bears, and each bear has a place at the table, a chair, and a bed. She tries father bear's porridge – too hot. She tries father's chair – too hard. She tries father's bed – too high at one end. She tries mother bear's porridge – too cool. She tries mother bear's chair – too soft. She tries mother's bed – too high at the other end. She tries baby bear's porridge – and eats it all up. She tries baby's chair – which fits, but breaks under her. She tries baby's bed – which is just right and she sleeps. But the bears return – each is critical of intruder; baby bear squeaks; Goldilocks wakes and jumps out of the window, and goes back wherever she came from.

(ii) Hansel and Gretel

A brother and sister hear their parents talking about being unable to feed them. Mother leads them out into the forest and leaves them but Hansel has dropped white stones and they find their way back. Mother later tries again; Hansel drops white bread but the birds eat it up, so they cannot find their way back. A dove leads them to a gingerbread house and Hansel and Gretel start to eat it. A voice within asks: 'Who is nibbling my little home?' A witch comes out and invites them in. She feeds them well, and provides pretty little beds; but she is fattening them up for the oven. Hansel tricks her into getting into the oven and they burn her to death. They inherit her jewels and make their way home. They have to cross a wide lake and Gretel calls a white duck to help them, warning Hansel that they cannot both ride the duck together. They cross separately, and come home to live in joy.

(iii) Sleeping Beauty

A king and queen had to wait a long time for a child, and when the princess is born they invite twelve fairies to the christening. The fairies bless the child, but a thirteenth fairy comes and curses the child – that when she is fifteen she will prick her finger on a distaff and die. But the twelfth fairy turns the spell from death to a long sleep. The king tries to remove all distaffs from the kingdom. But on her fifteenth birthday the princess

Exercise 4.5: Continued

ascends a spiral staircase, unlocks a room and enters to find an old woman spinning. She asks: 'What is that funny thing (the distaff)?' She pricks her finger and falls into a sleep. Thorns grow round the palace and keep princes away; until one day a prince arrives, the thorns turn to roses, and he enters and wakes her with a kiss. And they live happily until their death.

(iv) Cinderella

Cinderella's mother dies and her father marries again. She lives with step-mother and two step-sisters. Cinderella is made to sweep up the cinders/ashes, to do the dirty jobs, and she sleeps by the hearth. She plants a twig on her mother's grave and waters it with her tears. The twig grows into a tree which grants her wishes for a dress and slippers to go to the ball. Her step-mother makes her perform 'impossible' tasks before she will let her go, but she is helped by the birds. Cinderella goes to the ball three times; each time she leaves early and hides from the prince. The third time she leaves her glass slipper behind stuck in pitch which the prince has put down. The prince searches for the girl whose foot will fit the glass slipper. The step-mother gets one daughter to cut off her big toe and the other her heel, in order to fit the slipper. The prince is deceived, but the birds tell him each time that the foot in the slipper is bleeding. He returns once more, and sees Cinderella in rags, and fits the slipper himself upon her foot. On the way to the wedding, the step-sisters each lose an eye, pecked out by the birds.

(v) Jack and the Beanstalk

Jack lives with his poor mother. Their cow stops giving milk, and Jack takes it to market, but on the way he exchanges it for magic seeds. His mother is very angry and sends him to bed without food. That night a beanstalk grows outside his room. He climbs it three times, and is hidden by the ogre's wife when he is under threat, in an oven and a copper. Jack steals a bag of gold, a hen that lays golden eggs, and a golden harp that speaks and wakes the ogre. The ogre follows Jack down the beanstalk and Jack calls to his mother to cut down the ogre. But she cannot, and he takes the axe, and brings the beanstalk to the ground, so that the ogre falls and dies.

(vi) Little Red Riding Hood

Little Red Riding Hood sets off with food to visit her grandmother; her mother warns her not to stray from the forest path. She enjoys the beauty of the forest, and picks flowers. She meets a wolf, who talks about the flowers, and asks where her grandmother lives. She tells him and he leaves, and arrives before her, eats

Exercise 4.5: Continued

grandmother, and takes her place. Red Riding Hood arrives, and gets into bed with 'grandmother'. 'What big ears, eyes, teeth you've got', she says. The wolf eats Red Riding Hood up too. A hunter arrives, and cuts open the wolf, rescuing Red Riding Hood and her grandmother. Red Riding Hood sews stones inside the wolf's belly, so that when it wakes, it collapses and dies. Grandmother enjoys the cakes Red Riding Hood has brought.

Instructions

1. A useful way to start this exercise is to tell a different fairy story from any of those included in the exercise, and to draw out some areas of significance from it. A particularly good one is the modern children's story *Where the Wild Things Are.*[13] But other modern stories, as well as traditional tales, often contain rich allusions to developmental material and to children's conflicts and fears.
2. Divide the class into small groups. There are story-lines for up to six groups, although where there are more, two groups can take the same story and compare notes when reporting back.
3. Give each group copies of their 'story'. They are to apply to it as a whole, and to the images in the story, what they imagine to be a classical Freudian interpretation. Emphasize that there are, of course, different possible interpretations, since the beauty of the best stories is that we all learn different things from them. Advise the groups that the story as outlined may contain elements of the 'original' which have been lost in modern story-books.

Debriefing

After twenty minutes' working in small groups, bring the groups together, and ask each one to interpret its story for the rest of the class. Following each interpretation, the tutor can add any elements which have been missed out but are included in the interpretations put forward in Bettelheim's book of fairy tales, *The Uses of Enchantment.*[14]

Comment

Fantasy plays an important part in trying to construct meanings, especially when there is as yet little knowledge by which to judge and understand what happens to us. Indeed, the fantasy world of the baby is perhaps the first way in which the child tries to make sense of good and bad experiences. Fantasy remains important throughout

Exercise 4.5: Continued

childhood and into adult life, relieving frustration, helping us to work through inner stresses and conflicts, and providing a sense of hope.

The stories which we tell our children before they go to sleep help calm the day, and prepare them for the dreams of the night. Many of these stories, whether they are fairy tales or more contemporary children's fiction, portray the inner world of the child via the characters and their fantastic adventures. Of fairy stories Dickens wrote:

> I may assume that I am not singular in entertaining a very great tenderness for the fairy literature of my childhood . . . It would be hard to estimate the amount of gentleness and mercy that has made its way among us through these slight channels. Forbearance, courtesy, consideration for the poor and aged, kind treatment of animals, the love of nature, abhorrence of tyranny and brute force – many such things have been first nourished in the child's heart by this powerful aid.[15]

Bettelheim, in the book upon which this exercise is drawn, writes similarly:

> The figures and events of fairy tales also personify and illustrate inner conflicts. But they suggest ever so subtly how these conflicts may be solved, and what the next steps in the development toward a higher humanity might be . . . Far from making demands the fairy tale reassures, gives hope for the future and holds out the promise of a happy ending . . . The fairy tale is therapeutic because the patient finds his own solution, through contemplating what the story seems to imply about him and his inner conflicts at this moment in his life.[16]

Exercise 4.6: Creating fantasies

Purpose

To give students an opportunity to play with their own fantasies, and to see how projection can reveal aspects of their own lives and personalities.

Duration

30 minutes.

Exercise 4.6: Continued

Method

Pairs of students are shown an indistinct picture together, and write a story around it. Having fixed their own story in their mind they then tell each other their own stories, and contrast them, particularly looking at what each person's interpretation of the picture might say about them.

Materials

For this exercise it is necessary to have a set of pictures, similar to those used in certain projective tests, such as the Thematic Apperception Test or the Object Relations Test. There are restrictions upon these who are not qualified as psychologists, making it difficult for some trainers to have access to or use of these actual test pictures, even though they are not used in this particular exercise as a clinical diagnostic tool. The alternative is to make a set of pictures, taken from magazines and colour supplements, which are sufficiently 'vague' to provoke imaginative story-telling. The ideal picture is one which could be portray the start, end or any middle point of a story, and which does not dictate by its composition what the story-line has to be. It should be able to give rise to a number of different story-lines. Enough pictures (or in large groups duplicates of them) are needed to have one for every two people.

Instructions

1 Form the class into pairs, sitting in a large circle, one partner facing outwards, looking at the other person facing inwards.
2 Give one picture to each pair – if possible a different one to each pair.
3 Without speaking to each other, the pair have five to ten minutes to look at the picture, and to write a story around it, where their picture represents either the start, or a middle point or the end of the story. They may make notes, but do not share their story with each other.
4 The person on the outer ring moves two places clockwise round the circle, taking the picture with him or her. That person tells their story to the new person they are sitting with. They have five minutes for this. If their story finishes before time is called, the listener may ask questions of the story-teller, to flesh out the details of the story; the story-teller uses his or her imagination to answer those questions, and adds the detail where appropriate to their story.
5 The picture is then returned to the original partner, who uses it to tell their

Exercise 4.6: Continued

story to their new partner for a further five minutes, with time for questions about detail as before. The purpose of this part of the exercise is to 'fix' the story in their minds, so that in retelling it to their original partner, the second is not influenced overmuch by what the first person has said.

6 The person on the outer ring now moves two places anti-clockwise, back to the original partner and back to their picture. Each person in turn now tells the 'finished' version of their story about the picture to the other – this will take about ten minutes.

7 The pair then compare their respective stories (those they composed, not those they have just heard). What were the differences between them? What might the different features of their story be saying about them? Were the characters in the story representative of aspects of their own external or inner worlds? If, as is likely, they imagined different stories and moods about the same picture, what might this tell them about themselves?

Debriefing

If there is time, small groups can share what they have learned about themselves from the use of projection and fantasy.

Comment

Standard projective tests usually recognize certain interpretations of the picture by the subject, the inclusion or lack of which is an indication of psychological maturity or psychopathology with regard to certain affects. It needs to be made clear that projective material is not in this case being used in this way. There are no right or wrong answers: it is what each person sees, especially where it is distinctive, which might provide insight for them into themselves.

Exercise 4.7: Imaginative exercise on infancy

Purpose

This exercise can be used to sum up the theme of trust and dependency, by drawing upon knowledge coming from reading, experiential learning and observation, and using it in the form of a guided fantasy.

Duration

1 hour.

Method

Pairs of students write an imaginative description of an hour in the day of a six-month-old child, and then take another pair through a guided fantasy.

Materials

None.

Instructions

1 Form pairs, and give them thirty minutes to write an imaginative description of an hour in the day of a six-month-old child. The finished 'story' will probably take about five minutes to deliver, at a slow pace.
2 They should decide what pleasant and unpleasant experiences to incorporate into the 'hour in the day of . . .'. They write the experience in the second person (e.g. 'You wake up from sleeping, and enjoy the sensation of your thumb on your gums and lips . . .'). Obviously the exercise uses words which the six-month-old child has no knowledge of; but essentially they should keep the description simple, concrete and vivid.
3 Each pair joins with another pair. Where at all possible they should find a quiet and comfortable spot to meet. One partner in the first pair asks the others to relax, to close their eyes, and imagine they are a six-month-old child; taking them through the imaginary hour, and the different experiences within it. This needs to be taken slowly enough to let the participants feel their way

Exercise 4.7: Continued

into the situations described – the whole 'hour' will probably be condensed into about five minutes in all. After a brief pause, one of the partners in the second pair takes the others through their imaginative description.

Debriefing

The foursome finish by discussing the experience together for about fifteen minutes, also comparing notes on the content which each pair chose to include.

Exercise 4.8: Role-plays

Purpose

The following three role-plays illustrate various aspects of trust and dependency issues, and provide practice in counselling skills as well as in relating developmental issues around trust and dependency to the client's presenting material.

Duration

60–75 minutes for any one role-play. It is suggested that each role-play lasts for forty minutes, with up to twenty minutes allowed for 'time out' (see Chapter 1).

Method etc.

See Exercise 1.2, Chapter 1, for method, materials, instructions and debriefing. Comments on possible handling each of the situations appear after the last script. Debriefing and analysis of the counsellor's work, are of course, essential and may take a further thirty minutes after the role-play.

Exercise 4.8: Continued

(i) Briefing for Gerry (aged twenty-five)

You have an urgent decision to make, whether or not to have an abortion. Six months ago your husband left you because, he said, he was fed up with your fussing over him. He said that he felt overwhelmed by your love, and felt like a child. As you see it you always tried to be a perfect wife, caring about what he felt like, what he ate, how hard he was working, etc. You had been married for three years.

Two months ago he suggested you go out for the evening together, and you finished up in bed together, with the result that you are now pregnant. He doesn't want anything to do with this new situation, and now says he wants a divorce. You do not know whether he has any other close relationship at present, since he resents any questions you ask.

You realize that it is unwise to go ahead with the pregnancy, because you are not sure you can keep your job, and make a new life for yourself as a potential single parent. But your feelings are as strong as your thinking: you want the baby, partly because it is 'part' of your husband, and partly because you desperately need to have a child to pour your love upon. You do not see the baby as a way of getting him back, because you recognize that the marriage is over.

This is the main story-line. As a person, you are demanding and overwhelming, and if you can do it you keep up a barrage of complaint that no one cares, including your counsellor. No one will give you the love you always give to others, no one cares for you as you do for others, etc. If you wish to, you can elaborate your story with references to your own childhood, where you felt deprived of love, and always had to care for others in the family – develop this story-line as you wish.

(ii)(a) Client's briefing for Jean (aged forty-five)

You have been seeing your counsellor for six months. Because of this your counsellor has been given all the information in the next paragraph of your notes before the role-play starts, so that you can assume that it is shared knowledge. This role-play starts with a 'time out' (when you are absent from the group) so that the counsellor can brief the group about this knowledge, and work out how to handle this situation. After any and every later 'time out' taken, you must assume that you are coming back to the next session a week later.

You came to see the counsellor six months ago because you were (and still are) depressed, and you got (and get) panic attacks whenever demands are made upon you with which you feel you cannot cope. These happen at times at the office where you have a part-time job as a clerical assistant. This job is one you took after your husband left you two years ago. You have two teenage children, both of whom are due to leave

Exercise 4.8: Continued

home in a few weeks' time, one to go to college, the other to a job in another part of the country. They have been your mainstay since your husband left, although your counsellor has also become a lifeline over these last few months, even if you are hardly any better than when you first came.

You will need to convey in this role-play that your counsellor is the only person you can really talk to, the only person you feel safe with. You can, of course, say this. You also keep asking questions like 'What's the matter with me? Will I get any better?', though try to avoid questions about what you should do. When the counsellor says things, try and convey how grateful you are, for everything she or he gives you – how helpful the counsellor's remarks are, how you hadn't seen things like that before, etc. So you are both demanding but also dependent, hanging on every word. You may come across, therefore, as quite agitated, and perhaps only calm down and become more genuinely constructive if, first, your counsellor can contain your feelings without panicking herself or himself; and particularly if she or he is able to help you get in touch with your anger at everyone (including the counsellor) for leaving you so much of the time to cope with things on your own.

(ii)(b) Counsellor's notes on Jean (not to be shown to person playing Jean)

In this role-play Jean, aged forty-five, has been seeing you for six months. You are given the same information in the next paragraph as Jean has in her briefing notes. This role-play starts with a 'time out' (when Jean is absent from the group) so that you can brief the group about this knowledge, and work out how to handle a situation which has arisen and which Jean does not yet know about. That is that you are due to go on holiday in four weeks' time for a fortnight. You are aware that the only thing that keeps her going is her weekly session with you, which she has attended faithfully since you started seeing her. Also in this role-play, if you take further 'time out', each time you call Jean back you must assume that a week has passed. Jean has also been briefed about this.

The person playing Jean has the following information and knows that you have it, too: that she came to see you six months ago because she was (and still is) depressed, and got (and still gets) panic attacks whenever demands are made upon her with which she feels she cannot cope. These happen at times at the office where she has a part-time job as a clerical assistant. This job is one she took after her husband left her two years ago. She has two teenage children, both of whom are due to leave home in a few weeks' time, one to go to college, the other to a job in another part of the country. They have been her mainstay since her husband left, although you have also become a lifeline over these last few months, even if she is hardly any better than when she first came.

Exercise 4.8: Continued

(iii) Briefing for Eddie (aged fifty-five)

If this character is played by a man simply alter gender details in the case material. Share the first paragraph below with the person playing the counsellor before you start the role-play

Last week you rang the counsellor you are about to see having been given her or his name by another agency. On the phone you told the counsellor that you had seen a lot of people/agencies over the years, and none of them had been able to help you. You told the counsellor that you were afraid that your grandson would commit suicide, as your son did some years ago. You thought you were just going to talk on the phone, but the counsellor suggested you meet together to talk at length; and you are now seeing her or him for the first time.

The following background information is reserved for you to relate to the counsellor, as and when you think appropriate during the role-play:

You get into your story quickly, and you talk freely. You live alone, having separated some fifteen years ago; you and your husband split up partly because you were drinking heavily at the time. This is a continual problem for you, although over the last year you have controlled your drinking rather better. You had a son and a daughter, but your son died of an overdose of drugs some ten years ago, when he was twenty; you think it was suicide. You still have a daughter, who is thirty-five, married, and has a son of fifteen. But she will not let you visit her home; she says this is because when you are there you are always souring the atmosphere. You are afraid (as you have already told the counsellor on the phone) that her son, your grandson, will get into drugs and overdose, too.

When you are in your stride, and the interview is going along smoothly, spring this question on your counsellor: 'What sign are you?' By 'what sign' you mean what sign of the zodiac. You can go on to speak quite freely about your strong belief in astrology and the stars, that you are 'scorpio', that you have visited several astrologers and fortune-tellers, all of whom have in one way or another forecast another tragedy in the family. And you believe it: you can't alter the paths of fate, etc.

Deep down, behind all your worries, there is a fear that it was your own drinking that drove your husband away, that drove your son to drugs and suicide, and that keeps your daughter at a distance. You are afraid deep down that everyone you come into contact with is in danger of being harmed by you, as if you carry a sting in the tail like a scorpion. You are afraid you will damage your helpers, and therefore do not stay long with any of them. You feel a sort of fatalism that means that you (like fate itself) are all powerful, and can only do harm. It will take a very skilful and insightful counsellor to get hold of this and allow you to share all this information in one session, but share what you feel comes naturally within the counselling relationship.

Exercise 4.8: Continued

Comment

Gerry's story bears some resemblance to one case cited in *The Presenting Past*,[17] although the presenting problem has been changed to provide a different dimension, and the added complication of the urgency involved in pre-abortion counselling. Inasmuch as a potential birth is involved this situation contains the seeds of the first developmental stage; but in fact it is the dependency needs of the oral stage theme which is the real reason for placing the role-play at this point.

The decision about an abortion is an urgent one, and always difficult for a counsellor used to proceeding patiently. The counsellor cannot, of course, make or force a decision. What he or she can do is to help Gerry see some connections between her need to care and her need to be cared for; that there may be other ways of meeting her own needs to be cared for; and that the counsellor's own inability to give advice is being felt as uncaring. By tapping Gerry's feelings about this last point in particular, Gerry may be helped to realize that being cared for is not always found in activity, in doing or in having (perhaps much of the reason for her wanting to be a mother), but rather in being (a quite different aspect of motherhood).

The situation does not imply that an abortion is necessary. Single-parent women, particularly when they have a good support network, can only welcome their pregnancy, and enjoy bringing up their child or children, with, of course, the same strains as two-parent families, and with some gains and some losses.

Jean is a very dependent client, and it is the forthcoming break which is the essential point in the second role-play. In the initial 'time out' the counsellor will probably realize this, and want to work out how to convey this break to Jean. Jean, of course, does not know, and the news, when it comes, often comes as a genuine shock, almost like the real thing.

What tends to happen in this role-play is that the counsellor puts off telling Jean, partly because Jean is so effusive when the session starts, and partly because the counsellor (rightly) fears Jean's reaction. And, of course, each 'time out' means that the next session that starts is one week nearer the break! The other mistake counsellors make is to try and make the whole situation into something very positive, and to provide reassurance, advice or alternative help: 'I am sure you will manage very well for two weeks', 'Why don't you write a diary each day which you can then tell me about later?', 'Would it be a good idea if we planned different things you could do instead of seeing me?', 'Perhaps I could give you the name of someone else you could see when I am away'. Although careful management is sometimes necessary, and emergency arrangements may need to be considered, most clients, well prepared for a break (starting at least three or four weeks before) and given the opportunity to ventilate all their feelings of disappointment, anger, rejection, envy, etc., find that they

Exercise 4.8: Continued

cope satisfactorily, and gain confidence from the fact that they are not as unable to manage without the counsellor as they had imagined.

What the counsellor therefore needs to do is, first, to take the initiative at the start of the first session (four weeks before the break), and announce his or her intentions, giving Jean plenty of time to work on her reactions to it. If she does not respond, then the counsellor needs to make references to the break thereafter; if she does, then the counsellor needs to allow her to express all her feelings, and not to provide false reassurance or promises. The counsellor needs to take all the anger that may be heaped on him or her. Linking in the impending break and Jean's feelings of rejection, anger, etc., with both her husband leaving, and her children shortly moving away from the home are also valuable interventions to make when the time seems right.

Eddie provides a particular problem, not so much perhaps in the immediate situation, as in trying to make a relationship with her which will survive into a second, third and subsequent sessions. Her fear that she drives people away or kills them off, and furthermore that there is nothing she can do about it since it seems out of her control, comes through in what she says. The skill of the counsellor is to help her express this anxiety in relation to the counselling relationship too, and to create a sufficiently trusting and safe relationship for Eddie to risk making a long-term commitment to counselling. There are positive signs (her control of her drinking); but some of other apparently positive signs (such as asking about the counsellor's birth sign) may not be friendly as much as highly suspicious as to whether the two of them are compatible. The way the counsellor handles that question, and understands its significance, is crucial.

5

Authority and autonomy

Introduction

The theme of autonomy and authority is first seen clearly in what the psychoanalytic model of human development calls the anal stage. Erikson's expansion of this phrase to 'anal-muscular' makes it much more complete, immediately including even earlier developments than toilet training which similarly raise questions of autonomy and authority. The gradual co-ordination of the muscles and limbs is seen first in the way a child can raise her head and exercise obvious control over the neck muscles; but such muscular control begins to raise the issues of this developmental theme more obviously when a child begins to manipulate objects (and therefore pull them apart!); or to crawl, stand and walk and so reach into places where breakable, precious and dangerous objects are capable of being touched, knocked, handled or grabbed (forcing parents into a completely new lifestyle, where the placing of everything has to be watched!). All this precedes and overlaps with the more standard restricted understanding of the anal stage, and its battles over bowel and bladder control. Each one of the achievements of the child that comes through increasing muscular development leads to some sort of negotiation between child and parents of what is and what is not possible. The foundations of autonomy, and of confidence in one's abilities, are laid in the way parents exercise their power, authority and control over their young child, and in the way the child both initiates and responds.[1]

The majority of the exercises on this theme reflect various aspects of authority and power, autonomy and self-confidence, but in adult life rather than in childhood. Exercise 5.1 takes the form of a different type of role-play. Simulations used in experiential learning are of many kinds, including role-plays which attempt to replicate the original situations as far as possible in the use of real characters and roles, in the problem areas represented, and in using real time. Other simulations involve games – sometimes board games, but more often team games, designed to illustrate the dimensions of a particular problem or of ways in which people relate under certain conditions.[2]

A simulation can also take the form of a role-play which has some similarity to the game, often because it involves some competitive element. It uses various characters, but it is not a miniature version of the real-life problem. Instead the simulation employs fantasy and play to act out a problem or aspects of relating, set in a completely different context. All such types of simulation need careful unpacking in order to draw out the lessons that may be learned from them. Although such simulations involve fantasy and play, they can become remarkably real, as if participants really are fighting over life and death issues. The intensity of such feelings in a play situation can occasionally disturb participants, and trainers need to be aware of over-reactions leading to anxiety and to guilt.

The reader may notice that the more typical role-plays in this chapter involve mainly male characters (although admittedly two of them can be represented by either gender); and that in Chapter 4 the role-plays involved mainly female characters (with one which could be either gender). This split is not insignificant, and in its own way reflects clearly some of the gender issues found, first, in our culture; second, in the feminist psychodynamic writing on the psychological differences between men and women;[3] and third, in the way men and women present in counselling and therapy. The men in the role-plays on the theme of autonomy and authority predominantly show difficulties with relinquishing power, with trusting themselves or others to another person, and with being in some way dependent upon someone else. Their self-confidence seems to be based on how far they feel and are seen to be in charge or in control. The women in the role-plays on trust and dependency present difficulties of taking power, of exercising an independent role, and of finding their own strength and authority without the traditional expectation that they need to depend upon men.

This division of gender characters and roles between the two themes is not, I hope, an indication of my own sexism, conscious or unconscious. Indeed, I trust it is the opposite, that I find myself wanting to illustrate through the role-plays the problems men and women have in moving out of stereotypical roles and attitudes. Men and women seem to become traditionally over-identified with a particular set of developmental themes. Authority and autonomy and doing are culturally seen as male strengths, trust and dependency and being as women's. The role-plays suggest that many male clients need to be able to relinquish their fixation on autonomy and authority, and to become more confident with issues of trust and dependency; and that many female clients need to move beyond questions of trust and dependency to become more confident with the issues of autonomy and authority. Of course some men and some women are able to incorporate both ways of being into their inner and outer lives. But many clients will be in the position of still needing to discover the strengths of another developmental dimension.

Exercise 5.1: The palace revolution[4]

Purpose

To experience and observe the difficulties of exercising power and influence when part of an authoritarian milieu; and to examine the way in which authority is claimed, used and responded to in small groups.

Duration

45–60 minutes.

Method

A simulation in which some participants act out an imaginary situation involving attitudes to authority, while others observe in order to assist the debriefing.

Materials

Set out a large table and seven chairs around it, with observers' chairs in a large circle around the central table and chairs. A stop-watch and a watch or clock, will also be needed.

There are four briefing sheets. Make one copy of (i), three each of (ii) and (iii), and as many copies of (iv) as there are students remaining.

(i) The palace revolution

The scene is the Council Chamber in the ancient kingdom of Ruritania. The Council has met with the authoritarian monarch to discuss plans for the best diplomatic marriage of the monarch's only issue into one of the other royal families in Europe.

Exercise 5.1: Continued

You play the monarch, and it is your task to conduct the Council in the way you think an authoritarian monarch might.

(ii) The palace revolution

The scene is the Council Chamber in the ancient kingdom of Ruritania. The Council has met with the authoritarian monarch to discuss plans for the best diplomatic marriage of the monarch's only issue into one of the other royal families in Europe.

But other forces are at work. There is a plot to overthrow the monarch. A fiendishly clever professor has invented a device which has been placed beneath the monarch's chair. It measures every second during which the monarch speaks, and when the monarch has spoken for a cumulative total of eight minutes, the miniature device will activate a powerful laser which will dematerialize the royal chair and the royal personage and consign them non-violently to a new kingdom in the sky.

You are one of those involved in the plot. So your task is to get the monarch to speak as much as possible, so that the device can be activated. But unfortunately for you and your co-conspirators, you heard just before the Council meeting began that the inventor of the device has been arrested by the secret police, and may spill the beans any minute. So there is no time to waste! You will have to get the monarch talking!

(iii) The palace revolution

The scene is the Council Chamber in the ancient kingdom of Ruritania. The Council has met with the authoritarian monarch to discuss plans for the best diplomatic marriage of the monarch's only issue into one of the other royal families in Europe.

But other forces are at work. There is a plot to overthrow the monarch. A fiendishly clever professor has invented a device which has been placed beneath the monarch's chair. It measures every second during which the monarch speaks, and when the monarch has spoken for a cumulative total of eight minutes, the miniature device will activate a powerful laser which will dematerialize the royal chair and the royal personage and consign them non-violently to a new kingdom in the sky.

You are one of the monarch's loyal supporters, so you must as far as is possible in such a meeting prevent the monarch from speaking. You heard just before the Council meeting that the inventor of the device had been arrested by the secret police, and may spill the beans any minute about who is involved in the plot, some of whom are sitting round the Council table. But you want to identify who they are, so that when the Chief of Police arrives the whole lot can be rounded up. You cannot tell the monarch about the plot, but if you can stop the monarch talking for the cumulative total of eight minutes you will save the monarch's life and unmask the conspirators. So there is no time to waste!

Exercise 5.1: Continued

(iv) Observer instructions

In this simulation you are watching for the way in which people cope with authority in groups. Authority figures in groups may or may not be formally designated as such. Three of the participants are trying to undermine the monarch's authority, and three are trying to support it – although it is not quite as straightforward as it seems, since all the participants are trying to undermine the authority of those whom they detect to be 'against' them!

Concentrate upon the person you have been asked to observe, and make notes on the way she or he copes with the situation. You may wish to include among your observations:

(a) How, and how well, does she or he assert herself or himself?
(b) How does she or he cope with other people who are assertive or over-assertive?
(c) How does she or he react to the chairperson (the monarch) compared to other members of the group?
(d) What gambits/tactics does she or he use to get attention?
(e) How far does she or he try to use 'rules of procedure' or the designated authority figure (the monarch) to get her or his own way?
(f) Does she or he spot who are the potential allies, and who the enemy?
(g) Does she or he use the allies in any way?
(h) How does she or he cope with any rising anxiety/conflict/disruption in the group?

After the simulation ends you will help this person debrief, so you may ask the same questions of her or him, and then share your own observations.

Together, or in small groups, you may then go on to ask how what you have observed applies to behaviour in the exercise of power, authority, tactics for manipulation, group work, on committees, in individual counselling, etc.

Instructions

1 The exercise needs seven participants, and ideally about seven observers. If there are less observers they have to work harder, concentrating on the group as a whole, more than upon one individual member of it. If there are more than fourteen in a class there will obviously be a surplus of observers, unless numbers are sufficient to run two separate simulations – in different rooms, since the noise level, and even the physical exertion can be considerable!

Exercise 5.1: Continued

2 Set out a table and seven chairs, one of them at the head of the table, and ask for seven volunteers to take part in a simulation of a royal council meeting. Ask the volunteers who would like to be the authoritarian monarch. This description of the monarch helps draw out those who fancy themselves as such – although the exercise needs someone firm or very firm if they are to survive!
3 Sit the observers in a circle round the participants' table, where possible giving each observer one participant to observe, as well as the observer's instructions to help them in their task.
4 Hand out the participant sheets: (i) to the monarch, and (ii) and (iii) randomly to the six council members, so that you do not set up obvious 'sides'. Ask all the participants to read their instructions through, and to take the tutor on one side if they are not clear about their task. They are not told how long the exercise lasts, but they are told that the tutor will stop it at an appropriate point.
5 It is vital for the tutor to have, and be able to use, a stop-watch (as on many digital watches) – one which accumulates time, not the lap counter. What is necessary is that each time it is switched on it starts from the number of minutes and seconds when it was stopped, adding the new amount of time to the total. When it is switched off the watch must stop counting (unlike the lap counter which goes on recording the passage of time). It is very important to understand the different functions and to use the cumulative stop-watch, not the lap counter!
6 Each time the monarch starts to speak the stop-watch is turned on; as soon as the monarch stops it is turned off. The last complication is that a second watch or clock is necessary to set the 'deadline' of twenty minutes for the simulation. However, if the monarch's total number of speaking seconds adds up to eight minutes, the simulation is stopped by the tutor with some sort of 'zapping' noise! If the simulation survives for twenty minutes, the tutor brings it to a halt by declaring the monarch 'rescued'. It is actually rare for monarchs to be dematerialized!

Debriefing

The exercise is likely to generate a lot of noise, and even give rise to physical exertion, so that a two-minute 'breather' straight afterwards might be welcome. Before bringing in the observers it is often interesting to ask the person who played the monarch who he or she felt were allies and who were enemies. But move quite quickly to the debriefing, matching the observers with those whom they observed individually. The

Exercise 5.1: Continued

observers can use the questions on their briefing sheet to help debrief those taking part in the simulation. Following this discussion (in pairs or threes) it may be valuable to move on to small-group discussion of what the participants and observers have learned about power, authority, the tactics used in manipulating meetings, group-work and individual work.

Comment

This simulation is designed to show how people handle power and how they react to those who try to exercise authority in small groups, particularly in those with some formal structure and task, like a committee. Those who wield authority may or may not be formally designated as leaders. So the monarch in this simulation is like a chairperson, with the councillors ranged on different sides of an argument and, like many groups, not using real arguments as much as verbal tactics in order to get their way.

This parallel need not be fully explained before the exercise, although it may be important to draw attention to it later. There may be some questions about what the exercise has to do with counselling. Apart from the ability of counsellors to overcome verbal or verbose 'tactics' on the parts of some individual clients, the exercise provides some insights into groupwork; and also into what clients themselves experience when they are members of groups, committees, etc.; or when they try to challenge authoritarian figures, whether they be bosses, parents or partners.

Exercise 5.2: Imaginative exercise on being a toddler

Purpose

This exercise can be used to sum up the theme of autonomy and authority, by drawing upon knowledge coming from reading, experiential learning and observation, and using it in the form of a guided fantasy.

Exercise 5.2: Continued

Duration

1 hour.

Method

Pairs of students write an imaginative description of an hour in the day of an eighteen-month-old child, and then take another pair through a guided fantasy.

Materials

None.

Instructions

1 Form pairs, and give them thirty minutes to write an imaginative description of an hour in the day of an eighteen-month-old child. The finished 'story' will probably take about five minutes to deliver, at a slow pace.
2 They should decide what pleasant and unpleasant experiences to incorporate into the 'hour in the day of . . .'. They write the experience in the second person (e.g. 'You are having a lovely time spooning your dinner on to the floor, and watching it spill and splash all over the carpet, when suddenly there is a loud shout from across the room which shakes you . . .'. Obviously the exercise uses many words of which the eighteen-month-old child has little knowledge; but essentially they should keep the description simple, concrete and vivid.
3 Each pair joins with another pair. Where at all possible they should find a quiet and comfortable spot to meet. One partner in the first pair asks the others to relax, to close their eyes and imagine they are an eighteen-month-old child; taking them through the imaginary hour, and the different experiences within it. This needs to be taken slowly enough to let the participants feel their way into the situations described – the whole 'hour' will probably be condensed into about five minutes in all. After a brief pause, one of the partners in the second pair takes the others through their imaginative description.

Exercise 5.2: Continued

Debriefing

The foursome finish by discussing the experience together for about fifteen minutes, also comparing notes on the content which each pair chose to include.

Exercise 5.3: Role-plays

Purpose

The following four role-plays illustrate various aspects of autonomy and authority issues, and provide practice in counselling skills as well as in relating developmental issues around authority and autonomy to the client's presenting material.

Duration

60–75 minutes for any one role play. It is suggested that each role play lasts forty minutes, with up to twenty minutes allowed for 'time out' (see Chapter 1).

Method

See Exercise 1.2, Chapter 1, for method, materials, instructions and debriefing. Comments on possible handling each of the situations appear after the last script. Debriefing and analysis of the counsellor's work is, of course, essential and may take a further thirty minutes after the role-play.

(i) **Briefing for Mr Bull** (aged fifty)

In this situation it is essential that the 'counsellor' is a senior teacher (using counselling skills rather than counselling as such). You know from the records that Mr Bull, who has asked for an appointment to talk about his son, Clive, is the managing director of his own small business. Enquiries amongst other staff in the sixth form indicate that Clive appears to be doing well with his A-level courses, having got reasonable marks in his GCSEs.

Exercise 5.3: Continued

Before starting the interview, inform your counsellor of the information in the previous paragraph, particularly the name of the person you are playing, and your age, and agree where and when the interview is taking place. The information below is yours to reveal as and when it feels right, and depending on how sensitive your counsellor is.

You are very angry, which is why you have made a time to see this senior teacher at Clive's school. Your son, Clive, says he is struggling rather with one of his A-level courses, and that he is being taught by a young new member of staff in that subject. You are unimpressed with what you have heard about the member of staff's teaching ability – and she's a woman – and you have heard other parents complain about her, too.

It is the last straw, and you will need to invent your own list of things that are wrong with the school, which you have heard from parents and students. (If you wish you can write some headings down to take into the interview with you; this would not be unusual.) If you are given the opportunity to talk freely, and the 'counsellor' is not too defensive, or does not try to argue with you, or is not too obviously counselling you, you calm down as you talk about this list of things. If the 'counsellor' tries to argue, or defend, or talk down to you, your voice rises and you get more and more angry and forceful. What is important is that the 'counsellor' listens and acknowledges just how angry you are, and meets your anger head on rather than backs away from it.

If the tutor helps you to talk calmly, so that you get through your list of complaints, you can then begin to share some of your anxiety about the pressures on young people to do well. You know only too well yourself just what a competitive world we live in, as the managing director of a small business; as someone who has had to fight to make good; as someone who knows that you can never afford to miss a trick, etc.

(ii) **Briefing for Ian or Jan** (aged twenty-three)

You are a very pleasant person, you talk freely, you appear co-operative and interested in what the counsellor says. It is your first session at a counselling centre. The situation is that you have a decision to make, and you are unable to make it. You trained, after a degree, as a librarian, but you have only been able to get a temporary job up to now. The opportunity has arisen for you to apply for two jobs within the Library Service, but in neighbouring counties. You cannot apply for both since the interview dates are likely to be some weeks apart; if you apply for and get the first you cannot really apply for the second, and yet it is the second you really want, yet the second is not one you are likely to get, etc. It should soon become clear to the counsellor that you are very indecisive.

Exercise 5.3: Continued

The following information will extend your story-line

Your present temporary job is going to be made into a permanent post, and you stand quite a good chance of getting it. It is rather dull, weeding out old stock in the basement of the main library, but it is at least permanent, and helps you get experience.

The second job is one you have heard about on the grapevine, and you believe will be advertised soon. It is much more interesting. In another county, it involves running a mobile library service. You will get out and about, and it sounds challenging. But you lack the experience for it, and you have not held a driving licence for very long – you failed your test three times because you were over-cautious. The mobile library job is the one you really would like, but it is highly unlikely you will get it.

You talk over the facts and the decision with your counsellor, perhaps deluging her or him with factual information about the jobs. You are eager to listen to what your counsellor says, but you keep saying (especially if your counsellor tries to guide your decision) 'Yes, but . . .' – 'Yes, but the second job is more interesting . . . yes, but I am unlikely to get it . . . no, but the present job is more in my reach . . . yes, but the present job is so dull . . .'.

You are clearly not confident about making decisions, and this should make your counsellor aware that the second job asks for more responsibility than you seem able to take at this stage of your life, and that you are probably not ready for the challenge yet. But really your counsellor should help you begin to see this for yourself, and take responsibility for your own decision, to which you might then reply, if you are feeling very awkward, 'Yes, I know I have to decide myself, but . . .'!

You can develop (should you need it) a family background/history for Ian or Jan, one which underlines that it has been difficult both to be autonomous, and to stand up and argue for yourself.

(iii) Briefing for Geoffrey Brown (aged forty-five)

You are unemployed. You worked as a printer before you were made redundant, but you have been unable to find a suitable opening now for two years. You come for counselling because you are depressed. As your counsellor helps you to speak (it's not easy to admit any 'weak' feelings as you see them) you say more about your situation, although you will probably only reveal the last sentence on this sheet if you feel you can really trust your counsellor not to belittle you or to put you down.

You are married, and your wife Jean is a relatively well-paid teacher. You have two children: Alan, aged twenty-two; and Wendy, aged seventeen. Alan is also unemployed. He plays snooker and darts at a local centre for the unemployed, but when he hangs around the house there is often conflict between the two of you. You may

Exercise 5.3: Continued

even wish to start by focusing your problems on Alan, and only move on to your own when your counsellor helps you to talk about your own unemployment.

You are tired, you don't eat much, you can't sleep. Life is worthless, although you do not hint at any kind of suicidal feelings.

When you were in work things were OK. You are something of a macho man, who as long as you earned as much as your wife felt secure enough to 'rule the roost'. But it is not nearly so easy now you have no independent income. You feel you 'live off' her. There has been a reversal of traditional roles, and you cannot adjust to that.

The last area you might reveal (if your counsellor helps you feel OK about it) is that you are also impotent.

(iv)(a) **Briefing for Alex or Alec** (any age)

In this particular situation you are not a client but a trainee counsellor seeing an independent assessor for an interim assessment of your training. *Do not play yourself*, although you can draw upon your present experience of counselling and of work in groups. Your assessor has been briefed about Alex or Alec by fictional course staff, so needs no further instructions, other than your name. If your name happens to be Alex or Alec change it to another to avoid confusion and identification with the character you are playing.

Your character, Alex or Alec, is very keen to do well on the course. He or she tries to do everything perfectly, and to a large measure succeeds in being perfect. (In fact he or she is almost too good!)

Every student has a mid-term assessment with an independent assessor, and you are going for such an assessment. You expect to be told that you have done well – which is what you believe yourself – and you are not aware of any adverse comment that could be made upon your work.

In fact (though it might be difficult for you to admit this) you are too much of a perfectionist, rather too precise and particular, even impatient with clients, or with anyone else who doesn't know what he or she is doing, whether it is those you are responsible for or those you are responsible to. But this will be difficult to admit, because you want to do well in this assessment.

If you feel you are gently led into acknowledging how difficult it is for you to accept yourself as less than perfect you might then be able to respond positively to what you fear are otherwise negative aspects of this assessment. If your assessor is too blunt, or in your eyes 'incompetent' then you may get impatient and defensive. Play it by ear; feel your way through this assessment as a rather 'prickly' person might. But if your assessor makes it possible, try letting some of the defensiveness go.

Exercise 5.3: Continued

(iv)(b) The 'assessor's' brief for assessing Alex or Alec

In this particular role-play you are not a counsellor as such, although you use your counselling skills. You are an independent assessor seeing a trainee counsellor for an interim assessment of her or his training. This person is not playing himself or herself but a fictional character.

You have been given a verbal report by the (fictional) course staff about this trainee. In many ways it is difficult to fault Alex/Alec. She or he works well, has a lot of theoretical knowledge, is technically very correct, and understands situations clearly. But this student is also very independent, not really taking notice of others, not consulting with them, and in fact rather precise and particular, even impatient with clients who don't understand or change, and rather powerful in the counsellor's position. And the trainee appears to resent the advice and help of the permanent staff.

In conducting an assessment you use much the same skills as you do in counselling. Imagine yourself conducting an assessment as an external assessor might do for anyone on a real counselling or therapy course, like one you are perhaps attending. You are trying to help Alex or Alec to make her or his own self-assessment; but you may need to confront her or him where necessary with negative aspects of her or his work, either that you pick up in the assessment, or that have been hinted to you beforehand by others; it will be particularly important to do this if they are not mentioned by the trainee.

Comment

Hurricanes need to blow themselves out, and Mr Bull must be allowed, at least to begin with, to vent his angry concern. Understanding his underlying anxiety that his son has to face the pressures that he himself has had to struggle with; encouraging Mr Bull to talk about his fight to 'make it'; and recognizing the pressures on him even now, may help Mr Bull in turn to be more understanding towards those whom he regards as very junior or even inferior to him – his son, women etc.; and may help him to exercise less pressure on others. He will not, of course, be told: he will need to find it out for himself, but he may do so when the person listening to him subtly acknowledges the strains on such a man. Beneath the bravado and the chauvinism Mr Bull may be a lonely and even a frightened man.

Ian (or Jan) is one of those 'Yes but . . .' characters who can become infuriating to the counsellor and to others. The script for the second role-play draws attention to the unsuitability of such an indecisive person for a job which requires initiative and decisiveness, at least at this stage of his (or her) life. It is quite in order for the

Exercise 5.3: Continued

counsellor to point out the way in which Ian (or Jan) sabotages all the counsellor's efforts to help, in the end making the client's life more difficult than the counsellor's. The obsessive type of personality, represented in part in this character, often needs a firm lead from the counsellor: not telling him or her what to do, but cutting through circular thinking, or dominating but comparatively irrelevant problems.

It is possible Geoffrey Brown will not find it easy talking to a counsellor whose work is a source of paid employment; and it is quite probable that he will not find it easy talking to a woman; if the woman is employed as a counsellor, then he will no doubt feel as threatened, defensive and inferior as he is at home. This parallel is very important, and the session will begin to take off once these issues are raised with him. It may be helpful to explore with him how it feels to be talking to someone who is paid as a 'counsellor'; or whether he feels in any way worried about appearing dependent. But it is especially important, if it applies, to explore what it feels like to be talking this way to a woman.

A woman counsellor may feel very angry with Geoffrey, and have to handle counter-transference feelings as well as his own explicit or implicit hostility. Her own anger may be a reflection of Geoff's anger about his present position, and in the end can be a way through to empathizing more fully with him. The way Geoffrey feels is what many women have felt for a very long time. Rather than use this as a stick to punish him with, or with which to take revenge, a woman counsellor is in a very strong position to show that she understands him; and out of such understanding help him to look at his difficulties about both being dependent upon his wife and accepting her independence and autonomy.

The perfectionism which Alex or (Alec) displays has a strongly defensive quality to it. It keeps people at a distance – technique is fine, but on the level of relationships, real understanding may be much more limited. Perfection prevents criticism, but in so doing it also prevents growth. In this instance it is necessary to concentrate upon the defence first – to look at her or his need to do so well, and to wonder what she or he would fear about making a mistake, doing it wrong, and hence even about taking a risk. The skill of the assessor (and, in other situations, of the counsellor or therapist) is to do all this, and to convey criticism without being felt to be judgemental. Tone of voice clearly helps; choice of words is very important; but references such as 'You may take this the wrong way, and think I am being very critical of you; and to some extent of course I am, but not in the way you think . . .' will also be frequent prefaces to what in the end are (of course) critical comments. The assessor, counsellor and therapist, too, must not be afraid of making mistakes, as long as he or she can own them; and, needless to say, is not required to model a perfect performance!

6

Co-operation and competition

Introduction

The third major theme which is presented by clients in counselling and therapy is linked to the third stage of development, which is known variously as the 'phallic', 'genital', 'locomotor-genital' or 'oedipal' stage. In *The Presenting Past* I expanded the genital emphasis not only to include the broader term 'oedipal' (which stresses triadic relationships, rather than physical sexual differences as central to this stage). I also added 'social relationships' and 'rivalry' as other key terms that had to be included if the fuller implications of this period of life were to be recognized. In refining my thinking I now prefer to summarize the main themes of this stage of development in the briefer and more comprehensive phrase 'co-operation and competition'; and were it not already long enough, the summarizing phrase might also include 'complementarity'.[1]

Co-operation and competition provide a convenient way of describing issues and concerns at this particular point of a child's life. As themes they continue to be influential into what Freud styled the 'latency' period (see below), through adolescence and throughout adulthood. Genital differences (to take the original Freudian emphasis) sometimes lead to competitiveness, towards one's own as well as towards the opposite gender; although genital differences can be both transcended (in most relationships) and enjoyed (in a few special relationships) through co-operativeness and complementarity. More importantly than the genital, close relationships also hold co-operation and competition in some sort of tension – a tension which can be creative or destructive depending on which of the two qualities is in the ascendant. The triadic situation which is symbolized in the classical Oedipus story and in the oedipal tensions in some families illustrates one of the central facets not only of the growing child's relationships but also of many adult relationship patterns. Furthermore, co-operation and competition extend into the field of learning (begun in a major way at this stage of development) and into the major arena of adult life, the workplace. Competition is inevitable at certain key points in life; but co-operation has often been neglected because of an over-emphasis (at least in the male world, which so dominates society) on competitiveness.

The exercises in this chapter provide possibilities for insight into different aspects of co-operation and competition. Three-person situations and gender issues are complemented by some attention to the relevance of the themes for learning situations and for team work. Those who know the Erikson 'Eight Ages' will observe that the fifth stage of latency[2] does not get a special chapter in this book. I would wish now to give greater emphasis to a latency *mode* (a state of mind) than to the latency *stage*: the latency mode is entered whenever we find ourselves in a learning environment, or whenever we evaluate or reflect upon a series of events, and learn from our experience. Although I call latency a mode rather than a theme, like a theme it not only extends through the years at school and, for some people, into further and higher education, but also continues throughout adult life, with special periods of particular learning or relearning. At many points there is the possibility of informally engaging (consciously or unconsciously) in a latency mode; every situation presents an opportunity for learning. It scarcely needs saying the latency theme also applies to the three pre-latency stages: the early years of life involve a phenomenal degree of learning through experience. What blocks, prevents or hinders learning at any stage, as I make clear in *The Presenting Past*,[3] is the interference of difficulties arising from any or all of the three major themes of trust and dependency, autonomy and authority, and co-operation and competition. It is these issues, especially those of co-operation and competition (the former generally enhancing and the latter for most people destroying opportunities of learning) which two of the exercises (6.3.1 and 6.3.2) seek to simulate.

Exercise 6.1: A fictitious election[4]

Purpose

This exercise simulates the tensions in three-person relationships, particularly looking at what tactics people adopt which result in such situations, and how it feels to be included or to be the 'odd one out'.

Duration

1 hour.

Method

A simulation using an imaginary historical setting in which, after a period of preparation, three people vie as to which two will form an alliance, and which will become the leader, while the third is forced out. The feelings evoked by these experiences are examined in small groups.

Materials

Four sets of briefing papers, each to be distributed to a quarter of the class.

(i) Observer's briefing

In this simulation we are looking at the way in which 'two may be company, but three a crowd', or the way in which alliances (between individuals) are made and broken. Three people meet, any two of them must form an alliance, with one of the two as the dominant partner; this inevitably means that the third person will be left out. How does this take place? What does each person do or say, or not do, which leads that person either to be the dominant partner in the alliance, or the second 'junior' partner in the alliance, or the one who is left out?

The simulation is simple: each of the three participants represents the leader of a semi-historical political party, each of whom has won a third of the seats at an election. Their (completely unhistorical) manifestos mean that there are equal chances of any two becoming allies, so that no one has an unfair advantage before the simulation starts. What tactics does each person use to get into the alliance, and get

Exercise 6.1: Continued

power (one has to become the prime minister of a two-party alliance)? Watch the three negotiating and record your observations below:

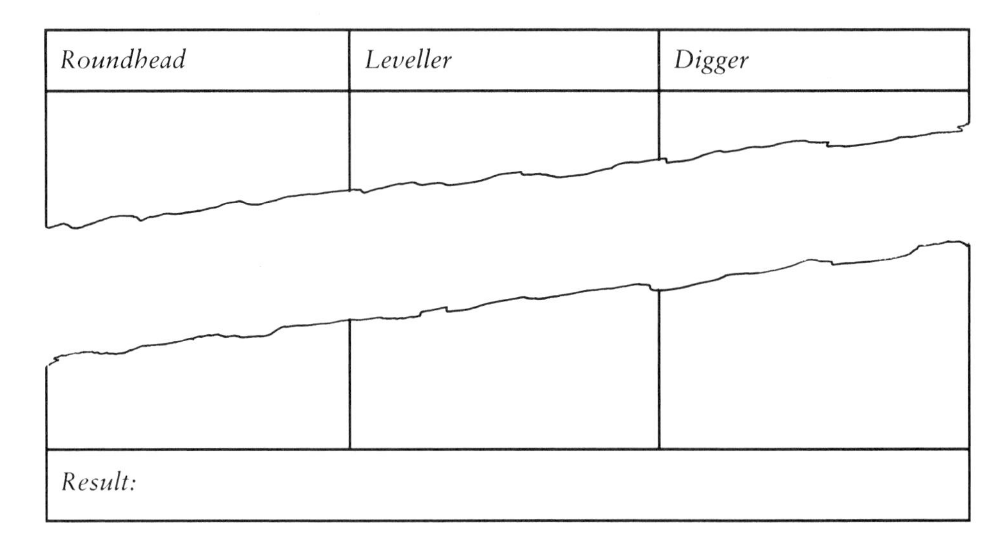

Roundhead	*Leveller*	*Digger*
Result:		

(ii) The Roundheads

It is 1648 and there has just been a general election in which the three parties – the Roundheads, the Levellers and the Diggers – have each won exactly one-third of the seats. There is now a period of negotiation, out of which a coalition must be formed by two of the parties; a coalition which must include an agreement by the two parties concerned as to which of them shall nominate the prime minister.

After the initial party meeting to discuss the situation, you will become the leader of the Roundheads; in the allotted time, use whatever negotiating skills (and tricks) you have in order to decide with which of the other two leaders you are going to form a government, and who is going to lead it.

Your party was elected on the following manifesto:

1 to confine the King to the Isle of Wight;
2 to license witches and wizards;
3 to withdraw troops from the American colonies;
4 to raise the ship tax;
5 to make attendance at chapel compulsory;
6 to levy a potato tax on imports from Ireland.

Exercise 6.1: Continued

But you were firmly opposed to:

(a) finance for research by alchemists;
(b) closer links with the Low Countries;
(c) the communal ownership of sheep.

(iii) The Levellers

It is 1648 and there has just been a general election in which the three parties – the Roundheads, the Levellers and the Diggers – have each won exactly one-third of the seats. There is now a period of negotiation, out of which a coalition must be formed by two of the parties; a coalition which must include an agreement by the two parties concerned as to which of them shall nominate the prime minister.

After the initial party meeting to discuss the situation, you will become the leader of the Levellers; in the allotted time, use whatever negotiating skills (and tricks) you have in order to decide with which of the other two leaders you are going to form a government, and who is going to lead it.

Your party was elected on the following manifesto:

1 to raise the ship tax;
2 to make attendance at chapel compulsory;
3 to levy a potato tax on imports from Ireland;
4 to finance research by alchemists into turning base metals into gold;
5 to forge closer links with the Low Countries;
6 to bring about the communal ownership of sheep.

But you were firmly opposed to:

(a) confining the King to the Isle of Wight;
(b) licensing witches and wizards;
(c) withdrawing troops from the American colonies.

(iv) The Diggers

It is 1648 and there has just been a general election in which the three parties – the Roundheads, the Levellers and the Diggers – have each won exactly one-third of the seats. There is now a period of negotiation, out of which a coalition must be formed by two of the parties; a coalition which must include an agreement by the two parties concerned as to which of them shall nominate the prime minister.

After the initial party meeting to discuss the situation, you will become the leader of the Diggers; in the allotted time, use whatever negotiating skills (and tricks) you have in

Exercise 6.1: Continued

order to decide with which of the other two leaders you are going to form a government, and who is going to lead it.

Your party was elected on the following manifesto:

1 to finance research by alchemists into turning base metals into gold;
2 to forge closer links with the Low Countries;
3 to bring about the communal ownership of sheep;
4 to confine the King to the Isle of Wight;
5 to license witches and wizards;
6 to withdraw troops from the American colonies.

But you were firmly opposed to:

(a) raising the ship tax;
(b) making attendance at chapel compulsory;
(c) levying a potato tax on imports from Ireland.

Instructions

1 Divide the class into four groups, three of which must be of equal size, although it cannot be helped if the fourth is slightly smaller or larger. This fourth group consists of the observers, who are given the observers' briefing sheet (i). The role of the observers is crucial to this exercise, inasmuch as they can spot and later describe the reactions of the combatants to each other (aggressive, manipulative, co-operative, passive, defeatist, etc.) and also the strategies they adopt. Where the observer group is one person smaller than the other three groups (the political parties), the tutor can make up the numbers. If the observer group is one person more, two observers can watch one of the simulations.
2 The three equal-size groups are political parties, the Levellers, the Diggers and the Roundheads. Although they are not unhistorical groups, they each have a manifesto, included in the briefing sheets (ii), (iii) and (iv), for a purely fictitious election. Once the party groups have been formed, each party member receives a copy of her or his party's manifesto (and that manifesto alone).
3 The party group meets on its own for ten minutes to decide how they will go about their task, while the observers also prepare together for their role. If these groups are too large they can be subdivided for this ten-minute period.
4 After this period of preparation, form small groups consisting of four people: one Digger, one Leveller and one Roundhead; and one observer. From this

Exercise 6.1: Continued

point onwards each party member is the leader of her or his political party.

5 The three party negotiators in each small group have twenty minutes in which to decide which two parties are to form the coalition, and of those two which one party will nominate the prime minister. The tutor needs to remind groups of the passage of time, especially in the last five minutes. It is essential to insist from the start, and to go on insisting as the negotiation period comes to a close, that a solution must be found before time runs out: there must be two parties who have formed a coalition, and one of the two party leaders must be the prime minister.

Debriefing

When the end of the simulation time is called, the observers take five to ten minutes to share their observations with the threesome to which they are attached.

Then three new groups are formed: the prime ministers, 'junior' partners in the coalition, and those who have been excluded (or who, more positively, see themselves in opposition). The observers form their own group and share notes.

In this debriefing it is valuable to look at how people got into their particular group – prime ministers, partners, and excluded. What did they do or not do? What did they feel at the time, and how do they feel now? What do they think of the others for their tactics? In what ways does this exercise remind them of the ways things happen in threesomes, in families, etc., where so often it seems 'two's company, three's a crowd'.

The third group, those who are left out, may need to be affirmed in their determination to stand by what they believe, although often they have seen it for themselves and feel proud of it.

Comment

This exercise can help the participants experience vividly what it is to be caught up in three-person situations, and can demonstrate the way in which children and/or adults, whenever they find themselves in triangular relationships of any significance, use obvious and devious tactics in their attempts to gain the position they want. The old phrase 'Two's company, three's a crowd' sums up the exercise. Erikson's description of 'the infantile politics of nursery school, street corner and barnyard'[5] is an equally poignant phrase, although he would be the first to admit that on the whole younger children cope with making and breaking alliances rather more resiliently than adolescents and adults, and that the most damaging 'infantile politics' takes place among those who imagine themselves to be 'grown up'.

Exercise 6.1: Continued

There are a number of features in the outcome of this exercise which merit comment. It is important to notice how the group of those who are 'left out' frequently consists of people who stick to their principles and are not prepared to compromise. Such a trait might be seen by others as foolish or as noble: but whichever way the reader interprets it, it does appear that many of them feel so strongly that they were elected on the basis of a definite set of promises, that they are not willing to play the political game of dropping or changing them in order to gain power. Of course, a few of them have been unable to put up a strong case, and are defeated by the sheer verbal or argumentative powers of the other two participants; but experience suggests that these are rarer than one would imagine.

The 'middle' group, the junior partners in the alliance, are sometimes people who have been persuaded to sell themselves short by a forceful prime minister in order to gain a share of power; but they can also be the real agents in this situation, those who have the deviousness to say 'I'll make you prime minister if you let me get in on the action'. Moreover, this is an extremely powerful position to occupy, because the prime minister is the one who will be criticized if things go wrong; the so-called 'junior' partners live to fight another day. There is sometimes some concern in this group at the degree of power they have wielded, and at just how manipulative they have been.

The group of students who may well be pleased with themselves is the one where all the prime ministers have come together; but they sometimes also take stock and realize that a few of them have been put there and have not got there simply by virtue of their ability to argue their case, or by their charm. They may also feel guilty at knocking the third group out, without having the compensation that those in the third group have that they at least showed integrity.

Finally it is worth seeing what happens to the men in the class in this exercise. On one particularly memorable occasion the exercise was conducted with nine small groups of party leaders, seven of which consisted of one man and two women, the others of three women. (There were also a few men as observers.) The first question to be asked is whether the men, in deciding which threesomes to join, avoided being in one which would bring them into rivalry with another man. But what was even more remarkable is that when the final groups formed, the prime ministers' group consisted of seven men and two women! The two women came from the groups of three women, and therefore had to be represented: that all seven men had become prime minister from their threesomes was something they themselves did not notice until it was pointed out to them!

Exercise 6.2: The judgement of Paris

Purpose

The exercise deliberately raises issues about gender stereotyping, in order to examine the conscious and unconscious attitudes held by clients and counsellors alike.

Duration

At least 1 hour.

Method

Single-gender discussion groups look at the stereotypes they have of the other gender, and the stereotypes which they think the other gender has of them. These are compared and contrasted and feelings about carrying such stereotypes examined.

Materials

A briefing sheet for all participants as follows:

The Judgement of Paris

'The Judgement of Paris' is a favourite subject for painters. Three women stand before Paris and Hermes who sit on the ground looking upon their nakedness. The Greek myth which gives rise to this portrayal of the Judgement of Paris begins when Eris, the personification of strife, rivalry and competition, at a feast of the gods, throws down a golden apple inscribed 'for the fairest'. The three goddesses among whom the apple was intended to cause strife are unable to agree which of them should have the prize. They are therefore taken by Hermes, the messenger of the gods, to be judged as to who is the fairest, by Paris, reputed to be the most handsome of mortal men.

It sounds too much like the first Miss World! But the myth contains some interesting aspects. The three goddesses were Aphrodite, the goddess of sexuality (who won the apple); Athena, the goddess of wisdom; and Hera, the goddess of motherhood. It is interesting that they represent the three-way split into which stereotypes of women often fall – the sex object, the intelligent woman ('just like a man'!), and the mother figure. Stereotypical men sometimes split their women into partial stereotypes, not allowing women to be whole persons.

Exercise 6.2: Continued

But suppose the myth had been the other way round – three gods judged by a woman, representing the different stereotypes which the stereotypical woman has of men? What would they have been the gods of? Ares (or Mars), the god of war? Zeus, the father of the gods? Dionysius, the god of fertility? Eros, the god of love? Apollo, the god of poetry and music?

The object of this exercise is to try and identify the stereotypes which men and women have of each other, or which they may have been brought up with. Bearing in mind that Greek gods and goddesses are often personifications of human *qualities*, the separate groups of men and women need to do two things:

(a) Make a list of five qualities which they think a 'typical' man might look for in a woman whom he sees as a potential partner.
(b) Make a list of five qualities which they think a 'typical' woman might look for in a man whom she sees as a potential partner.

Instructions

1. Divide the class into single-gender groups of four or five members each. In a typical class there are likely to be more groups of women than of men. Hand out the briefing sheets.
2. It is important throughout this exercise, including in the briefing, to remind students that they are trying to look at what the stereotypes are – not what an apparently enlightened class of 'new men' and 'liberated women' think!
3. The single-gender groups have twenty minutes to draw up both lists. Once they have agreed their lists they note them down.
4. Take feedback from the groups, writing these up clearly so that the lists can be compared and contrasted. The comment section below contains an example of such a composite record. What the men's groups think women look for in a man is set alongside what the women's groups report. What the women's groups think men look for in a woman is set alongside what the men's groups report.

Debriefing

Following the reporting, the single-gender groups first reflect on what it *feels* like to be perceived and treated in these stereotypical ways. Following this, mix the men and women up so that small groups have representatives of each to share these feelings from the women's and from the men's point of view. How have stereotypes/sexist

Exercise 6.2: Continued

attitudes been perceived? How does it feel and how do they respond when this happens? Do they just soak up these attitudes? How would they like to respond?

Comment

This exercise started life as a simulation.[6] But it became increasingly clear when it was run that as a simulation it carried with it the danger of reinforcing the very behaviour and attitudes it was designed to highlight and question. The original situation has therefore become the vehicle for a discussion of gender stereotyping, and a reminder that such issues are as old as the gods (and goddesses).

The following is a sample of some of the findings coming from single-gender groups when the present exercise has been used:

Men's stereotypes of women (as women perceive them)
Men look for a woman to be:
gentle rather than aggressive
placid/non-competitive/undemanding/compliant
caring/sympathetic/tolerant
intelligent but not too intelligent
motherly/practical/dependable
a good household manager/home-maker/cook
sexually responsive to him and him alone
a virgin who learns quickly
a friend
equal 60–40 in his favour
and to have:
physical beauty animated by attractive personality
good child-bearing hips – to continue his line
a sense of humour
Men's stereotypes of women (as men perceive them)
Women should be or show:
physical attractiveness
sexual faithfulness
intelligence but not too much
home-maker
a sense of humour
partner not competitor
mother/keeper
umbrella companionship

Exercise 6.2: Continued

Women's stereotypes of men (as men perceive them)
Women look for a man to be:
protective/dependable
assertive/decisive
attentive
a father/provider
a boy child – though obviously a man
and to have:
physical strength
good looks
intelligence
Women's stereotypes of men (as women perceive them)
Men should be or show:
physical attractiveness including strength
strength of character
social status
protective and supportive – of family as well
kind but not too gentle/caring
a friend
a knight on a white charger
sexual chemistry
financially reliable/successful
faithful
romantic
machismo/power/virility
knowledge/wisdom
vulnerability
a father
capacity to provide material comfort

It may be noticed that the women's groups provide a much fuller and more varied list in both instances than the men's, as though they are much more familiar with the experience of being stereotyped.

Exercise 6.3: Co-operation in learning

Purpose

These two exercises look at how far people are prepared to co-operate in learning or in problem-solving, raising issues of co-operation and competition in groups. The first raises the problem of whether people are prepared to be co-operative at all; the second, having established that co-operation is allowed, looks at how well people work together when jointly involved in solving a problem.

Duration

Exercise 6.3.1, 30–45 minutes; Exercise 6.3.2, 1 hour.

Method

Depending on the size of class, the group can be split into two equal halves, each half taking it in turn to be participants and observers in the two exercises. A large class will need sub-groups within the two half groups. If there are two subgroups of participants in either exercise, there may be some rivalry between them, which adds a further dynamic.

Exercise 6.3.1: The puzzle

Materials

Up to ten cards are necessary for this exercise, each card containing the wording included on the sample cards below.

Card 1

Among the people who went to a conference in London were three men from Nottinghamshire. Their surnames were Smith, Jones and Brown, and their first names were Peter, Leslie and Sam, but not necessarily in that order. They came from Mansfield, Newark and Normanton in a Fiesta, a Nova and a Metro.

Exercise 6.3.1: Continued

From the following clues identify Peter, Leslie and Sam's surnames, where they came from and what car they owned:

> Mr Smith drove a Fiesta and Peter drove a Metro. Mr Jones came from Normanton, but Sam Brown did not come from Mansfield.

Card 2

Among the people who went to a conference in London were three women from Northamptonshire. Their surnames were Taylor, Baker and Brown, and their first names were Pat, Lillian and Sue, but not necessarily in that order. They came from Wellingborough, Blisworth and Kettering in a Fiesta, a Nova and a Metro.

From the following clues identify Pat, Lillian and Sue's surnames, where they came from and what car they owned:

> Ms Taylor drove a Fiesta and Pat drove a Metro. Ms Baker came from Kettering, but Sue Brown did not come from Wellingborough.

Card 3

Among the people who went to a conference in London were three women from Kent. Their surnames were Smith, Jones and Brown, and their first names were Gladys, Mavis and Glenys, but not necessarily in that order. They came from Dover, Canterbury and Tonbridge in a Rolls, a Daimler and a Bentley.

From the following clues identify Gladys, Mavis and Glenys' surnames, where they came from and what car they owned:

> Mrs Smith drove a Rolls and Gladys drove a Bentley. Mrs Jones came from Tonbridge, but Glenys Brown did not come from Dover.

Card 4

Among the people who went to a conference in London were three men from Sussex. Their surnames were Taylor, Fletcher and Jones, and their first names were Joe, Leslie and Mike, but not necessarily in that order. They came from Lewes, Worthing and Horsham in a Volvo, an Audi and a BMW.

Exercise 6.3.1: Continued

From the following clues identify Joe, Leslie and Mike's surnames, where they came from and what car they owned:

> Mr Taylor drove a Volvo and Joe drove a BMW. Mr Fletcher came from Horsham, but Mike Jones did not come from Lewes.

Card 5

Among the people who went to a conference in London were three women from Lancashire. Their surnames were Fletcher, Brown and Taylor, and their first names were Elizabeth, Mary and Joan, but not necessarily in that order. They came from Preston, Fleetwood and Wigan in a Maestro, a Cavalier and a Sierra.

From the following clues identify Elizabeth, Mary and Joan's surnames, where they came from and what car they owned:

> Ms Fletcher drove a Maestro and Elizabeth drove a Sierra. Ms Brown came from Wigan, but Joan Taylor did not come from Preston.

Card 6

Among the people who went to a conference in London were three men from Yorkshire. Their surnames were Cox, Williams and Pearce, and their first names were Peter, Leslie and Sam, but not necessarily in that order. They came from Leeds, Whitby and Skipton in a BMW, an Audi and a Volvo.

From the following clues identify Peter, Leslie and Sam's surnames, where they came from and what car they owned:

> Mr Cox drove a BMW and Peter drove a Volvo. Mr Pearce came from Skipton, but Sam Williams did not come from Leeds.

Card 7

Among the people who went to a conference in London were three women from Scotland. Their surnames were MacDuff, McCleod and Campbell, and their first names were Catriona, Flora and Fiona, but not necessarily in that order. They came from Perth, Glasgow and Aberdeen in a Fiesta, a Nova and a Metro.

Exercise 6.3.1: Continued

From the following clues identify Catriona, Flora and Fiona's surnames, where they came from and what car they owned:

> Mrs MacDuff drove a Fiesta and Fiona drove a Metro. Mrs Campbell came from Aberdeen, but Catriona McCleod did not come from Perth.

Card 8

Among the people who went to a conference in London were three men from Wales. Their surnames were Thomas, Jones and Lloyd, and their first names were David, Dylan and Edward, but not necessarily in that order. They came from Cardiff, Barmouth and Caernafon in a car, on a train and by coach.

From the following clues identify David, Dylan and Edward's surnames, where they came from and their form of transport:

> Mr Thomas came by train and Edward by coach. Mr Lloyd came from Cardiff, but Dylan Jones did not come from Barmouth.

Card 9

Among the people who went to a conference in London were three women from America. Their surnames were Feinstein, Goldberg and Miracello, and their first names were Marilyn, Debbie and Jayne, but not necessarily in that order. They came from Santa Monica, Washington and Miami by TWA, Virgin Atlantic and British Airways.

From the following clues identify Marilyn, Debbie and Jayne's surnames, where they came from and with which airline they flew:

> Ms Miracello flew with TWA and Jayne with Virgin Atlantic. Ms Goldberg came from Santa Monica, but Debbie Feinstein did not come from Miami.

Card 10

Among the people who went to a conference in central London were three men from the suburbs. Their surnames were Fletcher, Williams and Taylor, and their first names were Dave, Jack and Steve, but not necessarily in that order. They came from Dulwich, Hendon and Islington by bike, tube and bus.

Exercise 6.3.1: Continued

From the following clues identify Dave, Jack and Steve's surnames, where they came from and what form of transport they used:

> Mr Taylor came by bike and Dave by bus. Mr Williams came from Dulwich, but Jack Fletcher did not come from Hendon.

Instructions

1. It is important to say as little as necessary in introducing the purpose of the exercise, and in setting it up. It should *not* be introduced as an exercise in co-operation or competition in learning. It gains considerably from being a vehicle for all manner of assumptions by the participants and the observers.
2. Divide the class into two halves, with up to ten participants in the exercise, and an equal number of observers. The participants are seated in an arc, on chairs which are neither too close together, nor too far apart. (The participants need to be able to make up their own minds whether to work together or not, so the seating should try to be 'neutral'.) The observers are seated opposite them: each observer is asked to concentrate upon one participant. Observers are asked to note down everything that happens to the participant whom they are watching.
3. One of the cards is given to each participant. The *only words* that are spoken by the tutor are: 'The only rule is "Please do not write on the card"'. Those words are to be said as a clear signal to start, and no more is yet said, and no questions answered.
4. It is what happens next that is interesting. Do the participants work on their own? Do they look at each other's cards? How do they react when they discover that their cards are similar, then different, and then similar again? Does any pair co-operate, or is there any attempt to get the group to work together? How do people respond if this suggestion is made by one of them? If one finishes does she or he help another, and in what way? Do they solve it for them, or teach them?
5. It is often necessary, because the group members assume they are not allowed to work together, to repeat after a few minutes: 'The only rule is "Please do not write on the card"'. This seems to hint that they can co-operate, although sometimes the reminder of 'the only rule' has to be given a second time before some decide to work together. Of course there is also nothing to stop a participant going to their observer and involving them.
6. This part of the exercise does not have to run for too long. It can be called to a halt when it feels as if enough has happened to make feedback useful.

Exercise 6.3.1: Continued

Debriefing

In feedback each participant is given the opportunity to tell the group what went through their minds during the exercise; this is followed by their observer commenting on what they saw. As feedback is taken the lessons from the exercise can be drawn out, about competition, co-operation, styles of working, teaching, slavish obedience to the tutor, assuming rules which were not given, etc.

Comment

Solving problems is a frequent part of many learning situations. Typical of the attitudes engendered at school is one which assumes that each person is trying to be 'top' of the class, and, therefore, in helping someone else in the class, risks the other person doing at least as well as, if not better than him or her. Another typical attitude is one that assumes that the person who looks across for help is either 'cheating' or 'cribbing'.

Exercise 6.3.2: Who owns the canary?[7]

Materials

A copy of the conundrum below for each participant in the 'team' (not the observers).

Who owns the canary?

There are five houses in a row, each with a front door of a different colour, and with different trees in the garden. Each one is the home of a family of a different nationality, who own different pets, and have different favourite drinks.

The British family live in the house with the red door.
The Nigerian family own a dog.
Coffee is drunk in the house with the green door.
The Russian family drink tea.
The house with the green door is immediately to the right (your right) of the house with the ivory door.

Exercise 6.3.2: Continued

The family with a pine tree in the garden own a goat.
The family with a birch tree in the garden live in the house with the yellow door.
Milk is drunk in the middle house.
The Indian family lives in the first house on the left.
The family with an elm tree in the garden live next door to the family who own a goldfish.
Water is drunk in the house next to the house where the family own a cat.
The family with a willow tree in the garden drink orange juice.
The Japanese family have an oak tree in the garden.
The Indian family lives next to the house with the blue door.
The Nigerian family live next to the family who drink coffee.

Which family owns the canary?

Instructions

1 If this exercise is used in the same session as Exercise 6.3.1 above, reverse the participants and observers, so the observers now become participants and vice versa. The observers this time watch the whole participant group, although they may also wish to comment on the contribution of individuals in the group. The participants are clearly told that in this instance this is an exercise in teamwork.
2 Hand out the exercise 'Who Owns the Canary?' to the participant members, while the observers sit outside their circle watching them. When it feels as if this exercise has gone on for long enough, split the participants and the observers in two, so that they can share in two mixed groups what they feel happened in terms of co-operativeness and teamwork. Particularly look for any differences in the way women and men react, initiate, get taken notice of, lead, etc. It is not necessary to wait until the problem has been solved before stopping the exercise, although obviously a group which is very close to solving it might be given that pleasure.

Debriefing

The observers share what they have seen with the whole group, and discussion can take place on what examples there were of co-operation and competitiveness in trying to work together as a team. Following either exercise or both of them students can be given an opportunity in small groups to discuss their own experience of education, and how they function when they are in 'the latency mode'.

Exercise 6.4: Imaginative exercise on being a four-year-old

Purpose

This exercise can be used to sum up the theme of co-operation and competition, by drawing upon knowledge coming from reading, experiential learning and observation, and using it in the form of a guided fantasy.

Duration

1 hour.

Method

Pairs of students write an imaginative description of an hour in the day of a four-year-old child, and then take another pair through a guided fantasy.

Materials

None.

Instructions

1 Form pairs, and give them thirty minutes to write an imaginative description of an hour in the day of a four-year-old child. The finished 'story' will probably take about five minutes to deliver, at a slow pace.
2 They should decide what pleasant and unpleasant experiences to incorporate into the 'hour in the day of . . .'. They write the experience in the second person (e.g. 'You walk into the large noisy hall, holding your mother's hand. She passes your hand to a stranger and says "Goodbye, see you later" leaving you alone . . .'. Obviously the exercise might use a few words of which the four-year-old child does not yet know, but essentially they should keep the description simple, concrete and vivid, using a four-year-old's vocabulary as much as possible.
3 Each pair joins with another pair. Where at all possible they should find a quiet and comfortable spot to meet. One partner in the first pair asks the

Exercise 6.4: Continued

others to relax, to close their eyes, and imagine they are a four-year-old child; taking them through the imaginary hour, and the different experiences within it. This needs to be taken slowly enough to let the participants feel their way into the situations described – the whole 'hour' will probably be condensed into about five minutes in all. After a brief pause, one of the partners in the second pair takes the others through their imaginative description.

Debriefing

The foursome finish by discussing the experience together for about fifteen minutes, also comparing notes on the content which each pair chose to include.

Exercise 6.5: Role-plays

Purpose

The following four role-plays illustrate various aspects of issues of co-operation and competition, and/or of sexual/marital relationships. They provide practice in counselling skills as well as in relating developmental issues of co-operation and competition to the client's presenting material.

Duration

60–75 minutes for any one role-play. It is suggested that each role-play lasts for forty minutes, with up to twenty minutes allowed for 'time out' (see Chapter 1).

Method, etc.

See Exercise 1.2, Chapter 1, for method, materials, instructions and debriefing. Comments on possible handling each of the situations appear after the last script. Debriefing and analysis of the counsellor's work are, of course, essential and may take a further thirty minutes after the role-play.

Exercise 6.5: Continued

(i) Working with couples: Madge and Frank Harris

(a) Briefing for Mrs Madge Harris (aged fifty)

The counsellor has a separate briefing sheet. Please note that the first paragraph below is common knowledge to you and your husband, Frank, but the second paragraph is only on your sheet. You may, of course, reveal any of this as you feel appropriate in the session. During 'time out' it is up to you whether you choose to speak to your partner or not, in or out of role, but you should agree this between you first.

Frank and Madge have been quarrelling a lot lately. Madge's widowed father was taken ill recently and will not be able to live by himself any more. He has asked to come and live with you, and is going to need a lot of care and attention. He has always been a demanding, complaining 'old bugger' (Frank's words) and Madge agrees, but Frank and Madge disagree about what should be done. Madge feels it is her duty as a daughter to have him (she has a sister who lives in Canada, but otherwise only an aged aunt). Frank bitterly resents the idea of his coming. Both had been looking forward to doing lots of things together now that the family have grown up and left home, and married. Frank is a teacher in the Art and Design department of a middle school, having got a job in teaching before the days when there were restrictions on those who had not been trained in teaching. He has done very well from humble beginnings. Over the last two years Madge (who has a part-time job in a local shoe shop) has been to evening classes and she has learned to paint. The two had planned weekends and tours away, residential classes, etc., where they could share their interest in art and travel together. The quarrels have got too much. Frank has gone very quiet recently. Madge spoke to a friend who recommended a counsellor. When she rang the counsellor, and said she was worried about her marriage, and wanted help because she was bursting into tears all over the place, the counsellor said that she or he would prefer, if it were possible, to see both Frank and Madge together. Madge has 'persuaded' Frank to come with her to the first appointment.

Madge: You feel dreadful. Life looked so promising and now you feel your marriage is in ruins. You can't turn your back on your father, but you are terrified that Frank will leave you rather than live in the same house as your father. Try to get the counsellor on your side, and try to get her or him to back up your sense of duty. But if the counsellor encourages you to speak directly to Frank about your worries, make a great effort to persuade Frank of the correctness of your position.

(b) Briefing for Mr Frank Harris (aged fifty-five)

The counsellor has a separate briefing sheet. Please note that the first paragraph below is common knowledge to you and your wife, Madge, but the second paragraph is only on your sheet. You may, of course, reveal any of this as you feel appropriate in the

Exercise 6.5: Continued

session. During 'time out' it is up to you whether you choose to speak to your partner or not, in or out of role, but you should agree this between you first.

Frank and Madge have been quarrelling a lot lately. Madge's widowed father was taken ill recently and will not be able to live by himself any more. He has asked to come and live with you, and is going to need a lot of care and attention. He has always been a demanding, complaining 'old bugger' (Frank's words) and Madge agrees, but Frank and Madge disagree about what should be done. Madge feels it is her duty as a daughter to have him (she has a sister who lives in Canada, but otherwise only an aged aunt). Frank bitterly resents the idea of his coming. Both had been looking forward to doing lots of things together now that the family have grown up and left home, and married. Frank is a teacher in the Art and Design department of a middle school, having got a job in teaching before the days when there were restrictions on those who had not been trained in teaching. He has done very well from humble beginnings. Over the last two years Madge (who has a part-time job in a local shoe shop) has been to evening classes and she has learned to paint. The two had planned weekends and tours away, residential classes, etc., where they could share their interest in art and travel together. The quarrels have got too much. Frank has gone very quiet recently. Madge spoke to a friend who recommended a counsellor. When she rang the counsellor, and said she was worried about her marriage, and wanted help because she was bursting into tears all over the place, the counsellor said that she or he would prefer, if it were possible, to see both Frank and Madge together. Madge has 'persuaded' Frank to come with her to the first appointment.

Frank: You do not know what counselling really is, and although you are fed up with the quarrels, and agree to see the counsellor, you are seething inside, withdrawn, and resentful that a third person (Madge's friend/the counsellor/as well as her father in the first instance) has to be brought in to your relationship – though your counsellor needs to see this parallel for you to admit it openly. If the counsellor helps you acknowledge how you feel, you may become more talkative, but then want to win the counsellor over to your side of the argument. Only if the counsellor encourages you to talk with Madge directly – and steers you away from getting the counsellor on your side – do you begin to express to Madge what you feel, and perhaps, if a way seems possible, your willingness to try and arrive at a solution.

(c) Counsellor's briefing for Madge (aged fifty) and Frank (aged fifty-five)

Madge spoke to a friend who recommended a counsellor. When she rang you, and said she was worried about her marriage, and wanted help because she was bursting into tears all over the place, you said that you would prefer, if it were possible, to

Exercise 6.5: Continued

see both Frank and Madge together. Madge and Frank have come for their first appointment.

The following general guidelines are particularly applicable to working with a couple, and may in some respects assist your work with Frank and Madge:

1. Work with the two partners together from the beginning: although this may mean you have an individual session(s) with each of them at the start, or at some later stage, each is given the same. Do not start couple work when you have seen one partner for a while already.
2. Work with the relationship between the two of them, and not with the two of them as individual clients.
3. It can be easier to work with a co-therapist; this enables you both to model a relationship which is mutually supportive, but which does not avoid conflict; and where there is open communication. It also means less danger of being pulled in on one side or the other. It enables you to step back and observe from time to time while the other is more active.
4. Use the seating to put yourself at the same distance from each partner, able to see both; and enable the couple to make eye-contact with each other easily, and to touch each other if they wish. A Y-shaped seating plan is useful:

   P1 P2 — partners

   C — counsellor

5. Use your own eye movements to encourage the partners to speak to each other rather than to you, by looking as much at the one who is not speaking as the one who is.
6. Couple work tends to mean more frequent interventions on the part of the therapist/counsellor: steering the communication, enabling them to hear each other and to respond to each other.
   (a) Point out when they are speaking to you more than each other.
   (b) Observe either talking about the other as if he or she were 'out there'.
   (c) Be prepared to interrupt and say things like: 'Stop there', 'You are not listening', 'What do you feel about that?', 'How did you see that?'.
   (d) Enable couples to test out the assumptions they make about each other.

(ii) Briefing for Betty (aged thirty-five)

Inform your counsellor of your name and age, and that you are coming for your first appointment. The following information is for you to use as you feel appropriate within the session. There is no reason why you should hold any of it back.

Exercise 6.5: Continued

You are married, with two children aged ten and twelve, who are both 'lovely kids'. Your husband, Andrew, is forty-eight, thirteen years older than you, and the marriage is a happy one. You love Andrew, who is a steady person, easy going, but also unemotional. The physical relationship between you is 'all right'. Each of you goes out to work.

Your 'problem' is that you have a 'boyfriend' (your phrase): Colin is twenty-five, ten years younger than you. You have known him for a long time, because you used to work together, and you have always got on well. Colin is married to Denise, who is about his own age, and they have just had a young baby son. They appear to get on well together.

A foursome friendship has developed between the two couples, encouraged by you and Colin. You, Andrew, Colin and Denise spend quite a lot of time together. The other two know how well you and Colin get on, but Denise is busy looking after her new baby, and Andrew is a sort of grandfather figure to Denise's son. Denise likes your friendship and the help and advice you give her. Andrew does not realize anything is amiss: in his 'maturity' he seems very stable, but perhaps a bit staid.

You have not made love with Colin, but that is partly because there has been no easy opportunity. You are afraid that Andrew and Denise are too indulgent, and give you and Colin too much 'permission' to be together. You are aware that matters might get out of hand, breaking up both marriages, and you do not want that. But you also like to have Colin's company whenever there is the chance, and he appears to feel the same. You (though not Colin) feel you ought to make some sort of break, but you cannot bring yourself to do so. You keep on returning to the make-or-break theme, unless your counsellor helps you to move on to what these relationships seem to mean.

Develop imaginatively as you wish any aspects of Betty's family background which you consider might be pertinent in this type of situation.

(iii) Briefing for Keith (aged thirty-five)

Inform your counsellor of the name of the person you are playing and his age. The information below is yours to reveal as and when it feels right, and depending on how sensitive your counsellor is.

You are married with two young daughters. You work in middle management for a large private company. You have been working there for many years, having started as a trainee manager.

Every Friday the same group of you go to the local pub for lunch, and sometimes you meet at the end of the day for a drink in the company's social club, before the long journey home. Just recently one this group (Sue) separated from her husband, and you have spent a lot of time supporting her and helping her through her distress.

Exercise 6.5: Continued

Two weeks ago there was a company celebration for a very successful year's business, which you carried on in the social club after work. Both you and Sue had plenty to drink and you felt strongly attracted to each other. You gave Sue a lift home, and accepted her invitation to go in for a drink. Before long you ended up in bed together, although eventually you went home.

The next Monday you and Sue met again, and you wanted to treat the incident as a one-off event, but Sue wanted more. She has started to pressurize you at work, and you are increasingly worried that someone will realize, and that word could get back to your wife. You do not know how to handle this situation, and you feel that you have let everyone down, including yourself.

(iv) **Mr or Mrs Wilson** (**age: late thirties**)

The counsellor needs to be someone whom the client could have approached about an educational matter – a teacher perhaps – but he or she is not someone who knows any of the Wilson family personally.

Inform your counsellor of the name of the person you are playing and his or her age. The information below is yours to reveal as and when it feels right, and depending on how sensitive your counsellor is.

You are worried about your daughter Jane, who is taking A-levels in about nine months' time, and needs to pass with good grades in order to get a place at university. You have noticed that she seems down-hearted about her chances of getting good enough grades, and you feel that she does not appear to put in sustained effort. She spends too much time listening to music, or seeing her friends. But when you try to speak to her about the need to work hard if she is to pass, Jane says things like 'Don't; please don't go on at me. You are only making me feel more nervous.' You approach your helper initially in the hope that she or he can see Jane and try and help her with her lack of confidence.

If your helper is perceptive he or she will not get caught up on the difficulties which Jane apparently has, except inasmuch as you are yourself part of them. You were not able to go to university yourself, because you were not clever enough, or so you think. You very much want Jane to pass because this will mean that you satisfy in yourself what you now feel is an opportunity you wish you had had. You had very little interest shown in your schooling or your academic abilities by your parents: as far as they were concerned the pressure was to get a job, or get married and have a family. In their own way they pressurized you in that direction as much as you are tempted to pressurize Jane in the direction of university.

So in your attempts to help Jane to get confidence, you find that you are in fact making things even harder, saying things like 'You'll only pass if you work hard' or

Exercise 6.5: Continued

'You mustn't think that you are not as clever as your friends'. You are transferring your own lack of confidence in yourself on to Jane, and you need to look at your experience of school in order to see what that does to your own relationship to her. At first also you put pressure on the helper – you want her or him to produce results, too. But you ease up and talk more about your own anxieties about exams and tests at school, as long as the helper can direct your attention away from Jane and on to yourself.

Comment

Counselling courses need to include some reference to working with couples, with families and with groups, and not just to one-to-one work, even though the attention that can be given to working in these other arenas is necessarily slight. The first role-play provides an opportunity to try out the different technique that is often required when working with a couple. The briefing given to the counsellor in this role-play about particular techniques that may be useful in seeing Madge and Frank can also be presented to the observers, to assist them in the guidance they give the counsellor during 'time out'[8].

In the second role-play Betty needs to be given a chance to explore the various triangles present in this situation: herself and Colin and Denise; herself and Andrew and Denise; Colin and Andrew and herself; herself and Denise and the new baby. There is also Colin's triangle: himself and Denise and the baby, which may be making Betty particularly attractive at present. The younger–older aspects are similarly strongly in evidence – father and daughter (Andrew and Denise, perhaps also Andrew and Betty); and mother and son (Betty and Colin). Notice also the frustration Betty and Colin feel with their respective partners – Denise gives a lot of attention to the baby, Andrew is rather unemotional. The counsellor cannot tell Betty what to do, but can help her look at the many dimensions of this complicated set of relationships.

In the third role-play Keith provides in some respects a male version of Betty. Blurred boundary issues and responsibility in the helping relationship, informal in this instance, but also present in some more formal therapeutic relationships, are also raised by this situation. It is appropriate that Keith should take responsibility for the abuse of his position, even though it obviously takes two to create such a situation. Keith needs to look at the way in which he may have put pressure on Sue, and not just look at what he perceives as her pressure on him.

Although the fourth role-play is similar to 5.3.1 it is more about education and learning than about power and commercial success. It has been included to provide students with the chance of looking at some latency-mode difficulties arising in those in education, partly as a result of their own pressures upon themselves, but also the

Exercise 6.5: Continued

result of parental pressures and anxieties. Students sometimes have to carry the educational flag for their parents. The role-play is also useful where counselling trainees are preparing for assessment or examination on their own course, since it introduces some elements which may also interfere with their own ability to put themselves under examination.

7

Experiencing adolescence

Introduction

Adolescent attitudes and behaviour, together with the strong emotions so often experienced at such a time, are not uncommon among those of greater chronological age. Given the opportunity to let their hair down, adults often relish the chance to enjoy the freedom from responsibility that adolescents usually have; but also in sombre, rebellious or petulant moments in later life it is not unusual to find parallels with the stormy or angst-ridden times of adolescence. And what is true of individuals is also true of groups: given the cause or the occasion some large groups (or sub-groups within larger groups) show clear evidence of adolescent behaviour. This section builds on this capacity to re-experience adolescence with exercises which simulate being adolescent as well as working with young people in counselling.

Exercise 7.1: Halcyon days

Purpose

This large-group exercise provides participants with the chance either of recapturing or of experiencing for the first time some of the features present or missing in their adolescence.

Exercise 7.1: Continued

Duration

At least 2 hours.

Method

A large simulation, consisting of a wide variety of roles, nearly all of which are playing teenagers, milling around the school hall during a rainy lunchtime. All that then ensues results from the briefing instructions, the way in which the participants embroider their instructions, and the direction in which the general situation develops. Some of those playing teenagers are later given the chance to talk about their experience (as teenagers) with a teacher who is exercising pastoral care.

Materials

The exercise is a little time-consuming to prepare, although not in proportion to the amount of time that it runs. Effective preparation makes it easy to set up and conduct; it is not as complicated for students (who have only one script to follow) as it may appear here. The group briefing sheets for five different sets (or 'gangs') of teenagers are included below; and in each case there is also an individual briefing sheet for one member (or in the blue group, two members) of each set. Each person will also need a different coloured badge or sticker to match the colour indicated on her or his briefing sheet; the individual member in each group will need the same coloured badge but with a black star or asterisk upon it. These badges or stickers assist identification during the exercise. There also need to be instructions and black badges or stickers for those who will role-play the teachers.

'Red' group

For the next forty-five minutes you are an adolescent, aged between fourteen and sixteen. You are at school; it is raining; it is lunchtime, and you are milling around indoors with the other students in your year. There are a few teachers 'supervising' you (they are wearing black stickers or badges, and in the second half of the exercise will become available as personal tutors/counsellors to those who are individually briefed in the groups). You can choose to have as many or as few friends as you like in any of the other groups.

All those with the red sticker or badge are members of a group of friends who are planning a party next Saturday at one of your houses. Two of your group (now

Exercise 7.1: Continued

wearing a blue sticker or badge, with a star on it) yesterday went off in a sulk and joined the 'blue' group, who are planning a party of their own.

'Red' group – individual briefing

For the next forty-five minutes you are an adolescent, aged between fourteen and sixteen. You are at school; it is raining; it is lunchtime, and you are milling around indoors with the other students in your year. There are a few teachers 'supervising' you (they are wearing black stickers or badges, and in the second half of the exercise will become available as personal tutors/counsellors to those who are individually briefed in the groups). You can choose to have as many or as few friends as you like in any of the other groups.

All those with the red sticker or badge are members of a group of friends who are planning a party next Saturday at one of your houses. Two of your group (now wearing a blue sticker or badge, with a star on it) yesterday went off in a sulk and joined the 'blue' group, who are planning a party of their own.

In addition to anything else that happens in this exercise, you need to see yourself as the younger of two siblings in your family, your elder brother having done very well at school, and gone to university, and you feeling a great lack of confidence about your chances of getting anywhere academically. Actually you would like to be able to do a very practical job, something which would let you use your artistic abilities, but your parents are always holding your brother up as an example of what you feel they expect of you. In the second half of this session you go to see your school counsellor about your feelings about this.

'Blue' group

For the next forty-five minutes you are an adolescent, aged between fourteen and sixteen. You are at school; it is raining; it is lunchtime, and you are milling around indoors with the other students in your year. There are a few teachers 'supervising' you (they are wearing black stickers or badges, and in the second half of the exercise will become available as personal tutors/counsellors to those who are individually briefed in the groups). You can choose to have as many or as few friends as you like in any of the other groups.

All those with the blue sticker or badge are members of a group of friends who are planning a party next Saturday at one of your houses. Two of your group yesterday joined you from the red group of friends, having fallen out with them over their party. (Each is wearing a blue sticker or badge with a star.)

Exercise 7.1: Continued

'Blue' group – individual briefing (two copies)

For the next forty-five minutes you are an adolescent, aged between fourteen and sixteen. You are at school; it is raining; it is lunchtime, and you are milling around indoors with the other students in your year. There are a few teachers 'supervising' you (they are wearing black stickers or badges, and in the second half of the exercise will become available as personal tutors/counsellors to those who are individually briefed in the groups). You can choose to have as many or as few friends as you like in any of the other groups.

All those with the blue sticker or badge are members of a group of friends who are planning a party next Saturday at one of your houses. Yesterday you and another friend joined them, having fallen out with the red group of friends over their party.

You really were very good friends with the people in the red group, and whatever happens you have got very upset (whether or not you show it) over the way in which the friendship seems to have folded. As the session develops you will be able to develop your own story, and in the second half you will be able to see your school counsellor or personal tutor about feeling so upset or angry over the break-up of this friendship.

'Yellow' group

For the next forty-five minutes you are an adolescent, aged between fourteen and sixteen. You are at school; it is raining; it is lunchtime, and you are milling around indoors with the other students in your year. There are a few teachers 'supervising' you (they are wearing black stickers or badges, and in the second half of the exercise will become available as personal tutors/counsellors to those who are individually briefed in the groups). You can choose to have as many or as few friends as you like in any of the other groups.

All those with the yellow sticker or badge are members of a group of boys who are kicking their heels because it is too wet to play football. One of you (with a star on the sticker or badge) has taken a fancy to the girl with the starred red sticker or badge, and may talk about this with his friends.

'Yellow' group – individual briefing

For the next forty-five minutes you are an adolescent, aged between fourteen and sixteen. You are at school; it is raining; it is lunchtime, and you are milling around indoors with the other students in your year. There are a few teachers 'supervising' you (they are wearing black stickers or badges, and in the second half of the exercise will become available as personal tutors/counsellors to those who are individually

Exercise 7.1: Continued

briefed in the groups). You can choose to have as many or as few friends as you like in any of the other groups.

All those with the yellow sticker or badge are members of a group of boys who are kicking their heels because it is too wet to play football. You have taken a fancy to the girl with the starred red sticker or badge, and you can talk about this with your friends. At this stage of the exercise that is all you know; but however the situation develops, bear in mind that you will nevertheless be anxious if she accepts your invitation to go out, and unsure of how you are meant to behave. The other boys around you probably show a lot of bravado, but you are not so sure yourself. This, and anything else which has or has not developed is what you will be taking to your school counsellor or personal tutor during the second half of the session.

'Green' group

For the next forty-five minutes you are an adolescent, aged between fourteen and sixteen. You are at school; it is raining; it is lunchtime, and you are milling around indoors with the other students in your year. There are a few teachers 'supervising' you (they are wearing black stickers or badges, and in the second half of the exercise will become available as personal tutors/counsellors to those who are individually briefed in the groups). You can choose to have as many or as few friends as you like in any of the other groups.

All those with the green sticker or badge are members of a group of girls who are chatting about one of your friends (who is not in the group) who has told you about having slept with her boyfriend for the first time. The member of your group with the green sticker or badge with a star on it has taken a fancy to the boy with the starred yellow sticker or badge.

'Green' group – individual briefing

For the next forty-five minutes you are an adolescent, aged between fourteen and sixteen. You are at school; it is raining; it is lunchtime, and you are milling around indoors with the other students in your year. There are a few teachers 'supervising' you (they are wearing black stickers or badges, and in the second half of the exercise will become available as personal tutors/counsellors to those who are individually briefed in the groups). You can choose to have as many or as few friends as you like in any of the other groups.

All those with the green sticker or badge are members of a group of girls who are chatting about one of your friends (who is not in the group) who has told you about having slept with her boyfriend for the first time.

Exercise 7.1: Continued

You like one of the boys in your year (wearing a starred yellow sticker), and at this stage of the exercise that is all you know. As the exercise proceeds things may or may not happen, so that by the time the second half of the session starts, you will have something to talk about with your school counsellor or personal tutor, to whom you will eventually go about your feelings for this boy.

'White' group

For the next forty-five minutes you are an adolescent, aged between fourteen and sixteen. You are at school; it is raining; it is lunchtime, and you are milling around indoors with the other students in your year. There are a few teachers 'supervising' you (they are wearing black stickers or badges, and in the second half of the exercise will become available as personal tutors/counsellors to those who are individually briefed in the groups). You can choose to have as many or as few friends as you like in any of the other groups.

All those with the white sticker or badge are members of a group who are in the same class, complaining about a project on 'families' which one of the tutors has set. The one wearing a white sticker or badge with a star on it has had a row with her or his mum and dad about not being able to stay out late.

'White' group – individual briefing

For the next forty-five minutes you are an adolescent, aged between fourteen and sixteen. You are at school; it is raining; it is lunchtime, and you are milling around indoors with the other students in your year. There are a few teachers 'supervising' you (they are wearing black stickers or badges, and in the second half of the exercise will become available as personal tutors/counsellors to those who are individually briefed in the groups). You can choose to have as many or as few friends as you like in any of the other groups.

All those with the white sticker or badge are members of a group who are in the same class, complaining about a project on 'families' which one of you tutors has set.

You have had a row with your mum and dad about staying out late. You will be able to develop the situation, and your family background, as you go through the first part of the session; in the second half of the session you approach one of the personal tutors/counsellors to talk about the situation at home.

Teacher briefing

For the next forty-five minutes and into the second part of the session you are a teacher at a school, surrounded by a lot of adolescents, aged between fourteen and sixteen. It is

Exercise 7.1: Continued

raining; it is lunchtime, and they are milling around indoors. There are a few teachers 'supervising' with you (they have black stickers or badges, too), talking among yourselves but also keeping an eye on the students. Later, in the second half, you will become a personal tutor/counsellor to one of the students. This will be set up for you with observers, etc. There is nothing preventing you in the first half of the session from joining in whatever happens as you want to (in role as a teacher).

Instructions

1 The prepared briefing sheets are handed out at random at the start of the session as class members assemble. Note that briefing sheets and stickers for the green group can only be given to 'girls'; briefing sheets and stickers for the yellow group can only be given to 'boys'; and the individual briefing sheet and starred sticker for the red group can only be given to a 'girl'.
2 The number of members in the training group dictates how many of the teenage groups are used in the exercise. Although the following information seems complicated, tutors need only follow the instructions for the particular size of their group:
   (a) Where there are between ten and fifteen in the class, only use white, yellow and green groups, plus two teachers (black). Omit the sheet for the individual 'girl' in the green group, but still hand out a green 'starred' badge or sticker to one member of the green group. Substitute 'starred white sticker or badge' for the reference to 'starred red sticker or badge' on the sheets for the yellow group. Give the individual sheet and starred sticker for the white group to a 'girl'. These changes will still enable the exercise to work with a smaller group.
   (b) Where there are between sixteen and twenty-five use four groups (yellow, green, red, and blue, but not the white group) and four teachers (black). Omit the sheet for the individual 'girl' in the green group, but still hand out a green 'starred' badge or sticker to one member of the green group.
   (c) Where there are between twenty-six and thirty use all five groups (yellow, white, red, blue, and green) and five teachers (black), omitting only the sheet for the individual 'girl' in the green group, but still hand out a green 'starred' badge or sticker to one member of the green group.
   (d) Where there are more than thirty use all five groups and six teachers.
3 As backing for this exercise it is very effective to use some really good modern music: loud 'heavy metal' or whatever the taste of the day is! With this music

Exercise 7.1: Continued

already playing, the exercise should start as soon as people arrive for the session, when each one is given her or his briefing.

4 The exercise runs for forty-five minutes in all (although this time could be lengthened or shortened depending on the size of the group: the larger the group generally the greater the activity and therefore the longer the time). During this period there will be much to observe, although only those playing the teachers are likely to be observers: even they will not necessarily be left alone, and they may have to intervene from time to time to keep order. (One common response to those asked to play the teachers is that they feel deprived of the opportunity to be adolescents. Perhaps this says something about people who choose to work with this age group!)

5 After forty-five minutes most members of the simulation are asked to engage in debriefing in pairs. How did they feel during the time? What did it remind them of in their own adolescence? However, for the second part of the exercise, both the teachers and the students who received individual briefings are going to engage in conventional role-plays, based upon the experience which the individual teenagers have had in role during the simulation. They therefore need to meet during this general debriefing in separate groups ('clients' and 'teachers') to debrief so far, but aware that they will hold on to their role for the role-plays.

6 After this debriefing (about fifteen minutes) the teenage 'clients' and their 'teachers' are paired together; and small groups of observers from the rest of the class membership join them for role-plays. These last for forty minutes with up to twenty minutes' 'time out'.

Debriefing

Following the role-plays in the second half of the exercise, 'teachers' and teenage 'clients' need very thorough debriefing, since they have been in role for nearly two hours.

Exercise 7.2: Casework vignettes

Purpose

Using vignettes from books or from day-to-day practice, specific questions are asked of understanding and working with adolescent clients.

Duration

Up to 1 hour.

Method

Examples of the presenting difficulties of young people are taken from such books as *The Presenting Past*[1] and in *Counselling Young People*.[2] Specific questions are addressed arising out of these situations.

Materials

The following are examples of the way in which tutors[3] have used some of the many vignettes in the above two books:

(a) Ulric had great difficulty letting go of his feelings and emotions. He could only express himself in a distant intellectualized fashion. He discovered what his early weeks had been like when his sister had her first child. He had visited her at the same time as their mother, and heard mother telling his sister off for not putting the new-born baby on the pot straightaway: 'You and your brother were put on the pot from the first day out of hospital.' Ulric was amused, relieved (he realized it was not all his doing) and somewhat angry as he told this to the counsellor. It certainly helped him understand his problem of not being spontaneous, when his early life had been so ordered.[4]

> How might you try and help Ulric?
>
> How might he feel about coming to see a counsellor?

(b) Doris was saying how restricted she felt in her digs. She could not play music late at night, because it disturbed people; but others also disturbed her, the walls were so thin. Doris was one of those who find it difficult to enjoy

Exercise 7.2: Continued

themselves. She always felt she ought to be working. Her parents were still protective of her, never allowing her proper freedom, in case she got hurt. What they said when she was with them continued to exert a strong influence upon her when she was on her own. 'Working' was the only safe activity. The counsellor used her words about her digs to suggest that there were thin walls within herself, too, and that when she tried to enjoy herself she heard her parents saying 'Do be careful', 'You should be working', etc.[5]

What transference might Doris bring to counselling?

What counter-transference might she evoke in you?

(c) Andrew had been the nominal head of his family for eleven years since his father's death when he was thirteen. He'd also been around the world, picking up whatever menial work he could, and had just finished a degree in sociology. His favourite word for other people was 'ridiculous' and his relationships were all tainted with anger and contempt. He wrote letters to newspapers and organizations incessantly, complaining about unsatisfactory service or monstrous social problems which could easily be solved with a little of his intelligence. But he couldn't get a job, and he never instituted any reforms. People were rude to him, he thought, but it never occurred to him that the problem might lie within himself.[6]

How might you feel if Andrew was your client?

Would you feel able to help him?

Instructions

1 Select casework vignettes from the sources mentioned, or from personal experience.
2 Hand out copies of the vignettes to be used, together with the questions addressed out of the situation.

Debriefing

None.

Comment

This exercise can be used in relation to other age groups or client groups, by selecting the relevant examples.

Exercise 7.3: Role-plays

Purpose

The following two role-plays illustrate various aspects of being adolescent. They provide practice in using counselling skills with young adults.

Duration

60–75 minutes for any one role-play. It is suggested that each role-play lasts for forty minutes, with up to twenty minutes allowed for 'time out' (see Chapter 1).

Method, etc.

See Exercise 1.2, Chapter 1, for method, materials instructions and debriefing. Comments on possible handling each of the situations appear after the last script. Debriefing and analysis of the counsellor's work is, of course, essential and may take a further thirty minutes after the role play.

(i) **Briefing for Peter or Peta** (**aged sixteen**)

Before starting the role-play, tell your counsellor the name of the person you are playing, gender, and age.

You are extremely courteous during the interview: perhaps that politeness masks a nervousness and lack of confidence. You open it by asking politely 'Have you got a family of your own?' and then either 'Do you let them stay out late?' or 'If you had would you let them stay out late?'

You then go on to describe how you feel the laughing stock of the school and of others outside school because you have to be in by nine o'clock in the evening wherever you go. No one invites you to do anything with them now because of this. At school you are slow but industrious; you do not play games; you have little confidence; and do not really mix with schoolmates or other potential friends.

You have never told anyone why. You do not like to think you may be ridiculed, especially because you imagine that other young people do not take much notice of their parents.

Your mother is a house-bound invalid, and has been as long as you can remember.

Exercise 7.3: Continued

She is very bitter, and suspicious of everything you do. Your father runs the home and has a full-time job, and absorbs the continual complaints from his wife. He tries to cushion you and support you in everything in which you show interest, but he dare not cross your mother on the question of the time you have to be in. She rules the roost, especially by drawing attention to how hard life has treated her.

If your helper gives you the confidence to say it, you eventually come out with what you are loath to admit, even to yourself: that although your mother is ill, she does not try as hard as she might, and that she is driving you and your father mad; and that your father's capitulation to her makes you so angry with him that you cannot even look upon him as an ally.

(ii) Briefing for Tim (aged nineteen)

Before starting the interview, inform your counsellor of your name, gender, and age. Agree with your counsellor what sort of helper it would be most appropriate and comfortable for her or him to play (a counsellor, teacher, social worker, etc.) and where the interview is taking place. The information below is yours to reveal as and when it feels right, and depending on how sensitive your counsellor is.

You have what you call a 'slight difficulty' to talk over with your counsellor. You have not got a girlfriend, and you very much want one. You are not sure what to do about it. If the counsellor gives you the opportunity, you go on to say that there is a girl who has been making it clear to you fairly directly, and also through others, that she likes you. This is really very exciting, but also very scary, because you have never had a girlfriend, and you don't know what to do. You are afraid that if you proceed too fast you will put her off; or that if you go too slowly you will show how timid you are and bore her. She has suggested you go to the pictures.

As your counsellor helps you talk, remember that you are equally anxious and reserved with her or him. You wonder how you ought to behave on the evening you are going out with her – all the questions which a rather younger person might wonder about. You are not actually worrying about sex itself, because as far as you are concerned it is the very simple things about first going out with a girl that worry you – whether she will accept you invitation to go out again, whether to hold her hand, and whether you should kiss her goodnight, etc. If your counsellor is insensitive, and takes this as being a sexual problem, then you (like you imagine the girl might be) are put off. What really concerns you is that as long as you don't make a move, she remains an object of fantasy; the risk is that once you start to test out this fantasy, she may say 'no' at any point, and you will feel so disappointed that it would have been better to stay clear in the first place.

Your parents aren't much help. Your mother particularly is sure to go round and tell

Exercise 7.3: Continued

all her relatives that you are virtually engaged to the girl, if you so much as mention her at home.

Comment

Peter's/Peta's politeness, and perhaps sadness, may render the counsellor pretty depressed and helpless, or even angry with Peter/Peta for being so submissive. Of course, the depression or the anger may be experienced by the counsellor as spilling over from Peter's/Peta's reaction to his/her mother. Yet another feature of this case that might be worth looking out for is the way in which Peter/Peta actually takes on the characteristics of the mother – making the counsellor feel that he or she cannot make a move either, that there is nothing that can be done, and that the counsellor feels as helpless as the father and Peter/Peta in the situation. So, despite appearances, Peter/Peta becomes very powerful in the counselling session, just as his or her mother becomes powerful in the family. She may lack power in ways which are none of her fault; but she could take responsibility for the way she uses her invalidity to invalidate others; and the way she uses her lack of physical mobility to exercise strength in other ways. Some of this may be experienced similarly in the counsellor–client relationship, which often reflects outside or earlier situations, even to the point of putting the counsellor in the client's position and the client in the position of 'identification with the aggressor'. The apparently weak, unconfident and timid Peter/Peta may also (quite unconsciously) lead the counsellor a merry dance!

One of the pleasures of working with many young people is that their difficulties are often 'growing pains'. Disastrous though their situation appears and feels to them, a supportive, encouraging, non-judgemental adult listener will often enable the adolescent to surmount the present hurdle, to gain some confidence, and to move rapidly ahead in developmental terms. The young person may come back, perhaps when another obstacle proves just too hard. But many adolescents wish to be independent of adult help, to find their own feet, and to 'do it themselves'. Tim in the second role-play is a good example. The counsellor who looks for underlying difficulties is likely to blow it. That is not to say that young people always present themselves in such straightforward ways: counsellors are aware of the increasing numbers of young people coming for help who have been abused, or who suffer severe eating disorders, or are extremely depressed, or are from the most dreadful family situations. But hopefully counsellors working in general settings will also have sufficient work of the 'Tim' variety to give themselves similar confidence to that which the young person will find, that some things work out relatively smoothly and relatively easily.

8

The ages of adulthood

Introduction

It is not an easy task to put the many years of adult life into a structure which acts as a guide to the understanding of human development. Freud's categorization of three stages of infancy is not reflected in his treatment of adult life, which appears to be only one stage. Erikson is more helpful in suggesting three stages of adult life: young and middle adulthood and old age.[1] But even these have an artificiality inasmuch as the main issues in each of them (intimacy, generativity and integrity) are not as age specific as Erikson's model seems to make them. Jung writes of the first and second half of life, including a long period of youth (up to forty years of age), with mid-life and old aged both placed in the second half of life.[2] But where the boundary is placed between any of these stages may depend not only on age but also on attitudes, both within oneself and towards one on the part of others collectively and individually. Attitudes to ageing, for example, are clearly seen in the results of the exercise which forms the basis of this section, and are present in every decade of life. Those who are in their twenties, for example, see those in their forties as being 'old', whereas those in their forties can often feel that they are still (at least in some respects) 'young', while those in their seventies can express despair about being old, or excitement at the opportunities which old age opens up. We are in one sense as old as we feel, and as old as other people make us feel.

The difficulty in studying these chronological stages in adult life led me in *The Presenting Past* to take the three Erikson issues in adult life as a whole, and translate them into 'themes', in much the same way as I take oral, anal and genital stages and convert them into oral (dependency, trust), anal (authority, autonomy) and genital (competitive, co-operative) themes. Thus I look at intimacy[3], generativity[4] and creativity and integrity[5] as life-long themes, even though they frequently have particular relevance as issues at certain ages. I illustrate aspects of these themes in Chapters 9 and 10.

Despite my reservations about concentrating too much on chronological ages, the following exercise has proved a favourite with students, and serves as a useful general introduction to the developmental themes of adult life. Indeed the results coming from this exercise, accumulated over ten years and included in the Comment on p. 165, provide a remarkably full account of attitudes to and at different ages, meriting a chapter to itself.

Exercise 8: The ages of adulthood

Purpose

This exercise serves as an invaluable introduction to the developmental approach to adulthood, enabling the issues and concerns typical of each decade of life to be identified. It also has a subsidiary purpose, that of examining the stereotypes about ageing, often diminishing anxiety about growing older.

Duration

2 hours.

Method

The class is divided into age bands, who address certain questions about themselves now, ten years ago, and ten years into the future. Reporting back from these questions by age bands provides a comprehensive picture of the issues, feelings, joys and concerns at various points in adult life.

Materials

Overhead projector slides, or some other means of displaying the questions addressed to age groups, set out in the Instructions below.

Exercise 8: Continued

Instructions

1 For this exercise it is necessary to have a fairly large class of mixed age (about twenty students is the minimum unless the age range is comprehensive).
2 The students are asked to divide into age groups – the twenties, thirties, forties, fifties, and sixties and over. If there is only one person in an age group they will need to join the nearest age group, where they can make their own contribution to the discussion, or if they wish, speak about their own age group. If one group is too large it can be split into two.
3 The groups are asked three sets of questions, divided into three slots of time, allowing about fifteen minutes for discussion in each time-period. All the questions in one section may be revealed at once, or four to five minutes given for each one. Each group will need a 'scribe' (perhaps a different one for each section) to record the group's findings. The questions asked of the groups are:
A The present:
What is it like being in your age group?
What are the issues that face men and women (alike or separately) in your age decade?
What are the pleasures of being your age?
What are the pressures/worries/problems of being your age?
B Look back ten years:
What was life like then?
What happy memories do you have?
What do you miss now that you had then?
What are you glad to have left behind?
C Look forward ten years:
What will life be like then?
What do you fear or dread?
What do you look forward to?

Debriefing

This takes the form of feedback from the age-band groups. It is best taken on separate overhead projector slides (especially since photocopies can be made from them for later distribution to the class). The OHP slides can contain the following headings, based upon the questions asked of the groups, which are completed as reports taken variously from the different groups, working through from the twenties to the sixties:

Exercise 8: Continued

(a) How the twenties see their teens:
How the twenties see themselves:
How the thirties see their twenties:

(b) How the twenties see the thirties:
How the thirties see themselves:
How the forties see their thirties:

(c) How the thirties see the forties:
How the forties see themselves:
How the fifties see their forties:

(d) How the forties see the fifties:
How the fifties see themselves:
How the sixties see their fifties:

(e) How the fifties see the sixties:
How the sixties see themselves:
How the sixties see the future.

The collated summaries of feedback from this exercise, which appear below, can be used as a resource by the tutor, should the class not have all the age groups represented. Where feedback is going to be missing due to the composition of the class, the summary material for that age group can be used instead: for example, if there are no students in their twenties in the class, the first two sections on slide (a) and the first section on slide (b) can be written up while the main questions are being discussed; they can then be spoken about during the feedback part of the exercise. The summaries might also be used to expand on any points not made in the group reports, although there may not be much time for this, since it takes about an hour to record feedback, especially if the class is large and all the ages are represented.

Comment

From using this exercise over a period of ten years, a valuable picture has been built up of the types of issue which different age groups consider important. What follows is a compilation of the feedback from the many times this exercise has been run. However, in using this material it is important to be aware of certain qualifications:

First, there are inevitably contradictory statements within the same section. But life is like that, and this is recognized in the psychological term 'ambivalence'.

Second, men and women in the same age bands may have quite different experiences – particularly where women shoulder the major responsibility for dependents, whether children (at one stage of life) or elderly parents (at another).

Exercise 8: Continued

Third, two key factors seem to influence the changing circumstances of the ages of adult life, making some experiences less dependent on the actual age of the subject than on the ages of their dependents. Thus parents (but particularly mothers) in their twenties with young children are likely to have many of the same pleasures and frustrations as women in their thirties with similar-aged children. Likewise, men and women in their forties (but again particularly women) with elderly and frail or infirm parents will tend to have the same constraints upon them as men and women in their thirties or fifties with similar parents.

Finally, these statements were made by mainly middle-class, mainly white, mainly fairly financially secure men and women, who were motivated sufficiently to explore themselves through the medium of adult education. There will be others in society, particularly those who are disadvantaged by poverty, colour, disability or lack of education whose lives are more bleak than the occasional sombre statement included below.

The teens: the twenties look back

Depression, loneliness, no one to dance with, shyness, insecurity, desperate feelings, lack of confidence, conscious of making mistakes; conflict with parents, outbursts followed by guilt; parental guidance and warmth; lack of independence from parents; exaggerated feelings, things out of proportion, emotional insecurity, as if things will never end; more sensitive, open, idealistic and optimistic about the future; holidays seemed better, more beautiful and more interesting; sense of discovery of the unknown; more image-conscious, high fashion, outrageousness; abundance of friends, group life, parties, pop idols; sporty, active, lots of energy; puberty, courting games, scared of sex, sexual excitement, new young love, confusion, getting attention; bitchiness, more aggressiveness; freedom, feeling 'adult' but also naive, as if life is no problem, lack of responsibility; independence on leaving home, bedsit life; lack of money.

The twenties

As the twenties see themselves

Reluctantly finding a niche; rebellious still, but less so; balance between youthfulness and growing maturity, conflict between 'ought' and 'must', commitment and self-desire; sense of expectation of parents and others, parents seen more as friends; close friends more important than acquaintances; looking for relationships; some still lonely; more risk in entering sexual relationships because there is more to lose; still exploring activities with other people; some feel more stable, some less stable; sense of

Exercise 8: Continued

freedom, independence, including financial independence, more money, though perhaps poverty for some; don't like pressure of being sucked into the system, pressure to conform; pressure from society to find long-term relationship; abundance of possibilities; not always taken seriously; more credibility, confidence and mobility; confidence in opinions, but not necessarily of capabilities; challenge and uncertainty still; in control of one's own destiny, becoming an individual, trying to establish oneself or one's persona; active giving and receiving of love; like being alive; looking forward with anticipation to future; realization of some of our dreams; physical well-being and attractiveness, fit enough to do anything, though aware already of physical decline and routines that come from responsibility, worry about getting old and parents getting old; mortgages and semi-detached; lot of changes – career, moving to another region; more stability in career; looking for work which is interesting, satisfying and long-term; protector of own children or of other people; decision of children versus career; some have families, some don't.

The thirties look back
Rosy, sense of freedom, irresponsibility, or less responsibilities and restrictions than later; endless energy and strength, wider view of time; choices, options, hopes and aspirations, with freedom to do as you please; fixed opinions, still seeing issues in black and white; frail and false sense of security, shyness, uncertainty, lack of confidence, identity as yet unfounded, indecision; selfishness, having to impress, competitiveness, peer-group competition; still concerned with what parents think, heavily influenced by others and authority figures, need to prove oneself in exams or job, conflict between own expectations and the hopes of others; earnestness and crusading spirit, big hopes and plans, many more openings, everything is possible, optimism, excitement about the future; holidays; physical well-being, feeling young, figure in proportion, good health; sexual freedom, height of romantic experience, developing sexual identity, high level of intimacy; socializing; difficulties in close relationships, not so sensitive to others; work identity not yet founded, work responsibilities, career-building; possession of 'wealth', more money, although also for some financial insecurities, and austerity if they have a family at this age; sense of isolation if they have young family, young demanding children, more ties, both fulfilling and boring.

The thirties

As anticipated by the twenties
Looking older, looking for a stable relationship; more crises; the final 'sell-out'; routine; dread of being static; hope for success, finding 'fame and fortune'; dream

Exercise 8: Continued

home, more time for ourselves; life less intense, less striving, less confusion, more self-acceptance; less sexually attractive, physical decline accelerates; a respected age, more esteem; building a career, settled in work, interest in work; 'have arrived'; secure, more comfortable financially; concern about society on behalf of one's children; less marketable; plenty of 'get up and go'; children – having them, and them growing up, though for some infertility; breaking away from parents; parents' ill health or death; time running out.

As the thirties see themselves

More alive than ever; not so assertive, more assertive; not as professionally compelled, not so competitive, hard work; financial and emotional security; established in career, promotion, crossroads of career, status in job, acquisition of material gains, want creature comforts, not so adaptable; resilient and affluent, major job decisions over, though career development for some; financial implications of career changes; personal achievement, demands come from self more than from others; stability, being one's own person, greater self-awareness, greater freedom, less sense of urgency, feelings are less intense, things less dramatic now, more open and tolerant, less black and white, more greys, less idealistic, more realistic; more outward-looking, prepared to learn more, more self-awareness, not afraid to be ourselves, less inhibited, can be 'stupid' and it doesn't matter, pleasure in being ordinary; value ordinary things; active social life, better relationships with spouse, children, and parents, more freedom from parental influence, realize one can't change one's parents; parenting helps resolve issues with one's own parents since one identifies with them; responsibility to ageing parents; feeling of having a past, like being treated as an adult, bridging the gap between young and older generations; no longer playing games, people consider you are grown up, authenticity, credibility from others; more able to see people as people; stress on partners' relationships which change as children grow older, divorce and new relationships; less sustained physical energy, interest in exercise and sport, still young, fit and healthy, awareness of ageing, aware of body image, and of wish to feel fit and attractive, larger fashion choice, aware of beer bellies, feel ancient in cinema queues, grey hair, wrinkles, feelings of loss, not being able to bear children becomes an issue for some women, biological time-bomb for women, health problems, aware of the forties coming up; children versus career; if still single then marriage and children remain an issue; bogged down with small children, a time of dependent children; like being trusted by young children; more freedom as children get older; more awareness of own needs and greater feeling that they might be obtainable; stick at things more in various roles – sexually, education, etc; sex gets better as you get older; loss of fantasy about life, re-evaluation; responsibility of finances, but additional responsibility can cause resentment; awareness brings dissatisfaction; changing roles an issue for men,

Exercise 8: Continued

hardening of identities; regret at lost opportunities, worries about the future, urgency of time; life gelling, coming to terms with oneself, more stable, more at peace with ourselves, increased self-confidence, think more deeply; sense of direction, self acceptance, greater competence, more balance, less introspective, more comfortable and content in oneself – in fact a bit smug!

The forties look back

Slimmer, conscious of appearance, looking in mirror and seeing one's mother, looking all right in the morning when made up, aware of first wrinkles; clapped-out cars, junk food; more energy, planning to do things in the future; financial security, need to make money; not liking some relationships, hard decisions to take, especially if there are life changes, quality of marriage changes, relationships ended; more opportunities; still insecure, still lacking in confidence; more social expectation, more pressure, competition, the 'rat-race', less selfish, less impetuous; financial dependency for some women, less able to earn money, though some women become more independent through their career; life too busy with children to make any plans; the feeling 'is this all there is to life?'; survival, coping, finding a balance, being busy, racing around, restriction of lifestyle by having a family, family responsibilities and constraints, no time for oneself, submerged in others, which for some feels all right, for others not; young or teenage children, somebody's mother or wife, not sure of own identity; lot of pleasure out of children growing up; consolidation, stable period, in harness at work, lost in work (especially for men); personal development experienced by some women, although also job aspirations shelved and some resentment of that; the agenda seems determined by circumstances.

The forties

As anticipated by the thirties

More conscious of health, which is good but perhaps deteriorating, losing one's teeth, feeling one's age, ill health, more grey hairs, putting away bikini for the last time, fear of running out of energy; looking forward to retirement; more aware of future; death creeping closer; being a grandparent, communicating better with one's own children; more time to be with one's partner, relationships come before anything else, unsure whether sex life will be poorer or better; freedom to travel, Caribbean holidays; doing things for oneself; greater freedom with loss of children on leaving home (positive and negative feelings about that); responsibility for ageing parents one may not get on with; worries about children when they are too old to control, dreading children's adolescence; bereavement, close family members dying; financial security and freedom, less mortgage to pay; irresponsibility, can say what one wants to say, be

Exercise 8: Continued

eccentric; settledness, greater creativity, greater skills, more interests, greater self-confidence, more experienced, greater acceptance, inner peace, greater control; building up career, settled in career, career diversification, inability to change career; less able to cope with change, fear of becoming rigid and inflexible, fear of being alone, unable to change with the times, less passionate (about all sorts of things), may not have found what one wants to do, but no longer have children as excuse for not doing it.

As the forties see themselves

Stability, strong self-identity, more confidence, self-acceptance, experience, truly middle-aged although is this in our heads or in the eyes of society, neither young nor old, bridge between the generations, able to mix with a wide range of people; comparing self when their age with younger generation, do not like being written off by the young; grown out of camping holidays, definite ideas on use of leisure; can be depressing, going downhill, things one cannot do because of decisions already made and out of one's control, regrets, sadness; physically healthy (though some are not), less energy and stamina, signs of ageing, aware of wrinkles, more weight, early signs of senility, aware that one is not at one's physical peak but this is not an issue, having to drop some sports, dread of illness; financial security and affluence, less financial commitment to family; new beginnings, more freedom to choose, time for ourselves to be ourselves, healthily selfish and irresponsible, not worried what others think, facility to be 'me'; happier, expected by others to be sombre and dignified but do not feel it; facing up to things, can admit bad things, more open, trusting own judgements, more positive in decisions and generally more in touch with others' problems, sorting people out boldly not just politely; being thought to be the fount of all knowledge is restricting; sense of power as a full person, respected, a leader in the family; have been through bad times and survived; more sense of purpose focused by time running out, sense of limited time and the need to use it, urgency to make long-term plans, many memories of the past but still hope for the future, regret over lost opportunities, awareness of mortality in one's own generation, first sign of the spectre of old age and death; new phase of life, new beginnings; fear that new beginning can be destroyed by dependency of parents, dread of parents getting older; questioning 'who am I?' the second time round, knowing oneself better, more clear about who you are and what you want; stability with partner, relationships can change if partner does not change, re-evaluation of relationships, confidence to change, everything open to change, tension about change, realization that a long relationship may have become a habit, depth of relationships greater, harder for men, some decrease in sexual need; more settled feeling (more so for men?), though still growing, women growing and leaving partners behind, women more likely to change; less awareness of gender, less division

Exercise 8: Continued

between male and female, male status going up, female status going down, differences for men and women over job and career, though women may feel more freedom whereas men may feel stuck; time to take stock at work, new goals, looking forward to retirement, fulfilment in job, career resolved, change of career; children more independent, more freedom as they leave home, conflicts with children on one hand and with parents on the other, pleasure in children growing up, trapped with teenagers, responsibility to help them to become independent, wanting them to leave home so I can be 'me', loss of children and the needs they satisfy, adolescent children can be a pain, reactivating one's own adolescence; awareness of spirituality, time of reflection, advancement of personal ideas, time of self-revelation, greater awareness of mental activity but also of lack of time to use it.

The fifties look back

Time of anger, aggravation, anxieties, teenagers, busy, pressure, responsibility for and worry about children, tensions, ferrying kids around, lending them the car, watching them have accidents, educational traumas of the children, parents' evenings, family rows, the financial cost of having teenagers, children at home a mixed blessing, affirmation of being needed by families, parental yet also adult-to-adult relationship with children, closer relationship with children even if traumatic; missing closeness of family, and sense of belonging with children leaving; support from parents when still alive; becoming grandparents changes relationships; financial tensions, buying and selling of houses; female (and male?) menopause, pre-menstrual tension, still physically attractive, with energy and stamina, health and career opportunities, fit, but also some ill health; more stress and responsibility (particularly for parents); more ambitious; complete reassessment, strong desire to grow and change, awakening spirituality, self-awareness, time to face yourself; pressure to succeed; need not be so absolute; a shifting time, more time to choose futures, sense of time as limitless; hopes, achievements and new challenges, enjoyment of freedom, companionship of siblings; more social contact; pretty awful, the most difficult period of our lives, glad to have left the forties behind.

The fifties

As anticipated by the forties

Not welcomed; private space, periods of peace and quiet, more leisure, further development, more cash, freedom to travel; enjoying the fruits of the forties; selling big house for a little one, financial freedom, even better lifestyle; being a twosome again; loss of sexual attractiveness; being alone if partner goes; ageing parents and dependent relatives, loss of friends and relations, death of parents and peers; failing

Exercise 8: Continued

health and physical prowess, putting on weight, disability, ageing, too old for anything, too close to the end, aware of our own mortality; more forceful, loss of tolerance, loss of mental faculties, may be thought 'frumpy'; children gone, not such a worry, fear children won't leave home, less demands as a parent; becoming the older generation, being grandparents, sense of parenting the world around (concern for the environment), children extending our life through theirs; work fitted into rest of life, less important, fear of redundancy, early retirement, loss of status and job; searching for other meanings, looking for different avenues, return to church, asking what life is about, taking stock, can let ourselves off the hook and be ourselves at last.

As the fifties see themselves

Very good and enjoyable, not what you thought; there is life after the menopause; a watershed, a time to celebrate, more comfort, life less of a struggle, life more for oneself; freedom financially though also responsibilities; more free sexually and emotionally, not concerned about sexual attractiveness, re-emergence of adolescence; loss of eyesight and physical ability; slowing down, but this does not matter, want to keep fit; doing the things have always wanted to; draw on experience and get things done more quickly; not the same concern about death as before although death more immediate concern; Saga holidays; meals out, new interests, can afford to do as one pleases; sense of being in transition, between the young and the old, becoming senior members of the family; getting on with both young and old; children leaving home, enjoying the friendship of own children, relationships more open and adult with children; more dependent on friends and relatives; family stress, family settled/ married; grandchildren; companionship of partner, reassessing relationship now back together on our own without children, beginning new relationships; responsibility to aged parents, seeing them age and realizing it will happen to you, death of friends, parents deceased; treated patronizingly; an ageless time, a new maturity; time of self-acceptance, more secure sense of identity, no need now to make excuses or conform, not having to pretend or play roles as much as before, don't care what people think about you, being yourself if you know who you are, finding out who you are, accept one's limitations, not having to prove oneself; more accepting and tolerant, though some think you are less tolerant, more in control of ourselves, more patient and understanding, more sensitive to others, less sensitive about other's opinions of ourselves; more flexible, calmer view of life, realization that it is not easy to change the world, more realistic expectations; more nervous, uncertain, vulnerable, a certain emptiness; lot of experience and not too late to use it; time to tie things up, resolve some things from the past, to say things before it is too late, can accept what has gone wrong; life opening up, finiteness of time obvious, demands of work greater, whether to retire or change jobs, more satisfaction for some from work, for others less, career

Exercise 8: Continued

limitations, difficult decisions, looking forward to retirement; time to think, more spiritual, living more for now, sense of value of the present moment, looking forward to the future, time short and passing quickly, reflecting on the past; different kind of memory (the past vivid, the short-term less vivid); deepening sense of the beauty of one's surroundings, no loss of passion about justice, in love for friends, etc.; retaining a strong commitment.

The sixties look back
Physical energy and ability to cope with anything when it came to the crunch; rich life of the workplace, job and companions at work, needed by many, defined and respected role in life, meeting new challenges, power and sense of responsibility at work; unpleasant and anxiety-provoking pressure, the 'rat-race', work frustrations, anxieties over having a senior position at work, possibilities of redundancy and loss of security; decent level of income, mortgage; looking and being attractive; anxiety and worries over children, especially the 'late developers'; family responsibilities and traumas about family decisions, partner returning to work, domestic adjustments, children getting married, grandchildren, loss of parents, restrictions on leisure.

The sixties and beyond

As anticipated by the fifties
Contemporaries dying, partner dying, being ill, humiliation through illness, loss of mobility, lack of worth or hope, senile dementia, physical limitations, lack of independence; classified and stereotyped as 'old' or 'elderly'; bus-passes, being a bore, repeating stories; being dependent, a liability, a burden or a worry to the family; loss of income, poverty, living on pension; independence and wanting to remain independent; the future less important than the present; less responsibilities; more leisure, more time for exploring and indulging interests, reading, etc.; time for embarking on fulfilling relationships, making new friends; partner retiring, own retirement, working less, able to do one's own thing, escape to freedom, freedom to do what you want to do rather than what you have to do, less stress; part-time voluntary work as providing new challenge, purpose and direction; enjoyment of grandchildren; knowing ourselves more, development and spiritual growth, wisdom.

As the sixties see themselves now and in the future
Some dimunition of power, energy and control, physical decline and disability; more aware of small bodily malfunctions; not in work, so loss of role, social contacts, income, status and of significance through work; very sharp contrasts in abrupt changes at retirement; loss of a larger home; sense of time running out; but also life

Exercise 8: Continued

goes on in the same way; time of great change; sense of life opening up; more accepting, not battling, less rush, sharp reduction in pressures, can sit and enjoy things, time to reflect; exploration of relationships with partner, living closer together than ever before, growing points still there in the relationship; good personal relationships, can relax and enjoy relationships; exciting, test of self-reliance, growing still; enjoy grandchildren from more relaxed point of view, visiting them, holidays with them, interest in the development of family members, enjoy our children looking after us; holidays (can choose when to go); nothing to lose, so let's have a go; far more flexible than ever in the past; time for leisure, hobbies, classes, reading, fun; still have responsibility, still in demand, taking on more, fresh activities; 'treats' are now simpler; more sense of being than doing; look back on successes and appreciate life; know so much more, accumulated wisdom; more relaxed view of death; do not like being thought of as 'old' by the young; have few regrets.

9

Some issues in adult life

Introduction

A developmental model which links present adult experience to past experience (particularly, although not solely, to childhood and adolescence) means that many of the issues of adult life which are brought into counselling or therapy are reflections of the themes which are included in Chapters 4–7. Loss and bereavement are given special attention in the next Chapter. Here I take three aspects of adult life (relationships, work and values) and examine them in relation to counselling and therapy. Apart from the role-play (Exercise 9.5), which illustrates all three aspects in a client, the exercises in this chapter concentrate attention upon the counsellor and therapist, and not on the client.

Exercise 9.1: Therapeutic relationships

Purpose

This exercise provides an opportunity to experience different types of human interaction, all of which are potentially therapeutic and/or anti-therapeutic. It also addresses questions about what relationships outside those in therapy or counselling have to teach the therapist or counsellor, and what the therapist's relationship has to teach those who find themselves helping others as parents, friends or colleagues.

Exercise 9.1: Continued

Duration

2–3 hours.

Method

There are eight mini situations, each of which has a similar theme but demonstrates a different type or style of relationship at work. By comparing and contrasting the feelings, thoughts, spoken words and actions in a series of mini situations, students are encouraged to consider what aspects of counselling and therapy are unique, and what are shared with other types of helping relationship.

Materials

Sufficient copies of the mini situations for the number of pairs using them; plus one copy of Chart 1 and Chart 2 for all participants.

Situation 1: 'marital' partnership

Partner A
You have had a bad day at work: you had delegated a major piece of work to a member of your staff. (Choose your own work setting, and develop what this situation might have been, so that where necessary you can expand on this story-line.) You had a lot to gain or lose by the way this piece of work was handled; you had thought your staff member was reliable, and you had overlooked one or two signs that might have indicated inadequacy or inability on that person's part. Today you had a meeting with her or him to find out how things were going, and discovered that she or he was not coming up to your expectations, and that your own assessment of her or his ability was gravely mistaken. She or he had taken little notice of your instructions, and has made a serious mess of the job. With all this in mind you arrive home. You exchange views of your respective days, and are in a mood to talk . . .

Situation 1: 'marital' partnership

Partner B
It is early evening; your partner arrives home from work after you, and you begin to exchange news of your respective days. Your partner wants to talk, although your day has not been at all good either. (Here decide what your work is, and develop your own

Exercise 9.1: Continued

story-line so that where necessary you can expand on this story-line.) You have made a number of silly mistakes during the day – nothing too serious, but all in all leaving you feeling quite depressed . . .

Situation 2: grandparent and grandchild

A: Grandchild
You are a teenager (aged fourteen) visiting your widowed seventy-year-old grandparent for tea on the way home from school, where you have had a bad day. You had chosen someone in your class as a partner in a project. (If necessary choose your own idea for a project, and develop it as you want.) You had a lot to gain or lose by the way in which this piece of work was done, and you thought you had chosen someone reliable and trustworthy to work with. In fact you now realize that she or he has always been much better at talking about things than actually doing them. Today you discovered that she or he has not done any of the things which she or he said she or he would do towards the project, and can only give you a lot of rather feeble excuses. Your grandparent asks you how things are going at school . . .

Situation 2: grandparent and grandchild

B: Grandparent
It is late afternoon, and your fourteen-year-old grandchild has come in for tea on the way home from school. You are pleased to see her or him, although you haven't had a very good day yourself. You live alone; and you have made a number of silly mistakes during the day – nothing too serious, but all in all leaving you feeling quite depressed . . .

Situation 3: therapist and client

A: Client
You have had a bad week at work: you had delegated a major piece of work to a member of your staff. (Choose your own work setting, and develop what this situation might have been, so that where necessary you can expand on this story-line.) You had a lot to gain or lose by the way this piece of work was handled; you had thought your staff member was reliable, and you had overlooked one or two signs that might have indicated inadequacy or inability on that person's part. Today you had a meeting with her or him to find out how things were going, and discovered that she or he was not coming up to your expectations, and that your own assessment of her or his ability was gravely mistaken. She or he had taken little notice of your instructions, and has made a serious mess of the job.

Exercise 9.1: Continued

You are at the start of your therapy session; you have talked about this type of situation before, although you did not then realize that this person at work was likely to let you down . . .

Situation 3: therapist and client

B: Therapist
Your client arrives for another session, and begins to talk. You vaguely remember her or him talking about this situation before; although it was on a day when you were pretty off-colour yourself. Your client did not appear to realize it, but you were not as alert then as you might otherwise have been . . .

Situation 4: work colleagues

A: Junior colleague
You have had a bad week at work: you had delegated a major piece of work to a member of your staff. (Choose your own work setting, and develop what this situation might have been, so that where necessary you can expand on this story-line.) You had a lot to gain or lose by the way this piece of work was handled; you had thought your staff member was reliable, and you had overlooked one or two signs that might have indicated inadequacy or inability on that person's part. Today you had a meeting with her or him to find out how things were going, and discovered that she or he was not coming up to your expectations, and that your own assessment of her or his ability was gravely mistaken. She or he had taken little notice of your instructions, and has made a serious mess of the job.

All this coincides with your annual appraisal. You are now sitting with your senior colleague, who asks you how you feel things have been going . . .

Situation 4: work colleagues

B: Senior colleague
A colleague, slightly junior to yourself, has come at your request for her or his annual appraisal. You start this by asking how things have been going. You are aware as she or he talks that you have yourself felt some concern in the past, about not giving your colleague enough guidance on staff management. But your own work programme has been so full that you have felt snowed under; and you realize that you have failed to be as helpful as you might be to your junior staff . . .

Exercise 9.1: Continued

Situation 5: teacher and child

A: Ten-year-old child
It is a bad day. One of the teachers with whom you thought you got on well told you off very severely this morning while you were queuing for lunch, for starting a scuffle: it actually began when some other children pushed their way in, and you protested that they were being unfair. The teacher did not even allow you to put your side of the situation, although your form teacher (whom you also like) has picked up that you are unhappy, because you were none too communicative to her or him at the end of the afternoon. You decide to tell her or him what it is all about . . .

Situation 5: teacher and child

B: Teacher
It has been a pretty rotten day – your lessons did not go well because you were too pushed to prepare them properly, the children seemed to be playing up partly at the end of a long term, partly because of the weather, and the head teacher has sounded off about standards at the early-morning staff meeting. But you still notice that one of your class in particular, who is normally quite chirpy and friendly to you and others, is less than communicative this afternoon, and you have the chance to let her or him chat before school finishes . . .

Situation 6: supervision

A: Trainee therapist
You have had a bad session with one of your clients. You had decided, on the basis of what you knew so far, that she or he was able to handle a particular situation which she or he had talked about. (Choose your own client, and invent a situation, developing it as you need.) You realize now that you had overlooked one or two signs that might have indicated inadequacy or inability on the client's part to cope with that particular situation. This week you saw her or him, and it all seemed to have gone wrong for the client; and you felt inwardly angry with the client for not having been able to cope as you thought she or he might.

It is the start of your supervision session. You have talked about this client before, although for the purposes of this exercise you may have to 'remind' your supervisor of the salient features of the case . . .

Exercise 9.1: Continued

Situation 6: supervision

B: Supervisor

Your trainee therapist arrives for a supervision session, and begins to present a case which she or he has talked about before. You only vaguely remember her or him talking about this case before, although it was on a day when you were pretty off-colour yourself. Your trainee did not appear to realize it, but you were not as alert then as you might otherwise have been . . .

Situation 7: parent and child

A: Five-year-old child

It has been a horrid day at school: one of those days when your best friend turns around and says you smell and she or he doesn't like you and won't be friends with you any more; a day when you spilt red paint over your clothes; a day when you were sick at lunchtime; and when even the childminder appeared to be cross with you when you got home. Your mother/father (a single parent) has just come home . . .

Situation 7: parent and child

B: Single parent

It is early evening; you arrive home from work to greet your five-year-old child, who has been cared for after school by the childminder. You have not had a good day either. (Here decide what your work is, and develop your own story if you wish.) You have made a number of silly mistakes during the day – nothing too serious, but all in all leaving you feeling quite depressed . . .

Situation 8: friendship

Friend A

You have had a bad day at work: you had delegated a major piece of work to a member of your staff. (Choose your own work setting, and develop what this situation might have been, so that where necessary you can expand on this story-line.) You had a lot to gain or lose by the way this piece of work was handled; you had thought your staff member was reliable, and you had overlooked one or two signs that might have indicated inadequacy or inability on the person's part. Today you had a meeting with her or him to find out how things were going, and discovered that she or he was not coming up to your expectations, and that your own assessment of her or his ability

Exercise 9.1: Continued

was gravely mistaken. She or he had taken little notice of your instructions, and has made a serious mess of the job. With all this in mind, you meet a good friend of yours on the way home and pop in for a drink . . .

Situation 8: friendship

Friend B
It is early evening; you have met a good friend on the way home and are having a drink together, after a day at work which has not been at all good. (Here decide what your work is, and develop your own story-line so that where necessary you can expand on this story-line.) You have made a number of silly mistakes during the day – nothing too serious, but all in all leaving you feeling quite depressed . . .

Therapeutic relationships exercise (Chart 1, p. 182)

During the five minutes for recording your mini situation, use the spaces provided on the chart for reflection on the three situations you role-play; the other five situations can be completed later when comparing notes with others in your group.

Under the heading 'said/not said', say what you wanted to say but could not say, what you did say but did not feel like saying, and what you did say that you wanted to say. If you 'dried up', why did this happen? Under the heading 'feelings', say what feelings you could actually express, what feelings you had to keep to yourself, and how you felt by the end of the situation.

Then on a scale of 1 to 10, say whether you felt:

distant (1) – close (10)
tense (1) – relaxed (10)
worse (1) – better (10)
unequal (1) – equal (10)
cautious (1) – trusting (10)

There is also space (A or B) for you to record your partner's ratings, to compare different experiences of the same situation.

Therapeutic relationships exercise (Chart 2, p. 183)

Space is given in Chart 2 to record ideas from your small group discussion about what features in each situation were therapeutic or anti-therapeutic, as well as what lessons each situation might provide for the relationship in therapy itself.

Exercise 9.1: Chart 1

Situation	*Said/not said*	*Feelings*	*Ratings*		
			A		B
'Marital' partners				distant – close tense – relaxed worse – better unequal – equal cautious – trusting	
Grandparent and grandchild				distant – close tense – relaxed worse – better unequal – equal cautious – trusting	
Therapist and client				distant – close tense – relaxed worse – better unequal – equal cautious – trusting	
Work colleagues				distant – close tense – relaxed worse – better unequal – equal cautious – trusting	
Teacher and child				distant – close tense – relaxed worse – better unequal – equal cautious – trusting	
Supervisor and trainee				distant – close tense – relaxed worse – better unequal – equal cautious – trusting	
Parent and child				distant – close tense – relaxed worse – better unequal – equal cautious – trusting	
Friends				distant – close tense – relaxed worse – better unequal – equal cautious – trusting	

Exercise 9.1: Chart 2

Situation	*Therapeutic features*	*Anti-therapeutic features*	*Lessons for counselling*
'Marital' partners			
Grandparent and grandchild			
Therapist and client			
Work colleagues			
Teacher and child			
Supervisor and trainee			
Parent and child			
Friends			

Exercise 9.1: Continued

Instructions

1 Since it is too much to ask students to play and hold in mind all eight situations, the recommended method is to divide the class into groups of six or eight, and to give each pair in the group *three* of the eight situations (e.g. pair one: 1,2,3; pair two: 4,5,6; pair three: 7,8,1; pair four: 2,3,4). There will be slight overlap between two pairs, giving a chance of further comparison in the group feedback.
2 The same partner always takes the A or B script each time (B is on balance the one who gives the help, although she or he may also need some help herself or himself). For each mini situation the timing is: a few minutes to read the script and get into role; ten minutes playing the scene; five minutes silently answering some simple questions on the experience (Chart 1), but not yet sharing these with the partner. If the mini situation finishes before ten minutes are up, both partners use the extra time to record their observations. The tutor calls for the start and finish of the mini role-play, and for the start of the next mini session.

Debriefing

Following their three mini sessions, the two people in each pair share their observations between themselves on the three situations they have taken part in, recording their respective 'scores' for different feelings (Chart 1). This may take up to fifteen minutes. Then the group of six or eight re-forms, and each person has the chance to share their observations about the different situations, and to record those which others discuss on their copy of Chart 1 (thirty to forty-five minutes).

After this, if time permits the exercise to be extended, the members of the small groups are given Chart 2 upon which to record their ideas about what features were therapeutic or anti-therapeutic in each of the eight different situations, as well as what lessons each situation might provide for the relationship in therapy itself (a further thirty to forty-five minutes). It is also possible to ask in what ways the therapy relationship itself had lessons to convey for the other types of therapeutic relationship illustrated in this exercise.

Comment

The relationship between a therapist and client is reckoned in most schools of counselling to be central to the process of change. For some (particularly person-centred therapists) it is the warmth, congruence, non-judgemental acceptance and

Exercise 9.1: Continued

genuineness of the counsellor which is essential. For others (particularly psychodynamic therapists) the understanding and use of transference and counter-transference (see Exercise 2.7 in Chapter 2) in the relationship between therapist and client is held to be vital. While both these aspects are probably necessary it is easy to forget that it is not only counsellors and therapists who enable people to grow and change. Starting with parents, a whole series of relationships throughout life provide nurture, support, confrontation and insight. As Searles so poignantly writes, 'any human interaction which is at all intense and prolonged is, in a very real sense of the word, mutually therapeutic (or anti-therapeutic)'.[1]

Exercise 9.2: Reflecting on work and life

Purpose

Questions for discussion look at the significance and satisfaction for the student of their day-to-day working life, whether or not in paid employment. The question is also addressed of long-term aims and what it will be like looking back on the opportunities people have had for personal and work development.[2]

Duration

30–45 minutes.

Method

Small discussion groups reflect on personal experience.

Materials

None.

Exercise 9.2: Continued

Instructions

Form small groups, who are given the following questions to reflect upon:

(a) What gives you satisfaction at the end of a good working day? (If not in employment, at the end of a good day?)
(b) What makes you feel dissatisfied at the end of a bad working day? (If not in employment, at the end of a bad day?)
(c) If you were not in paid employment and you were reasonably financially secure, how would you wish to spend your time?
(d) When it comes (as well it may) to the time when you look back over your (working) life, what would you like to have achieved?

Debriefing

Feedback can be taken from small groups if desired.

Exercise 9.3: What are counsellors made of?

Purpose

This exercise looks at the personal characteristics which might be necessary in a counsellor and/or therapist, compared and contrasted with various other occupations.

Duration

45–60 minutes.

Exercise 9.3: Continued

Method

A self-administered inventory of the degree of personal qualities necessary for various jobs provides an opportunity for students a chance to draw up a profile of what characteristics are most important in a number of different occupations, and an opportunity to rate themselves against the profiles they have drawn.

Materials

Copies of the instructions and the chart for each student:

Instructions for completing the self-inventory (p. 188)

1 Fill in the far right-hand box at the top of the grid with the title of your present job, or the last job you did when you were in paid employment; then fill in the box immediately to the left with the title of an occupation not listed in the other boxes, which interests you as a possible job.
2 Add to the list of personal characteristics any others which you feel describe you, or which you feel should be included as necessary for any of the jobs listed along the top of the grid.
3 Using the scale immediately below, take each of the personal descriptions in turn, and work across the five columns, rating how important or not it is for a person who is (say) a counsellor to have that personal characteristic; you will make some sort of comparison between the five occupations as you do this. Leave the narrow columns headed 'ST' clear for the time being.

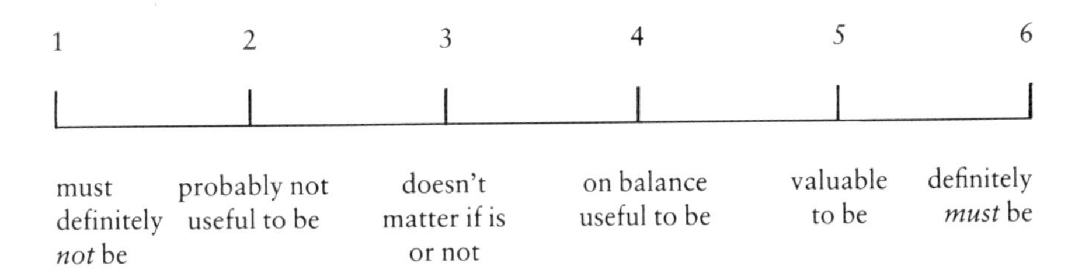

Exercise 9.3: What are counsellors made of? A self-analysis

Your self	*Qualities*	*Counsellor*		*Social worker*		*Teacher*		*A job you would like to have/do*		*Your present job or a job you have done*	
			ST		ST		ST		ST		ST
	patient										
	ambitious										
	creative										
	influential										
	numerate										
	versatile										
	self-reliant										
	articulate										
	assertive										
	unflappable										
	tactful										
	imaginative										
	sensitive to others										
	logical										
	competitive										
	persuasive										
	co-operative										
	determined										
	trusting										
	independent										
	authoritative										
		Total		Total		Total		Total		Total	

Exercise 9.3: Continued

4 Turn your attention now to the box on the left of the personal characteristics. Using the scale immediately below rate yourself on how patient, ambitious, etc. you think you *actually* are (not how you would like to be).

1	2	3	4	5	6
I am never . . .	generally I am not . . .	I am a little . . .	I am fairly . . .	I am . . .	I am *very* . . .

5 Compare the number you have rated or each characteristic in yourself with the scores in the five occupational columns. In every case subtract the lower figure (whichever it is) from the higher figure (or if equal subtract to make '0') and record this number in the narrow column marked 'ST' (sub-total) under each occupation.
6 Add up the scores in each of the narrow columns marked 'ST'.
7 Provided you have been able to make a fair assessment of yourself and of the characteristics required in each occupation, you should now find that the occupation where you score *lowest* is one which is temperamentally most like you. This does not mean, of course, that you necessarily have the right technical ability, skills or qualifications to follow this particular occupation.

This exercise is not a psychological test as such. It has not been tested widely enough to place too much reliance on the results, although when it has been used with people in settled occupations, there does appear to be some correlation between their lowest score and their chosen career. The exercise (which is a simplified version of the method used in repertory grids) is primarily designed to stimulate thought and discussion.

Instructions

The instructions on the papers given to students are self-explanatory. But the tutor will need to take the students through the various parts of the inventory, one part at a time.

Debriefing

This can take place in small groups following the exercise, particularly concentrating upon what qualities are necessary in a good counsellor. The issues are not as clear-cut as they at first seem.

Exercise 9.3: Continued

Comment

The exercise has no statistical validity, although the results give rise to interesting discussions and also to some surprises: for example, that the perceived profile of students' present occupations appears to match their own personal profile, or that their 'wildest dream' is not really them at all! The discussion of personal qualities in a counsellor and therapist also throws up some valuable observations about qualities other than those that are traditionally associated with the profession.

Exercise 9.4: Beliefs, attitudes and values

Purpose

This series of exercises gives students the opportunity to review their attitudes to different types of client; to consider their explicit and implicit values; and to begin defining what they see as the general aims of counselling and therapy.

Duration

The duration of each part of the exercise is indicated in the Instructions. The exercise as a whole usually takes even more time than allowed for, and may require in excess of 2 hours in all if all four parts are covered.

Method

Discussion of cases, of personal prejudices and values and of the aims of counselling and therapy, in pairs and small groups.

Exercise 9.4: Continued

Materials

Worksheets for each student as follows:

Exercise 9.4.1

Contrary values and beliefs
In counselling we are sure to meet clients who represent all the things we find most difficult. How do you find yourself reacting to these two clients (take them one by one)? What dilemmas and conflicts would they raise in you? How would you deal with each of them?

Case history A
Bernard is a student reading economics. He finds his fellow students lacking in intellectual and moral fibre: they are apathetic. He has strong views: he thought Margaret Thatcher was too soft. He would like to see greater discipline all round. Students should improve their standards of dress and conduct. There should be much firmer control of immigrants to this country and those already here should systematically be deported back where they came from. Bernard is also a practising Catholic strongly opposed to abortion and all artificial methods of contraception. Even some of the clergy and the bishops have become too permissive. You learn all this from Bernard when he comes to see you, since he treats you like a public meeting. He has come to see you because he can't sleep, and has difficulty concentrating hard enough on his work. And he is desperate to do well in his final exams.

Case history B
Roger is in his late thirties. He comes to you for advice. He wants to find the best way of persuading his fourteen-year-old daughter, Alison, not to divulge to her mother that she and her father have been having an incestuous relationship for the past fifteen months. He is worried because for the past few weeks Alison has been saying that she feels uncomfortable with her mother, and feels she ought to tell her about this very special relationship she is having with her father. Roger realizes now that what he has done is wrong, and he will stop; but he wants to know how to get it across to Alison that her mother would rather not know, that she would be very upset. He asks the counsellor how best to deal with Alison. If Alison tells this to her mother, she might also tell her that he has been masturbating her ever since she was a little girl. He says his wife is very proper, a beautiful woman, but cold towards him.

Exercise 9.4: Continued

Exercises 9.4.2 and 9.4.3

Exercise 9.4.2: Your nightmare client

(a) For a few minutes work out on your own what your nightmare client might be like – the person you would have the utmost difficulty in dealing with and relating to. What would he or she be like in terms of background; appearance; age; race; beliefs, attitudes and values; mannerisms; politics; social class; and presenting problem?

(b) Form pairs. Describe that person to someone else, and listen in turn to theirs. Do you both feel the same about your nightmare clients? Or is there some aspect of your nightmare client which is telling you something about a particular prejudice/bias/blind spot that you might have?

Exercise 9.4.3: Your own values and counselling

Think about your own values: what matters most in life to you? List your principal values, perhaps in some order of priority. How strongly do you hold them – do they influence your counselling? What do you feel about people (including clients) who contravene the values you hold most dear? You do not have to share your views with anyone else, but your views are likely to influence your contribution to the next part of the exercise.

Exercise 9.4.4

The aims of counselling and therapy

The following are some statements that have been made about maturity in terms of human development, or about the aims of therapy or counselling. Read them through, and then in your small group pool your ideas and write a short group definition of what counselling or therapy might try to achieve.

Some psychodynamic definitions of maturity:

Freud: To love and to work.

Guntrip: The peak of maturity [is] to be able to give oneself to the utmost in love, for convincing reasons, without loss of ego-integrity.

Guntrip: The grown-up child is free without anxiety or guilt to enter an erotic relationship with an extra-familial partner, and to form other important personal relationships in which there is genuine meeting of kindred spirits without the erotic element, and further to exercise an active and spontaneous personality free from inhibiting fears.

Exercise 9.4: Continued

Winnicott: The mature human being is neither so nice nor so nasty as the immature. The water in the glass is muddy, but not mud.[3]

Horney: To be without pretence, to be emotionally sincere, to be able to put the whole of oneself into one's feelings, one's work, one's beliefs.

Some expressions of the aims of counselling/therapy

Horney: To help the person regain his spontaneity, to find his measurements of value in himself, to give him the courage to be himself.

Maslow: To move from . . . splitting toward integration of seemingly irreconcilable opposites.

Freud: We try to restore the ego, to free it from its restrictions, and to give it back the command over the id which it has lost owing to its early repressions.[4]

Moreno: To free the spontaneously creative self.

Instructions

1 Hand out the worksheets for this exercise.
2 The instructions given on each worksheet are clear, but need to be repeated verbally before each exercise.
3 Start Exercise 9.4.1, which will take up to one hour. The second part of this exercise will arouse strong feelings, and it is important to bear in mind that inevitably there will be some members of any class who have been sexually abused as children. The issues arising are not straightforward, however strong the feeling against Roger.
4 Divide the class into pairs for Exercise 9.4.2, which will last about twenty minutes.
5 Students can work on their own for about ten minutes on Exercise 9.4.3, although the instructions can be altered so that they are invited to share their ideas in pairs before moving on to the last part of whole exercise.
6 Form small groups again for Exercise 9.4.4, which will take about forty-five minutes, discussion and feedback.

Debriefing

As indicated in the instructions above, this takes the form of feedback after two particular sections of the whole exercise (9.4.1 and 9.4.4).

Exercise 9.4: Continued

Comment

Whatever merit there is in the non-judgemental stance (and it is considerable), it is impossible to relate to a client without constantly touching upon values and moral judgements of one kind and another since they are present in both client and counsellor. Some of these will be commonly held beliefs, shared by counsellor and client, and by most people in society at large – such as the abhorrence of the abuse of children. Sometimes they will be beliefs shared by counsellor and client, but poorly represented in the way the majority of people act; for example, some gender issues about male power and dominance may be common ground for a feminist therapist and her client, but not generally perceived as having real significance in the eyes of much of society. On occasion a counsellor may find herself or himself at variance with the views put forward by a client, and will want to suggest an alternative way of looking at a situation. And on some occasions a counsellor may find herself or himself at loggerheads with attitudes which are so unacceptable as to make continuation of the work difficult. All these possibilities are likely to arise in the course of this exercise.

Exercise 9.5: Role-play

Purpose

The role-play illustrates various issues in mid-life.

Duration

60–75 minutes. It is suggested the role-play lasts for forty minutes, with up to twenty minutes allowed for 'time out' (see Chapter 1).

Exercise 9.5: Continued

Method, etc.

See Exercise 1.2, Chapter 1, for method, materials, instructions and debriefing. Comments on the possible handling of the situation appear at the end. Debriefing and analysis of the counsellor's work is of course essential and may take a further thirty minutes after the role-play.

Briefing for Freda (aged forty-eight)

You have been referred to the counsellor by your doctor, whom you consulted about arthritic pains in your hands. He told you and the counsellor that you also seemed tense and depressed. Before you start the role-play, inform your counsellor of your name and age, and the details above. What follows is for you to use in the role-play as you think fit:

You are pleased to see a counsellor, because the doctor's suggestion about tension made some sort of sense, although you do not know why you should feel tense.

You are married, and the marriage seems a good relationship to you; your teenage children have been no trouble to you. In fact, apart from your recent pain and tension, and the fact that over the last year you have lost some friends and relatives through death, life has treated you well. You talk freely with your counsellor about most of what follows, but the last paragraph only comes out if the counsellor gets close to it.

You have tried as a mother not to be like your own mother. She was always concerned about dirt and noise; she constantly wanted you to be neat and tidy, and to do well at school. You have encouraged your own children, but unlike her you have not given affection only on the basis of their achievements, as she did with you. You were as a child particularly gifted in amateur dramatics and on the piano, where you achieved a high grade in your music exams. You used to have to play the piano to cheer up your father, who often got rather depressed. You now play the piano for your local church, where your playing has always been much appreciated. Your counsellor may draw out from you that with arthritic pains in your hands it is becoming less easy to play well.

You react strongly to any hint of what you take as criticism of yourself as a wife, mother, pianist, etc. Praise is very important to you: you need it, although you like to give praise. You hang on every word the counsellor utters, looking for instructions how to live and how to be (although you do not actually ask for advice). You particularly want to please the counsellor, as you make clear when she or he says something that is genuinely helpful.

If your counsellor touches on it, you can begin to reveal that you are afraid of ageing and death, now that you are in the second half of life. The death of others close to you

Exercise 9.5: Continued

has brought home its actuality; your arthritic pains are a sign of some physical decline. Your religious faith has been tied up in doing things for the church, and now that playing the piano there is more difficult, you are afraid you will no longer earn praise for it. Your life and faith are governed by doing things well (linked to your relationship to your mother); you have no faith in just 'being', and so no sense of comfort about ageing and dying. All your life you have felt well, because you have been able to win sufficient praise to boost your self-image. But it has always been built on pleasing others, and that no longer feels possible.

Comment

This role-play highlights what is sometimes called 'the mid-life crisis'. It links together many of the themes previously illustrated, but in a way which only mid-life might throw up. It is important to stress that Freda presents a huge task in therapy, and she will probably need long-term help. This role-play can only scrape the surface and begin to raise some of the issues. She needs to move from an identity which has been built up on the basis of pleasing others to one which finds satisfaction in simply being herself. The counsellor who gets hooked on her description of her marriage and her children in positive terms (understandably wondering whether this is idealization, and that in fact things are not so good) may well have it wrong. The point is that Freda probably *has* made a good job of all that she has turned her hands to. But her hands will not allow her to go on doing this, either literally in playing the piano in church, or metaphorically in her constant need to be doing something for others.

There are a number of role-plays in earlier chapters which could also be used as examples of issues in adult life, although they have been related to early themes. These include Gerry (Exercise 4.6.i), Eddie (4.6.iii), Ian or Jan (5.3.ii), Geoffrey Brown (5.3.iii), Madge and Frank Harris (6.5.i), Betty (6.5.ii) and Keith (6.5.iii). Like so many role-plays these explore issues of relationship (intimacy themes) or work (generativity themes). The role-plays in the next chapter concentrate on obvious loss and bereavement in death, an inevitable feature of adult life.

10

Loss and death

Introduction

Working with issues around death and bereavement is a specialized area of counselling, met by an increasing number of courses which seek to meet the demand for interest in this field of work. It is not clear whether this interest is because of the concerns people have for counselling others, or for their own anxieties about loss and death. I hesitate to add to the existing literature, but the following exercises have proved useful in the context of courses on human development. They take students into some experiences of old age, and into reactions to illness; into areas of loss other than death, as a comparative exercise which has bearing on the many types of loss presented in therapy and counselling; into death itself, and into different reactions to the extreme pain and questioning that can be caused by the premature death of the young.

Exercise 10.1: Reactions to ageing and illness

Purpose

The exercise aims to provide insight into the experience of being old and being ill, and the different reactions to dependence. It also aims at providing some brief experience of visiting old people with these different reactions, giving some insight into how relatives and other ward visitors might experience these situations.

Duration

75 minutes.

Method

The exercise asks students to play four different types of person reacting to old age and to illness,[1] as well as someone visiting them in hospital.

Materials

There are two briefing sheets; the first given to one partner in pairs for the first four mini situations; the second to the other for the last four mini situations.

Briefing sheet 1

Imagine yourself aged about eighty, sitting in a chair by the side of your bed in a hospital ward. You will adopt a number of different moods and styles of being and relating, according to the situations described below. Each situation will last five minutes, during which time you will be visited by a different person. Stay in the same chair during all four mini situations. There will be a break of two minutes between visits to allow you time to read through the next role, and to get into the mood. After you have played these four roles, you will then become a visitor, immediately moving one place anti-clockwise, and thereafter one place anti-clockwise for each new situation. When the whole exercise is finished, you will have the chance to debrief, and reflect upon what it is like being each of these types of old person, and in turn being the visitor.

Exercise 10.1: Continued

1 The first time play the well-integrated type of old person, who has high self-esteem and an interest in life; who is self-aware and still enjoying a sense of responsibility; but who also likes tranquillity; who is realistic, with a sense of purpose and meaning to life; but who is in considerable physical pain.
2 The second time play the type of person who does not like old age and infirmity, and is, indeed, afraid of it; who normally compensates by being compulsively active, self-sufficient, over-controlled and fiercely independent; who is just about to be 'released' from hospital after having recovered from the illness.
3 The third time play the self-hating old person, who is despairing and pessimistic, who turns anger into self-contempt, who has very limited interests, and has such a negative view of the past and the present that death is looked forward to as a merciful release. And since this person is in considerable physical pain, he or she may feel as if that release will come, or needs to come, soon.
4 The last time play the type of old person whose mind is somewhere else, and who therefore seems to talk all the time in riddles. This might be difficult to play, so imagine you are a character in a book (such as *Alice in Wonderland* or *Through the Looking-Glass*) and converse with your visitor as though he or she were different characters in the book.

Briefing sheet 2

Imagine yourself aged about eighty, sitting in a chair by the side of your bed in a hospital ward. You will adopt a number of different moods and styles of being and relating, according to the situations described below. Each situation will last five minutes, during which time you will be visited by a different person. Stay in the same chair during all four mini situations. There will be a break of two minutes between visits to allow you time to read through the next role, and to get into the mood. After you have played these four roles, you will have the chance to debrief, and to reflect upon what it is like being each of these types of old person, as well as on what it was like previously being the visitor.

1 The first time play the type of old person who is hostile, and who directs anger outward, criticizing others, the hospital, the doctors and nurses, and who is envious of younger people; who is afraid of death; but is physically well and waiting to go home.
2 The second time play the sort of old person who is far away in their thoughts, mumbling to yourself, but not at all aware of the visitor who is with you; and

Exercise 10.1: Continued

saying things so quietly to yourself, that your words cannot be heard. But in your own way you really are quite content.

3 The third time play the self-hating old person, who is despairing and pessimistic, who turns anger into self-contempt, who has limited interests, and such a negative view of the past that death is looked forward to as a merciful release; but you are now physically well, and due to go home, so you have been 'cheated', even of dying.

4 The last time play the dependent type of old person, who is passive and likes to be looked after, who likes comfort, and is self-satisfied, not objecting to old age, or to the prospect of death, but determined to make the most of all the comfort that is going. You play this as being healthy again, but not particularly wanting to leave hospital where you like being looked after, and having everything done for you.

Instructions

1. The class is divided into two equal halves, seated in pairs in a large circle, the partners sitting in a position which is comfortable for talking and listening.
2. One partner on the left-hand side is given Briefing Sheet 1, and plays four mini situations.
3. The one on the right is given no briefing sheet during the first half of the exercise, but is given the instructions that he or she is visiting a number of 'old people' in hospital. Each visit lasts for five minutes, with two minutes between for the student playing the old person to get into the next mini-situation. During this two minute period the 'visitor' moves one place clockwise around the circle to the next 'old person', ready for the next visit. These visits take place four times.
4. The 'visitor' then becomes the 'old person', and is given Briefing Sheet 2. It is now her or his turn to stay sitting in the same chair. The other partner now becomes the visitor, moving immediately one place anti-clockwise, and thereafter one place anti-clockwise for the next remaining mini-situations. With a large enough group this way of moving will mean that no one pairing is repeated during the exercise.

Debriefing

Following all eight mini situations debriefing takes place in fours or small groups, particularly looking at what it felt like playing both each type of old person, and also the one visiting that old person.

Exercise 10.2: Mini role-plays on loss

Purpose

The exercise aims to compare and contrast the experiences accompanying different kinds of loss, as well as practice in counselling different types of loss.

Duration

1 hour.

Method

Short role-plays representing seven different types of loss provide practice in counselling, and also information about the various feelings involved in different situations, which are then compared and contrasted in small groups.

Materials

Briefing sheets for one in three of the participants, and a debriefing sheet for all participants.

Briefings for experience of loss

(a) Through an industrial accident at work you have lost the use of a limb, although you have been given a different job in the firm.
(b) You have recently moved to the area, leaving behind a part of the country and many friends whom you miss a great deal.
(c) You have lost your partner as a result of a separation, which you did not really want to take place.
(d) You have been made redundant – your job was highly skilled, and there is little prospect of finding another job in that area of skill.
(e) You have lost a close friend through his or her death.
(f) You are about to stop seeing your counsellor who has helped you through the most troublesome period of your life.
(g) You have been a fervent believer – in a religious way, or an active member of a political party or pressure group. But you have lost your faith completely in what you believed in before.

Exercise 10.2: Continued

Mini role-plays on loss: debriefing sheet

Compare and contrast the different feelings apparent in the seven situations involving loss – first by listing along the top line the feelings which emerged in one or more of the situations, and ticking off which situations these occurred in.

Exercise 10.2: Loss

Feelings seen or experienced												
Industrial accident												
Move to new area												
Separation/divorce												
Redundancy												
Death of friend												
Stopping counselling												
Loss of belief												

Instructions

1 Form threesomes: the threes need to decide among themselves who is to be the counsellor, who the client, and who the observer.
2 Each 'client' leaves the other two, and is allocated by the tutor a brief outline of a situation involving one type of loss (listed under materials above). During the next five minutes the client works out a story-line to fit the situation, and works out what feelings might be present in that situation.
3 In the meantime the counsellor and observer discuss the possible feelings which might arise as a result of a loss – at this point they do not know what kind of a loss the counsellor will be dealing with.
4 The client returns to the pair, and the counsellor has twenty minutes to work

Exercise 10.2: Continued

with the client – of which about seven minutes can be taken as 'time out', which the observer simply estimates. The client leaves as usual during 'time out', so that the observer can assist the counsellor.

Debriefing

At the end of the role-plays, there need to be about ten minutes set aside to discuss the role-play in the threesomes, particularly concentrating on debriefing the client, and on the skills shown by the counsellor.

Finally, form three groups consisting of the counsellors, the clients and the observers. In these groups they share what different and what similar feelings arose in each of the mini role-plays – all different kinds of loss. The debriefing chart is provided so that the different feelings noted can be listed for each situation, and then comparisons made between the different kinds of loss. Are there any feelings common to all seven situations? How do they differ, and what might the counsellor need to bear in mind in each particular situation?

Exercise 10.3: A death and a community[2]

Purpose

The exercise examines the impact of dying and death on different members of a family and upon a community, particularly looking at the denial of death and the effect this has on the person dying as well as on others.

Duration

1 hour.

Exercise 10.3: Continued

Method

A story of a young person's death is read to small groups, each representing one character in the story. The impact of the whole story on each character is discussed in the groups. The group members then meet with other group members, in 'family' groups, so that they can role-play what the different characters might have wished to express to each other.

Materials

The tutor needs one copy of case history below, which is read to the class at the start of the exercise:

A death and a community: a case history

I was asked by a nurse in hospital where I work as a medical social worker, if I could visit Shirley and her parents. It was mid-September. Shirley, a seventeen-year-old sixth-former had been admitted three weeks before, with a fever and general malaise. Shirley came from a market town some fifty miles away from our hospital, which was part of the medical school. The nurse told me that Shirley's parents had literally not left her side all the time she had been there.

I looked at the nursing notes before I went in, and discovered that Shirley was seriously ill with an unknown disease. Different subtler forms of cancer had been suggested, but all had been gradually ruled out. However, drugs which are usually used in treating some forms of cancer were being given to Shirley on an experimental basis, without much sign yet of any success. They were clearly causing Shirley a lot of discomfort. The nursing staff were obviously worried by the inability of Karen and Jim Parks (Shirley's parents) to leave her side. Jim used to go to the hospital cafeteria and buy enough food for himself and Karen, which they then ate in Shirley's room.

When I first stepped into the private ward I was startled to see it filled with flowers; 'get-well' cards covered a whole wall, overflowing on to a second; and there were even cards pinned to the window curtains. I spoke to Jim, Karen and Shirley together.

I paid them a number of visits, and got more and more troubled by the situation. It was certainly true that her parents almost never left her side. I thought at first that she must be an only child, but I learned that she had a twelve-year-old brother, Ben, who stayed in their home town with various family friends. Every evening from seven to nine, Ben went home and waited for a telephone call from Jim or Karen, telling him about Shirley's current condition. It was Ben's responsibility, among other things, to

Exercise 10.3: Continued

be the town's source of information about his sister. Her illness had attracted a lot of attention in the town, so Karen told me, and the weekly town paper printed reports about her on the front page of every issue. Shirley was regularly prayed for at every service of the United Reformed Church to which the Parks family belonged.

It so happened that I had been at university with Harold Brown, the minister of their church. Using this link I telephoned him to find out what I could about the Parks family, and the community's response to Shirley's illness. Harold was glad to be able to talk. Not just his church, but all the churches in the town were now deeply involved in prayers for Shirley's recovery. Shirley was about to start her final year at school. She was clearly very popular, and had already had early acceptance at a Cambridge college, the first girl from her school to have done so.

Harold was a little troubled by the way in which Shirley's illness had become a kind of cause in the small town. People were fighting over the opportunity to have Ben stay with them. The newspaper called Ben every evening after he had heard from his parents. Harold asked me whether I had seen the amazing number of cards in Shirley's room. He would look out for me on his next visit to the hospital, because he wanted to discuss further the way people in the town had made Shirley into a sort of heroine of faith. The word was going round that, with her faith and that of the townspeople, Shirley was certain to recover.

By now I was getting very puzzled. I discovered that Karen, Shirley's mother, shared the view of the townspeople that her daughter's marvellous faith, and the prayers of the town, and even further afield in the county, were sure to save Shirley's life. But I could also see that Jim was not so sure. And he was clearly very worried about the effects of the experimental medication on Shirley. He had, I learned, been opposed to a treatment which had only a slim chance of working and would certainly cause his daughter severe discomfort. He stayed in the hospital, he said, because Karen needed his constant presence and support. In fact I was once able to speak to him alone, outside the room, and he told me that was actually afraid that Shirley would not live.

At last I got the opportunity to visit Shirley alone – well, almost alone, because Jim and Karen were both asleep in their chairs. Shirley made it clear to me that she was having to put on an act for her parents and for her community at home. She knew just how serious her condition was, and she was so often in pain, or nauseated, or both, that she often didn't feel like smiling. She wasn't sure that she had the sort of faith that her mother and other people thought she had. She wanted to be left alone sometimes, but could not admit that. But she did say that the love shown by the home community was very impressive, and she wanted to respond to that love.

Harold Brown looked me up the next time he came to the hospital, and told me that a number of people in the church had organized a county-wide twenty-four-hour 'prayer crusade' for Shirley's recovery. He was rather dubious about such an exercise,

Exercise 10.3: Continued

but he felt that as pastor of her church he had little choice but to participate, and he would himself be leading the first four hours of the crusade that evening in his church. He had doubts, but he was nevertheless impressed by the concern that everyone was showing for Shirley.

During October Shirley improved. During the first two weeks of November she held her own. But on December 1st her condition began to get worse. She fell into a coma on December 10th, and died on Christmas Eve.

By 10 o'clock that night Jim and Karen had removed every evidence of their long occupancy of the room, and they left the hospital without a word to anyone.

I rang Harold after Christmas and learned that there was to be a memorial service for Shirley in his church in the New Year; and I went to it, because the manner of Shirley's death had touched me. It was very strange. The whole service focused on the joy of resurrection. One of Shirley's best friends spoke about Shirley's beauty and warmth, and said how much she would be missed. Harold Brown spoke some rather traditional words of comfort. But when I went back with him to his home for a meal afterwards, he told me that the service had been designed by Karen Parks, and reflected her opinion that as little reference to death as possible should be contained in the service.

I think Harold must have been through a lot, because he remained in touch with me for a while, and I learned from him some of the aftermath of Shirley's illness and death. Jim Parks had stopped coming to church. He had begun to say that there had been no hope all along, and that he was deeply angry with himself for having agreed to the experimental treatment. Karen and Ben were in church every Sunday, refusing to refer to Shirley's death, and acting as if life would go on just as if nothing had happened. Meanwhile, I gather that the community buzzed for a while with conflicting opinions of whether or not Shirley really had had enough faith. But the buzz died down, and the town, like Karen Parks, seemed to continue its usual existence as if nothing had happened.

Instructions

1 Form five equal-size groups. Each group is given the name of a character in the case history and is asked to listen to the case history from that particular character's point of view, monitoring how that person might have felt both in her or himself, and also about the others involved. These five characters are Shirley, Karen (Shirley's mother), Jim (Shirley's father), Ben (Shirley's younger brother) and Harold Brown (the minister of this family's local church).

2 The above case history is then read aloud by the tutor to the whole class.

Exercise 10.3: Continued

3 Once the account has been read, each group has between ten and twenty minutes to discuss how that character might have felt, both within herself or himself and about the others.
4 'Family' groups are then formed, by taking one person from each group and putting the five people together, consisting of the four family members and the minister. Where there are not equal numbers the 'Harold Brown' group can be smaller; and it may therefore not always be represented in the family group.
5 The family groups play out what they might have wanted to say to each other, had they been given the chance to be really open and honest. This part of the exercise can last from fifteen to thirty minutes.

Debriefing

Each person in each family group must have the chance to come out of role, to become themselves again, before returning to the original character groups to discuss what they have learned from the exercise about the experiences of the different people involved.

Exercise 10.4: Role-play

Purpose

The following role-play illustrates some aspects of bereavement, in a family who have lost an adolescent son, and can also provide practice in counselling a couple in a crisis situation.

Duration

60–75 minutes. It is suggested that the role-play lasts for forty minutes, with up to twenty minutes allowed for 'time out' (see Chapter 1).

Exercise 10.4: Continued

Method, etc.

See Exercise 1.2, Chapter 1, for method, materials, instructions and debriefing. Comments on the possible handling of the situation appear at the end. Debriefing and analysis of the counsellor's work is, of course, essential and may take a further thirty minutes after the role play.

Briefing for Mr and/or Mrs Williams (aged about forty)

Give the counsellor the information in the first paragraph below, along with your name(s) and age(s). The material in the second paragraph can be used as seems appropriate during the counselling session.

Your teenage son, Rob, was killed in a road accident, while riding his new motorcycle. He was seventeen, and had left school and gone into training with an engineering firm. You had great hopes for him.

As you are given the opportunity to talk you say more and more of the things that are on your mind. Young people can't be told – you had tried to put him off the idea of getting a motorbike, but only got into arguments about it, and he said he had a right to spend his money the way he wanted to. What else could you have said or done? You feel responsible in some way, but also helpless. And his poor little sister, Jane, aged fourteen, had quarrelled with him the night he went out. What can you say to her?

Comment

Other role-plays on the theme of bereavement appear in *Still Small Voice*[3] (Mr Clarke) and *Swift to Hear*[4] (Mrs Fisher). Each of these involves the death of a spouse, one in old age, the other in mid-life. The role-play above, like Exercise 10.3, concerns the death of an adolescent. It can involve either parent, or both, depending on the emphasis which the tutor wishes to give to the situation.

11

Drawing together: The Evil Man

Introduction

The final exercise is unusual but extremely effective with advanced-level students. It assumes a good working knowledge of the three major themes introduced in Chapters 4–6, and of the way in which they are seen in presenting problems and in the counsellor–client relationship.

It is closely based on a case history included by Masud Khan in his book, *Hidden Selves.*[1] The exercise tries to represent something of the relationship between client and therapist that comes through in the record of the twists and turns in the case. It does this through its structure but also in the way in which the tutor conducting it relates to the small groups. On one level the tutor represents the client's presentation and responses to the small groups, who try to put themselves in the therapist's position. In its own way this relationship between tutor and small groups reflects the client and the therapist, and in its turn this reflects the client's own history, although aspects of this do not become clear until almost the end of the therapy.

It is also an unusual case study inasmuch as Masud Khan was himself unusual, sometimes pushing at the limits of how the therapist works with the client. The result in this case (as in others of his) is that his interventions are sometimes not those which students of counselling or psychotherapy would first imagine. He was at times extremely cautious, aware of the delicacy of his client, far more careful than many counsellors would be; but at other times he was more daring, opening areas, or setting out his views in ways which a counsellor might think were too risky. This means that, given mainly the multiple-choice answers in this exercise, the small groups sometimes get what seems like the obvious response wrong, or fail to go for the one which will yield a breakthrough. What is essential is that the groups begin to monitor what is happening to them, as the tutor responds to them, since this mirrors the way the client treated the therapist, and the way the client has been acted upon (and indeed acts) himself. If that sounds mysterious at this point, I confess that I am deliberately holding back anything which might anticipate each new event and the final denouement. What I can say is that this is an exercise which proves both fascinating and frustrating.

Exercise 11: The Evil Man

Purpose

This exercise aims to draw together all the major themes covered in the exercises in this manual, and found in more detail in *The Presenting Past.*[2]

Duration

At least 4 hours, preferably divided into two 2-hour sessions.

Method

Working in small groups on a case study, with questions mainly posed in multiple-choice form. The groups are scored for the aptness or not of their answers.

Materials

A summary of the three major themes for each member of the class. A fuller version summarizing these themes can be found in the Appendix of *The Presenting Past.*[3] One set of information sheets (1–18) for each small group taking part in the exercise.

Summary of the main features of the three major themes

OS: oral, dependency, trust themes. These include issues such as feeding, demanding, spitting out, biting, being held, black/white splitting, persecutory feelings, self/other/world boundaries, destructive rage, transitional

Exercise 11: Continued

objects, part objects, powerful fantasy, being cut off from others, in pieces, disorganization (internally), envy, exclusivity, capacity (or not) to be alone, tolerance of frustration, integration of good/bad, self-esteem (in basic self), being.

AS: anal, authority, autonomy themes. These include issues such as control, aggression, rebelling, battles of will, passive aggression, sadism, masochism, holding in, soiling, spoiling, mess, perfectionism, disorganization (of externals), conformity, order, rituals, intellectualization, rules, advice, judgementalism, criticism, shame, self-esteem (in what one can do), doing, performing.

GS: genital, competitive, co-operative themes. These include issues such as sexuality, rivalry, social relationships, oedipal issues, three-person relationships, jealousy, primacy, giving not just receiving.

Information sheet 1

It is April. Your client is a man aged forty-five, who is tall, suave, and elegantly dressed in a hand-tailored suit, but his clothes hang on him. He is polite but extremely reticent. He has a crumpled, damaged right hand, which he neither hides nor openly displays.

At this early stage does he present in OS, AS or GS themes? Give your reasons.

Information sheet 2

Score 1 for AS or OS, none for GS (there is no evidence yet). If you have given reasons, score 1 mark for AS reasons (reticence, politeness (withholding), neat appearance); 3 marks for OS reasons (clothes don't fit, looks as if he has lost weight, probably not eating). If both AS and OS then all marks count.

The doctor who referred him to you has told you that the man is married, with children, and had a successful job and contented family life until about three months ago, when he suddenly sank into an acute depression, and has been unable to go to work. He had refused up to now all suggestions of therapy or counselling.

The doctor also told you that what most worried him was the man's refusal to eat, and that he would only take food in liquid form.

The man says, after a brief pause: 'I am an evil man and there is no cure for that.'

Do you reply:

(a) 'No cure for that?'
(b) 'What have you done that is evil?'
(c) 'Do you want to tell me what makes you say such a damning thing?'
(d) 'What happened three months ago?'

Exercise 11: Continued

Information sheet 3

(a): 1 (very standard, safe response!)
(b): −3 (too probing – accepts word 'evil' at face value)
(c): 3 (gives him choice as to what to tell you: useful paraphrase of evil, ascribed to his words)
(d): −5 (too near the knuckle – in time you will see why; also uses outside information indiscriminately)

The man says nothing. He then asks what the doctor has told you. Do you:

(a) say nothing?
(b) say 'Nothing'?
(c) tell him all you know?
(d) tell him part of what you know – if so, which part?

Information sheet 4

(a): 0 (dodging the question, but safe!)
(b): −5 (lying!)
(c): −1 (completely honest, but see (d) below)
(d): 1st paragraph of doctor's information, 2 marks (you reveal enough to satisfy, but don't let on about 2nd paragraph)
(e): 2nd paragraph, −2 marks (because you let him know he can't eat, which implies he is regressed and out of control; and he is already showing you he is uncertain about letting any of that side of himself show)

The man says nothing more. After a silence, do you:

(a) stay silent?
(b) ask: 'What sort of work do you normally do?'
(c) say: 'I notice your damaged right hand. How did you manage that?'
(d) ask: 'What happened three months ago?'

Information sheet 5

(a): 1 (safe)
(b): −3 (you'll see why in due course!)
(c): 5 (brave, and not risky because he has neither hidden nor openly displayed the hand)
(d): −10 (You've already been told this is a penalty area!)

Exercise 11: Continued

Since it was all right to ask about the hand, we will assume you did! The man replies, 'I didn't manage it; it happened to me.' Do you say:

(a) 'What happened?'
(b) nothing?

Information sheet 6

This man is reticent, and somewhat awkward! He indicates he is not to be drawn, so why press on along a pointless path? So for (a) score −2; whereas refusing to be drawn yourself and staying silent (b) earns you 2 points.

He breaks the silence, but he doesn't give you much. He leaves the topic of the hand, and talks about his concern lest his 'condition' is distressing his children's preparations for A and O levels. He has two sons and a daughter. But little else is said of any consequence for a number of weeks. You feel as if you are being kept in suspense. Monitor how you also are feeling as a group at this point. Might this be telling you something about what the therapist was experiencing, and therefore something about this client as well? The question you are asked to answer is: Is this man at this point of showing OS, AS or GS themes (provide some evidence)?

Information sheet 7

If you said OS, AS or GS without reasons, then no mark. You could say OS because he is not feeding you with anything, not trusting, etc., and for this you get 2 marks. Or AS because he is controlling, and punitive, and has you in his power, etc., for 3 marks. Or now you can add GS because there is perhaps an element of teasing (which may be a little sexual?), or rivalry in the relationship, for 2 marks. For any combination of all three stages add the scores together,

Thirteen weeks have now gone by since you started seeing him. You know nothing more significant than what is presently to hand. He reports that he has started work again, and asks to change his time with you for that reason; and you agree to this. His wife meanwhile rings to tell you what a relief it is because her husband has started to eat proper meals again. Next time you meet him do you:

(a) suggest to him that it is a good time to finish counselling?
(b) tell him his wife has told you about the eating?
(c) tell him you are still puzzled about what happened about his hand?

Exercise 11: Continued

Information sheet 8

The answer has to be (b), because you must not talk about a client behind his back, without letting him know. Otherwise you will lose his trust and confidence. So (a) scores −2 (this is defeatist, and anyway he asked to change the time – he wants to go on); (b) scores 2 (hopefully you didn't tell him before that you knew he was not eating); (c) scores −5 (what are you doing allowing yourself to get hooked on to that again? You know by now he just doesn't want to tell you things if you make the running!)

Time passes, and the sessions continue for a while with nothing special to tell you. It is now the last session before a six-week summer break (your holiday and his). He says: 'You once inquired how I managed to damage my right hand. On a wintry day I was cycling home. It was a rainy day and the country lane was narrow and slippery. A car hooted to warn me it wanted to overtake and I tried to pull in, but the cycle skidded, and I fell under the car – it crushed my right arm. The next thing I remember was waking up in hospital, my arm in plaster. I returned home after a week, but the arm did not heal, and I had four changes of plaster under anaesthetic. Once I heard the surgeon whispering to my father that there was an infection in the bone, that he feared gangrene and that the arm might have to be amputated.' He has got into his stride. The hour has gone, although his is the last appointment of the day. He obviously still wants to say more. He pauses. Do you:

(a) tell him you have to finish there?
(b) allow him to continue?

Information sheet 9

(a): 2 (technically correct, but you're missing a golden opportunity; at last he has decided to talk)
(b): 5 (if you understand what you are doing, and what is happening to you, that he is pushing you on boundaries, then fair enough!)

Normally you would want to stop, but he was at last speaking and you can be forgiven for letting him go on.

In fact, in the next half hour (which you give him) he tells you that he was fourteen years old when he had this accident. The arm did not have to be amputated, but a friend of his father suggested that he have treatment from a famous Swiss surgeon. He was flown to Switzerland, and stayed in the friend's chalet. After three months the arm was out of plaster, and he started physiotherapy. He had the use of his thumb and second and third fingers, but the other two were stiff and crumpled.

Exercise 11: Continued

Monitor how you are feeling as a group, and what this tells you about the therapist and perhaps also about the client. How do you understand the relationship between you now?

(a) Are you being taken for a ride?
(b) Is it a battle of wills?
(c) Are you testing each other out?

Information sheet 10

(a): *0* *(be more confident; you chose to give him more time!)*
(b): *1* *(this is a possibility)*
(c): *2* *(that's more how it felt: he's testing you on boundaries, and you are testing him on whether he will use the extra time)*

It is after the summer break. He returns from his holiday. He has been dreaming a lot about the accident and the year after. He has written one of the dreams down and reads it to you. 'I am cycling down a country lane – I don't know which country – and two young girls overtake me, racing each other. As they pass me, I spank the one nearest to me with my right hand on her bottom.' He pauses, and then says something about returning to work again next week. Do you:

(a) ask him what the dream means to him?
(b) observe to him that in his dream he seems to be able to cycle and use his right hand?
(c) say nothing?
(d) ask him what his work is?

Information sheet 11

(a): −2 *(he changes the subject at the end: he doesn't want to take it up himself)*
(b): −4 *(It's too early to make such a comment, it isn't the client's interpretation of his dream, and anyway he seems not to want to talk any more about the dream)*
(c): 2 *(you're getting the hang of it)*
(d): −5 *(you were warned about this penalty area earlier – you will see why!)*

The next week the client begins to talk much more freely about himself both before and after the accident. He was the third child of five, with two elder brothers and two younger sisters. He was a buoyant and hyperactive child before the accident. But after

Exercise 11: Continued

the accident, in hospital he refused to let the nurses feed him, and only permitted his mother to feed him. He began to draw away from his siblings, and felt helpless and dependent, and humiliated at being so. It was even worse when he went to Switzerland because he did not know the language, and he was unable to do much for himself. But gradually the operations and physiotherapy helped his arm and hand, although he was still unable to write. The surgeon then suggested he have drawing lessons. From this he found he was quite a talented artist, and the hand began to improve, and with it his ability to eat with the right hand, too. He became more sociable with others, although he continued to remain reticent and controlled, as he had been since the accident.

For several sessions he fills in this type of background, until the last week before the Christmas break, he tells you about an event that changed his whole life. He was walking back home during the last week in Switzerland, after a drawing lesson. It was a wintry, snowy day. Two girls cycled past him racing each other, each wearing tight white shorts, sweater and socks. This sight excited him, and when he got back to the chalet he drew his first doodle of a girl on a cycle. That night he dreamed that two girls in white shorts were racing past him, and with his ruler in his right hand he playfully smacked the one nearest him on the bottom; she turned and winked at him. The dream woke him and he had had his first nocturnal emission. From that dream onwards he began to draw cycles and girls on cycles, and evolved a fantasy.

He finishes his tale five minutes before the end of the session. As he puts on his coat he says: 'I don't think you know what I do? I specialize in making and designing furniture, I'll tell you about it after the break.'

How do you understand what he has told you in this session?

Information sheet 12

Score 1 mark for each useful point you made: such as the dream linking to the earlier dream he told you about; his difficulty telling you about sex; his not eating then and in the time before he first saw you; his teasing you at the end of the session with words about his work; the way he uses ends of sessions and last sessions before breaks (and it was the last week in Switzerland when this happened), his controlling the pace, etc. A special extra score of 3 marks for the girls overtaking him being like the car which overtook him, or the two girls perhaps like his two younger sisters.

After the Christmas break your client tells you he and his wife have an opportunity to go to the Far East for a year from next September. But his wife wants his treatment to have first priority. He asks you what he should do. Do you tell him:

(a) that it is his decision?

Exercise 11: Continued

(b) that he really needs another two years with you (which you actually believe is necessary)?
(c) that you recommend meeting twice as often each week and stopping in the summer?
(d) that you will stop at the summer break, since a lot can be done with his co-operation?

Information sheet 13

(a): 0 (a very tame, far too casual response – he has asked you, for the very first time, for your opinion)
(b): −1 (you are trying to pressurize him to stay)
(c): −3 (this will increase his dependency as you come to the end)
(d): 2 (you use the time in the way you know he uses time – making the most of 'ends', shortage of time; and you are responding to his wish to work with you rather than against you)

He asks you to guide him as to what to talk about first. Do you:

(a) politely decline to do this?
(b) ask him to tell you more about his work?
(c) ask him to tell you more about his dream?

Information sheet 14a

If you answer (a), you are penalized −2 points and you are asked to reconsider your answer. You invited his co-operation, and you should co-operate, too. This is rare that he actually wants you to guide him.

Information sheet 14b

It was good to ask him something because he is inviting your co-operation. But since you asked about his work, you get 0 marks, but the following free information.

When he got married, his father gave him an old warehouse in which he set up his own furniture design business. He had been to college to learn about manual crafts. But it was really that Swiss dream that had set him on that path. No more is forthcoming.

Would you now ask him about the dream?

Exercise 11: Continued

Information sheet 14c

Since you asked about the dream (much more in line with what he has been telling you) you get 1 mark, and the following information. If you previously answered that you asked about his work, and have now gone for the dream as being potentially more productive, well done. It's never too late, and you are right to admit your mistake!

On his return from Switzerland he asked to be tutored in languages and sciences. His parents said science was impossible with his handicap, but he insisted and he had his way. He still felt very lonely, and apart from his lessons, bored. One day he saw his sister's bike up against the wall, and he drew it. He began to draw bicycles as a pastime. He was also invited to his godfather's for a weekend, where he was allowed to use his carpentry tools, and he made the decision then to go to college to learn manual crafts. After college, and when he got married, his father gave him an old warehouse in which he set up his own furniture design business. 'The Swiss dream freed me and gave me my vocation,' he says.

How did it do that?

Information sheet 15

Score 1 mark for each useful point you made. Particularly note the confidence the dream-drawing gave him, and the sense of control that he then got back in his hand. This clearly led to his being able to work at science, and then woodwork, and so helped to shape his career.

In the sessions that follow he tells you how drawing cycles developed (when he became a student) into drawing girls on cycles, and he experienced more excitement then. At the same time he gradually developed a fantasy which accompanied the drawing, that he is cycling down a country lane on a sunny day when a girl in white shorts overtakes him on a bicycle. He catches up with her and they talk. He invites her to visit him when the family are away, and he persuades her to come to his studio where in his fantasy he has a bicycle carved in wood. In its final form, the fantasy involved the girl getting on the wooden cycle but being just unable to reach the pedals. He bets her she can't reach them by shifting in the seat, and that if she can't he will strike her with his ruler, which he does, but no more than five times.

How do you respond to this? Again monitor how you are feeling in this exercise. Do you:

(a) link in the sisters who in some sense overtook him as a result of his accident and handicap, and one of whose cycle he drew?
(b) ask him whether he used this fantasy to masturbate?

Exercise 11: Continued

(c) observe the playful quality of the fantasy?
(d) say that you feel tantalized and suspended by him like the girl in his fantasy?

Information sheet 16

(a): −3 (incestuous fantasies, which may have been there, but are not openly on show, are not easy to bring out, especially at this late stage)
(b): −1 (haven't you noticed how reticent he still is about sexual terms? This question is too intrusive)
(c): 2 (you need to relieve the rage in the fantasy – the vengeance over the car, now taken out on the two girls who overtook him. He may feel strong guilt over this rage, leading to his being depressed)
(d): −1 (though correct this is risky since you are identifying your relationship as having this sexual component, too, which might arouse sexual anxieties in him about the relationship with you)

In fact, as a result of your using the expression 'playful' about the fantasy (a niçe *double entendre*) he tells you that he got a lot of pleasure from masturbating when completing a girly drawing (as he called them), but not when he thought simply of the fantasy. The playfulness of the fantasy makes it a kind of transitional object, through which he begins to master his latent vengeful wishes against the car that knocked him down, his helplessness and inability to exercise control of his arm and hand, the frustration of the (white) plaster on his arm, etc. It is now the Easter break, and you have been seeing him a year. Do you now know what made him say he was an evil man?

Information sheet 17

Be honest, and stop trying to be omniscient: you haven't any real knowledge about why he thinks he is an evil man. So −1 mark for every guess; but you can have 5 marks if you guessed that the fantasy became real: it is an intelligent guess, but there is no evidence yet, of course. But if you answered that you do not know, then you score 10 for being absolutely honest!

You, and the therapist, have little or no idea of any facts about recent events. It is now after the Easter break, with three months to go before you finish. At last, perhaps because of the pressure of time, he is able to tell you what happened three months before he saw you.

That weekend his family had gone to their country home, leaving him to go to a

Exercise 11: Continued

conference dinner in London. Seated at his table were four colleagues and a young woman he did not know, a journalist who knew of his work. Only when they got up from dinner did he notice she was wearing very tight white trousers. They parted, and at the end of the evening he left to go for a taxi. It was raining. He did not have his own car because he did not wish to have to display the words 'Handicapped Driver'. After a short while a small car drew up, driven by the young woman, who asked him if he wanted a lift. As they drove she said she would like to see his workshop, and they went there. She noticed his private studio, asked to see inside, and there she saw a full-scale wooden cycle which he had made long ago. People joked about it as his toy. She got on the cycle, but could not reach the pedals. Everything then moved very quickly – he found himself petting her, she teased him about fantasies and said she had them, too, of being beaten before intercourse. He asked whether she would like it now, and she said she would. He went outside to find a stick, and when he came back she was undressed, again sitting on the cycle. He said he would give her one stroke each time she failed to reach the pedals. He beat her ten times, and was horrified to see he had drawn blood. She insisted he 'fuck' her (her word), which he did 'with a diabolical ferocity of lust' (his phrase). Then they dressed and she drove him near to his home. He went to sleep with his clothes on, and woke about midday. He went to sleep again and awoke the next morning with the statement 'I am an evil man' vivid in his mind, as if he had dreamt it.

How do you now understand this case? What are the OS, AS and GS elements?

Information sheet 18

Again you score 1 mark for every useful observation: the fantasy came true, and not only ceased to be a fantasy (in itself frightening), but also became a situation where he lost control of his arm and hand, rather than gained control of them – as he did through his fantasy drawings. See also the information below.

In the remaining weeks, because he had now told his story, and had been given his own control of the pace at which the whole story emerged, client and therapist were able to work together on understanding what had happened, reconstructing his life from the accident, through his achievements in overcoming the handicap, and the parallels in the events that night that had threatened to smash all his achievements. The therapist observed that it was not all his doing, that the young woman had set it up as well, and in fact she took control of events sufficiently to damage his hard-won sense of control and mastery of his handicap. The client's last remark to the therapist was: 'I have learnt that one evil act doesn't make an evil man. Each of us is capable of it.'

Exercise 11: Continued

Instructions

1 Divide the class into small groups, preferably those in which they are used to working.
2 The groups are told that they will be given a small initial amount of information about a client: they are to imagine they are the counsellor or therapist, and they need to work out what is happening, or choose one of a number of alternative responses, which will be given to them as the case progresses. They bring their answer(s) each time to the tutor, who will present them with the client's next response or action. If they give a good answer they score points: the more helpful the answer the higher the points. On occasion they may score nothing, or, if their answer is particularly unhelpful or tactless, they may even receive minus points. They should keep a running total of their score for themselves. They will be given a further information sheet after they have answered, which will also explain the score they have been given.
3 The exercise itself takes at least three hours, if not more; it then requires at least one hour for class discussion and feedback. Because of its length it will probably need to be spread over two separate sessions of two hours each. The break between sessions can be used to advantage, by aiming to bring all the groups to the questions at the end of information sheets 9 or 11, since both represent points of breaks in the therapy itself. Within ten minutes of the end of the first session bring all the groups to the same point, by reading (and then giving out to those who have not yet got them) all the information sheets which the slower groups have not yet had, up to and including sheets 9 or 11. Any group receiving a sheet in this way scores nothing for those sheets, since they have not got on to answering them – they may, of course, be spared a minus score this way!
4 All the groups then start at the same point the following session, ready to think about their answer to the questions addressed to them in either sheet 9 or 11. Groups take a long time to discuss their answers (especially when they have had one rap over the knuckles with penalty points!), and two hours will scarcely be long enough for even the quickest to get far beyond sheet 10 in the first session. Similarly, in the final session it will probably be necessary (and indeed particularly appropriate given the way the case went) to bring the exercise to a close by catching the groups up to the position of the leading group; and then to take them through to the denouement – again without scoring the sheets they have not worked on. In fact the denouement is so startling (and yet comprehensible) that the exercise normally ends without anyone bothering to ask about scores. The points system has served its

Exercise 11: Continued

purpose, both in making the groups think carefully about their answers, but in illustrating the way the therapist was treated by the client. Students are generally far more interested in the case than in their own relative merits.

Debriefing

Comprehensive discussion in the small groups and in the class as a whole of the complete case, as well as of the feelings evoked by the tutor's attitudes, is necessary to round off the exercise. It is very important to convey the significance of the reflection of the client's history in the therapist–client relationship, and of the therapist–client relationship in the exercise itself: for example, the way the tutor's responses represent the twists and turns of the client, who needs all the time to maintain control; the apparent punishment of the groups reflecting the sense of punishment and self-punishment in the client; the way information is given at the ends of sessions or withheld right until the end, just as the client does; and the almost total control which the tutor has over the groups in the way the client needs to exercise this over the therapist and over his own life. Finally, it needs to be stressed that the more experienced a therapist becomes, the more possibility there is of responding (when it is necessary and when the likely outcome is able to be anticipated) other than in the ways taught as the conventional wisdom of technique. The experienced therapist or counsellor is able to respond with, and to initiate, a whole range of interventions which do not necessarily 'go by the book'.

Notes to chapters

Chapter 1

1. See, just as a small sample of an ever increasing list of manuals for trainers and/or students of counselling, Dainow and Bailey (1988); Egan (1986a; 1990); Inskipp (undated); Meier (1989); Nelson-Jones (1983); Okun (1986); Priestly and McGuire (1983); Redman (1988); and Tschudin (1982).
2. See, for example, Truax (1963).
3. Jacobs (1988, pp. 28–33).
4. Jacobs (1985, pp. 13–14) contains exercises to illustrate the basic guidelines for listening and responding, as well as some role-play techniques, also described in this chapter, and some role-play situations which, with one exception, are not reprinted in this book. An earlier book (Jacobs, 1982, pp. 159–67) also contains a few exercises, some of which also appeared in Jacobs (1985), and some appear in revised form in the early part of this book.
5. Egan's stages are succinctly set out in Inskipp (undated) for Trainers, and are found in full in Egan (1986b).
6. Jacobs (1985, pp. 77–81).
7. Ibid., p. 79.
8. Ibid., p. 79.
9. Ibid., pp. 75–6.
10. There is an example of such a record in ibid., p. 78.
11. This exercise, printed here in a much expanded version, first appeared as 'A Family Flare-up' (Exercise 19.9) in ibid., pp. 86–7.
12. Yalom (1989).
13. Ibid., p. 180.
14. Ibid., p. 182.
15. Ibid., p. 184.

Chapter 2

1 This exercise and Exercise 2.2 have been inspired by Preston Bogia (1985). While the exercises themselves are my own, the introductions to them both draw heavily on that work. These exercises can also be used in basic skills training, following perhaps the two exercises in my basic manual (Jacobs, 1985, pp. 50–4). Exercise 12 in Jacobs (1985) is actually about practising keeping quiet, but it often illustrates the futility of a series of closed questions.
2 Laing (1965); Searles (1965).

Chapter 3

1 Among the vast literature on the facilitating of groups for therapy or learning are the following: Corey (1990); Corey and Corey (1987); Egan (1973; 1976); Foulkes (1982); Jacobs and Masson (1987); chs 5 and 6 of Jacobs (1985), on small and large groups, respectively; Jacques (1988a; 1988b); Yalom (1986).
2 Belbin (1981).
3 Robertson and Robertson (1976), available for hire or purchase from Concord Films Council, Nacton, Ipswich, Suffolk, England, IP3 9BJ; or the New York University Film Library, 26 Washington Place, New York, NY 10003.

Chapter 4

1 Jacobs (1986). Another valuable text for use in teaching personal development is Rayner (1986).
2 Erikson (1965). The important and extremely influential chapter which outlines his model is ch. 5 pp. 239–66. Erikson (1968: ch. 3) provides fuller treatment of the model.
3 Jacobs (1986, pp. 6–8, 20–2).
4 Erikson (1965, p. 265n).
5 Ibid., p. 253.
6 Ibid., p. 261.
7 Jacobs (1986, pp. 205–22).
8 Klein (1957).
9 Skynner and Cleese (1983, pp. 15–16).
10 Walrond-Skinner (1988). Not only does the author include two useful genograms, but the text covering Sara's genogram and its interpretation (pp. 19–22) is worth giving to students.
11 On the trust and dependency theme, characteristics of presenting problems related to the oral stage as described in psychoanalytic writing, and possible responses by the counsellor and therapist, see Jacobs (1986, ch. 3 and pp. 205–11).
12 Williams (1982, p. 353).
13 Sendak, M. (1970). For a summary of this story, see Jacobs (1986, pp. 52–3).
14 Bettelheim (1978). On 'Goldilocks and the Three Bears', see pp. 215–24; on 'Hansel and Gretel', see pp. 159–66; on 'Sleeping Beauty', see pp. 225–36; on 'Cinderella', see

pp. 236–77; on 'Jack and the Beanstalk', see pp. 183–94; and on 'Little Red Riding Hood', see pp. 166–83.

15 Dickens (1988).
16 Bettelheim (1978, pp. 26 and 25).
17 Jacobs (1986, pp. 12–13).

Chapter 5

1 On the autonomy and authority theme, characteristics of presenting problems related to the anal stage as described in psychoanalytic writing, and possible responses by the counsellor and therapist, see Jacobs (1986, ch. 4 and pp. 211–16).
2 The reader who is interested in the design of use of simulations of various kinds will find a growing literature on the subject. The following provide a start: Jones (1980; 1985); Tansey and Unwin (1969); Van Ments (1983).
3 On the feminist psychodynamic position on gender differences in the mother–child relationship and also in the psychology of adult men and women, see Chodorow (1978); Dinnerstein (1987); Gilligan (1982); Mitchell (1975). For an important modern psychoanalytic reassessment of the Freudian phallocentric understanding of male development see Fogel *et al.* (1986).
4 For the original version of this simulation, modified since in the manner of the monarch's dispatch, see Jacobs (1984, pp. 121–8).

Chapter 6

1 On the co-operation and competition theme (or genital-oedipal-rivalry-social stage as it is there called), characteristics of presenting problems related to the genital stage as described in psychoanalytic writing, and possible responses by the counsellor and therapist, see Jacobs (1986, ch. 5 and pp. 217–22).
2 Erikson (1965, ch. 5).
3 Jacobs (1986, pp. 123–31).
4 This and the following exercise first appeared in print in Jacobs (1984, pp. 121–8). Readers who compare the version of 'A Fictitious Election' in this chapter with that in Jacobs (1984) may notice the way in which violent references have been cut from the original. This is felt important for a number of reasons, not least that policies on capital punishment made the exercise more historically accurate but less psychologically defendable in those respects. The present version makes for more equal weighting in all three manifestos.
5 Erikson. E. (1968, p. 116).
6 For my original version of this exercise, see Jacobs (1984, p. 128).
7 I cannot trace the origin of this puzzle either to ask permission for its use, or to acknowledge authorship. I have in any case altered the original to make this version slightly easier to solve in the time available: but I have further altered it for publication from the conundrum I know as 'Who owns the zebra?'.
8 A videotape of the author struggling with a beautifully difficult pair playing Frank and

Madge can be seen on Demonstration Role Plays, available for hire or purchase from Audio-Visual Services, University of Leicester, Medical Sciences Building, University Road, Leicester, LE1 9HN.

Chapter 7

1 Jacobs (1986). Since most of my work when I was writing that book was with students, the examples are nearly all relevant to young people, as well as to adults.
2 Noonan (1983). This book also takes a psychodynamic approach, and includes many examples from her own work with young people.
3 Jane Taylor and Jackie Smith, both tutors on the Leicester Counselling courses, developed this exercise.
4 Jacobs (1986, p. 63–4).
5 Ibid., p. 67.
6 Noonan (1983, p. 25).

Chapter 8

1 Erikson (1965, ch. 5).
2 Samuels (1985, p. 170).
3 Jacobs (1986, ch. 8).
4 Ibid., chs 9 and 10.
5 Ibid., ch. 11.

Chapter 9

1 Searles (1965: 602–3).
2 Jacobs (1986, pp. 182–3).
3 Winnicott (1988, p. 138).
4 Freud (1962, p. 115).

Chapter 10

1 Jacobs (1986, p. 190).
2 This exercise is based on a case which has been adapted from an article by Mitchell (1982).
3 Jacobs (1982, pp. 164–5).
4 Jacobs (1985, p. 85).

Chapter 11

1 Khan (1983, ch. 8).
2 Jacobs (1986).
3 Ibid., pp. 205–22.

Bibliography

Belbin, R. M. (1981). *Management Teams.* London, Heinemann.
Bettelheim, B. (1978). *The Uses of Enchantment.* Harmondsworth, Penguin.
Chodorow, N. (1978). *The Reproduction of Mothering.* Berkeley and London, University of California Press.
Corey, G. (1990). *Theory and Practice of Group Counseling*, 3rd edn. New York, Brooks Cole.
Corey, M. S. and Corey, G. (1987). *Groups: Process and Practice.* New York, Brooks Cole.
Dainow, S. and Bailey, C. (1988). *Developing Skills with People.* Chichester, John Wiley.
Dickens, C. (1988). *My Early Times* (ed. P. Rowland). London, The Folio Society.
Dinnerstein, D. (1987). *The Rocking of the Cradle and the Ruling of the World.* London, The Women's Press.
Egan, G. (1973). *Face to Face: the Small Group Experience and Interpersonal Growth.* New York, Brooks Cole.
Egan, G. (1976). *Interpersonal Living.* New York, Brooks Cole.
Egan, G. (1986a). *Exercises in Helping Skills*, 3rd edn. New York, Brooks Cole.
Egan, G. (1986b). *The Skilled Helper*, 3rd edn. New York, Brooks Cole.
Egan, G. (1990). *The Skilled Helper*, 4th edn. New York, Brooks Cole.
Erikson, E. (1965). *Childhood and Society.* Harmondsworth, Penguin.
Erikson, E. (1968). *Identity: Youth and Crisis.* London, Faber and Faber.
Freud, S. (1962). *Two Short Accounts of Psychoanalysis.* Harmondsworth, Penguin.
Fogel, G. I., Lane, F. M. and Liebert, R. S. (eds) (1986). *The Psychology of Men.* New York, Basic Books.
Foulkes, S. H. (1982). *Introduction to Group Analytic Psychotherapy.* London, Marefield.
Gilligan, C. (1982). *In a Different Voice.* Cambridge, Mass., Harvard University Press.
Inskipp, F. (undated). *A Manual for Trainers.* St Leonards-on-Sea, Alexia Publications.
Jacobs, E. D. and Masson, R. L. (1987). *Group Counseling.* New York, Brooks Cole.
Jacobs, M. (1982). *Still Small Voice.* London, SPCK.
Jacobs, M. (1984). 'Erikson's Eight Ages of Man in Simulation' in D. Thatcher and J. Robinson, *Business, Health and Nursing Education.* University of Loughborough, SAGSET.
Jacobs, M. (1985). *Swift to Hear.* London, SPCK.
Jacobs, M. (1986). *The Presenting Past.* Milton Keynes, Open University Press.
Jacobs, M. (1988). *Psychodynamic Counselling in Action.* London, Sage Publications.

Jacques, D. (1988a). *Groups – Theory and Practice*. London, Routledge and Kegan Paul.
Jacques, D. (1988b). *Learning in Groups*. London, Routledge and Kegan Paul.
Jones, K. (1980). *Simulations – a Handbook for Teachers and Trainers*. London, Kogan Page.
Jones, K. (1985). *Designing Your Own Simulations*. London, Methuen.
Khan, M. (1983). *Hidden Selves*. London, Hogarth Press.
Klein, M. (1957). *Envy and Gratitude*. London, Tavistock.
Laing, R. D. (1965). *The Divided Self*. Harmondsworth, Penguin.
Meier, S. T. (1989). *The Elements of Counseling*. New York, Brooks Cole.
Mitchell, J. (1975). *Psychoanalysis and Feminism*. Harmondsworth, Penguin.
Mitchell, K. R. (1982), 'A Death and a Community', *The Journal of Pastoral Care*, vol. XXXVI, no. 1, pp. 3–6.
Nelson-Jones, R. (1983). *Practical Helping Skills*. London, Holt, Rinehart and Winston.
Noonan, E. (1983). *Counselling Young People*. London, Routledge and Kegan Paul.
Okun, B. F. (1986). *Effective Helping*. New York, Brooks Cole.
Preston Bogia, B. (1985). 'Responding to Questions in Pastoral Care', *The Journal of Pastoral Care*, vol. XXXIX, no. 4, pp. 357–69.
Priestly, P. and McGuire, J. (1983). *Learning to Help: Basic Skills Exercises*. London, Tavistock.
Rayner, E. (1986). Human Development, 3rd edn. London, Allen & Unwin.
Redman, W. (1988). *Listening Power: a Trainer Guide*. Dyfed, Management Learning Resources.
Robertson, J. and Robertson, J. (1976). *Young Children in Brief Separation: John, aged 17 months, for 9 Days in a Residential Nursery* (video). Concord Films Council, Ipswich; the New York University Film Library.
Samuels, A. (1985). *Jung and the Post-Jungians*. London, Routledge and Kegan Paul.
Searles, H. (1965). *Collected Papers on Schizophrenia and Related Subjects*. London, Hogarth Press.
Sendak, M. (1970). *Where the Wild Things Are*. Harmondsworth, Penguin (Puffin).
Skynner, R. S. and Cleese, J. (1983). *Families and How to Survive Them*. London, Methuen.
Tansey, P. and Unwin, D. (1969). *Simulation and Gaming in Education*. London, Methuen.
Thatcher, D. and Robinson, J., *Business, Health and Nursing Education*. University of Loughborough, SAGSET.
Truax, C. B. (1963). 'Effective Ingredients in Psychotherapy: an Approach to Unravelling Patient-Therapist Interactions', *J. Consulting, Psychology*, vol. 10, pp. 256–63.
Tschudin, V. (1982). *Counselling Skills for Nurses*. London, Baillière Tindall.
Van Ments, M. (1983). *The Effective Use of Role Play*. London, Kogan Page.
Walrond-Skinner, S. (1988). *Family Matters*. London, SPCK.
Williams, H. (1982). *Some Day I'll Find You*. London, Mitchell Beazley.
Winnicott, D. W. (1988). *Human Nature*. London, Free Association Press.
Yalom, I. D. (1986). *The Theory and Practice of Group Psychotherapy*. San Francisco, Harper and Row.
Yalom, I. D. (1989). *Love's Executioner*. London, Bloomsbury.

Index of exercises and subjects